Reasoning and Decision Making

Cognition Special Issues

The titles in this series are paperbacked, readily accessible, in some cases expanded and updated editions of the special issues of *COGNITION: An International Journal of Cognitive Science*, edited by Jacques Mehler and produced by special agreement with Elsevier Science Publishers B.V. The first six are available from M.I.T. Press.

VISUAL COGNITION   Steven Pinker, guest editor

THE ONSET OF LITERACY: Cognitive Processes in Reading Acquisition Paul Bertelson, guest editor

SPOKEN WORD RECOGNITION   Uli H. Frauenfelder and Lorraine Komisarjevsky Tyler, guest editors

CONNECTIONS AND SYMBOLS   Steven Pinker and Jacques Mehler, guest editors

NEUROBIOLOGY OF COGNITION   Peter D. Eimas and Albert M. Galaburda, guest editors

ANIMAL COGNITION   C. R. Gallistel, guest editor

LEXICAL AND CONCEPTUAL SEMANTICS   Beth Levin and Steven Pinker, guest editors

REASONING AND DECISION MAKING   P. N. Johnson-Laird and Eldar Shafir, guest editors

Reasoning and Decision Making

Edited by P. N. Johnson-Laird
and Eldar Shafir

BLACKWELL
Cambridge MA & Oxford UK

Copyright © Elsevier Science Publishers, B.V.,
Amsterdam, The Netherlands, 1993

This edition published by Blackwell Publishers, 1994

238 Main Street
Cambridge, MA 02142, USA

108 Cowley Road
Oxford, OX4 1JF, UK

Reprinted from *Cognition: International Journal of Cognitive Science*, Volume 49, Numbers 1–2,
1993. Blackwell Publishers have exclusive licence to sell this English-language book edition
throughout the world.

Library of Congress Cataloging-in-Publication Data

A CIP catalog record for this book is available from the Library of Congress.

ISBN 1–55786–601–5

British Library Cataloging in Publication Data

A CIP catalogue record for this book is available from the British Library.

Printed and bound at Hartnolls Ltd, Bodmin, Cornwall.

This book is printed on acid-free paper.

Contents

Contributors

Kaye Brown, National Center for Health Program Evaluation, Fairfield, Victoria, Australia.

Jonathan St B. T. Evans, Department of Psychology, University of Plymouth, UK.

V. Girotto, Department of Psychology, Università degli Studi di Trieste.

Reid Hastie, Department of Psychology, University of Colerado, Boulder.

Philip N. Johnson-Laird, Department of Psychology, Princeton University.

Joshua Klayman, Center for Decision Research, Graduate School of Business, University of Chicago.

P. Legrenzi, Department of Psychology, Università degli Studi di Trieste.

K. I. Manktelow, School of Health Sciences, University of Wolverhampton, UK.

Daniel Osherson, IDIAP, Martigny, Valais, Switzerland.

D. E. Over, School of Social and International Studies, University of Sunderland, UK.

Nancy Pennington, Department of Psychology, University of Colorado, Boulder.

Eldar Shafir, Department of Psychology, Princeton University.

Itamar Simonson, Department of Psychology, Graduate School of Business, Stanford University.

Edward E. Smith, Department of Psychology, University of Michigan.

Amos Tversky, Department of Psychology, Graduate School of Business, Stanford University.

1 The interaction between reasoning and decision making: an introduction

Philip N. Johnson-Laird, and Eldar Shafir

Department of Psychology, Princeton University

> In order to decide, judge;
> in order to judge, reason;
> in order to reason, decide (what to reason about).

Reasoning and decision making are high-level cognitive skills that have been under intensive investigation by psychologists and philosophers, among others, for the last thirty years. But, methods and theories have developed separately in the two fields so that distinct traditions have grown with little to say to one another. The aim of this special issue of *Cognition* is to encourage and help workers in these two traditions to understand one another's research and to reflect and enhance some recent signs of "crosstalk" between them.

It seemed to us high time to consider the growing interactions between reasoning and decision making for at least three reasons. First, the two abilities are often interwoven in real life, at least according to the common-sense view epitomized in the maxim at the head of this introduction. Second, their study has led to striking parallels in the conclusions that investigators have reached and to the recent signs of crosstalk. Third, the two fields have important lessons for each other. We will explore each of these reasons before we introduce the papers in this special issue. We begin with a sketch of the everyday assumptions that relate reasoning and decision making – a background that we will defend, though it is sometimes disparaged by philosophers as "folk psychology".

The "folk" psychology of reasoning and decision making

Human beings have desires and needs, and they use their knowledge to decide what to do and to infer how best to achieve their goals. They reason in order to make decisions and to justify them both to themselves and others; they reason in order to determine the consequences of their beliefs and of their hypothetical actions; they reason to work out plans of action. They make decisions about what values to treat as paramount; they make decisions about what actions to take; and they make decisions about what information to base their reasoning on. Hence, there is an interdependence between reasoning and decision making. They are, as computer scientists say, mutually recursive.

This account of reasons and decisions is part of "folk psychology", that is, the view that most individuals in our culture accept about mental life. Philosophers and others have a variety of views about folk psychology. Thus, at one extreme, Ramsey (1926/1990) brought together three of its fundamental concepts – truth, probability, and value – in a profound synthesis. At another extreme, however, certain philosophers reject folk psychology wholesale. Terms such as "belief" and "desire", they say, do not refer to any substantive entities. They are theoretical terms much like "phlogiston" or "ether", which will be replaced once science has succeeded in determining the real underpinnings of behavior. People may use folk psychology to predict their own and other individuals' actions, but, say the critics, the theory itself is incorrigible – it is not responsive to evidence; it is not a scientific theory. The proper study of the mind is instead brain, nerve, and synapse (e.g., Churchland, 1984; Stich, 1983). At the heart of these critiques seems to lie a common philosophical skepticism about 'intentional objects', that is, mental representations that have content and that are about something.

Students of reasoning and decision making do not generally regard assumptions about beliefs, desires, and values with total skepticism, but they are suspicious of one component of folk psychology; the myth of perfect awareness. Unlike cognitive and social psychologists, most people believe that their conscious feelings and judgments control their actions. The claim is a legacy of the Cartesian identification of the mind with consciousness. Nothing is easier according to this principle than to know the contents of your mind: introspection will deliver them to you as part of your immediate experience. But to what extent can you be aware of the causes of your behavior? There is probably no way to answer this question for any particular action. That is the problem that historians face. But the psychological study of reasoning and decision making has answered the question for replicable classes of action. Individuals are often not aware of how they reason, having at best only glimpses of the process. They are aware of the results, not the mechanism. What they say about their reasoning does not tally with its real nature (e.g., Wason & Evans, 1975). Likewise, as Nisbett and Ross (1980) have argued, people often are not aware of the real basis of their decisions. For example, Nisbett and Wilson (1977) asked shoppers in a mall to rate the quality of four nightgowns. Most subjects favored whichever was the last gown that they had examined, while attributing their preference to some property of the nightgown itself, rather than its position in the sequence. In a similar vein, psychologists have demonstrated that individuals' simplistic theories about the social roots of behavior pervade their attributions of causes for others' actions and emotions.

Yet, the imperfections of introspection do not imply that all aspects of folk psychology are illusory. Individuals do have access to goals, feelings, and values. Introspection makes available to them what they are thinking, and in this way, as Ericsson and Simon (1980) contend, it can provide clues to the underlying process. People regularly ascribe truth values to assertions. As long as this practice is not entirely suspect, then it is hard to see how there could be anything dubious about the idea that an individual holds an assertion to be true (or false). And thus the concept of belief remains in the domain of respectable discourse. It is true, nonetheless, that introspection is not a direct route to understanding mental processes, and, as far as we know, there is no direct route. That is why psychologists studying reasoning and decision making are committed to experimental investigations rather than to introspection and *a priori* analysis (also known as 'indoor ornithology').

Normative theories are not psychological theories

Normative theories have been proposed both for reasoning and for decision making. They are intended to specify what count as rational inferences and rational decisions. In the case of reasoning, the normative theory is formal logic, and many theorists have argued that it does indeed provide an account of human deductive competence (e.g., Beth & Piaget, 1966; Cherniak, 1986; Henle, 1962; Macnamara, 1986). There are, however, three difficulties with this proposal. First, which logic gives the normative account? Logic is not a monolithic enterprise, particularly if it is to embrace reasoning with modal terms such as "possibly" and "necessarily": there are probably an infinite number of distinct modal logics (Hughes & Cresswell, 1968). Perhaps none of them is relevant to human competence, because an assertion, such as:

It is raining, and possibly it is not raining.

is not a self-contradiction in any of these logics, as it seems to be in everyday language, which distinguishes between this assertion and the following "counterfactual" one:

It is raining, but it might not have been raining.

Second, logic gives no account of which valid conclusion to draw. From any set of premises, there are always infinitely many conclusions that follow validly; that is, they must be true given that the premises are true. Most of these conclusions are trivial, and it would hardly be rational to infer them. For example, given the following premises:

> If it is raining, then there is no need to water the plants.
> It is raining.

a sensible, rational, conclusion is:

> There is no need to water the plants.

But any of the following conclusions are valid too:

> It is raining or it is not raining.
> It is raining or it is snowing.
> It is raining or cats and dogs are falling out of the sky.

and so on.

Logic alone cannot determine which of the infinitely many valid conclusions are sensible to draw. Strangely, the theories that adopt logic as their account of deductive competence have almost universally overlooked this problem. Human reasoners seem naturally to infer conclusions that are parsimonious, that make information explicit that was not stated as such in the premises, and that do not throw information away by adding disjunctive alternatives (see Johnson-Laird & Byrne, 1991).

Whatever the definition of competence, human reasoners do make deductive errors. Yet, there have been many attempts to save the hypothesis that they are logically impeccable. The idea was first formulated by philosophers, perhaps on the grounds that humans are made in God's image. More recently, Henle (1962) has argued that apparent mistakes in reasoning do not impugn the underlying mechanism: individuals *are* reasoning validly, but they have forgotten a premise, reinterpreted a premise, or imported some additional premise. Similarly, Cohen (1981) has argued that the underlying competence cannot be at fault: there is merely a malfunction in the mechanism. The evidence suggests otherwise. Reasoners make errors in cases where there are no grounds for supposing that they have forgotten the premises, distorted them, or added new premises. Their errors are systematic and predictable, and they will even concede that they have erred. The phenomena do not imply that human beings are irredeemably irrational – after all, they are sensible enough to recognize their shortcomings and to devise formal logic as a device for testing the validity of their inferences. Systematic errors in deduction are compatible with the notion that deductive competence rests on the semantic principle of validity. According to this notion, an inference is valid if its conclusion must be true given that its premises are true. Human beings appear to grasp this idea (at least tacitly), but they do not always have the mental resources to pursue it properly, and so they fall into error. This idea lies at the heart of the mental model theory of reasoning, which is outlined in this issue (see the paper by Legrenzi, Girotto, & Johnson-Laird).

In the case of decision making, the classical normative account is expected utility theory (EUT), wherein the value of an alternative consists of the sum of the utilities of its outcomes, each weighted by its probability. Modern EUT was developed by von Neumann and Morgenstern (1947), who showed that if individuals' preferences satisfy a number of simple axioms, then their behavior can be described and justified as maximizing expected utility. Besides some more technical points, the axiomatic analysis reflects the following substantive assumptions about decisions (for further discussion, see Tversky & Kahneman, 1986, and references therein; in what follows we adopt their terminology, although these notions appear in a number of different guises elsewhere):

Cancellation: Any state of the world that yields the same outcome regardless of one's choice should be "cancelled", or eliminated from further consideration. Thus, choice between options should depend only on those states in which they yield different outcomes.

Transitivity: For any alternatives *x*, *y*, and *z*, if *x* is preferred to *y*, and *y* is preferred to *z*, then *x* must be preferred to *z*.

Dominance: If one option is better than another in one state of the world and at least as good in all other states, then the dominant option should be chosen.

Invariance: Different but logically identical representations of the same choice problem, or different methods of eliciting a choice, should yield the same preferences.

Just as the study of judgment has shown that humans are not intuitive Bayesian statisticians (see the papers in this issue by Klayman & Brown and by Smith, Shafir, & Osherson), so too studies of decision making have shown that people are not intuitive utility maximizers. Research in behavioral decision theory has documented systematic and predictable violations of the above assumptions. Perhaps the most basic assumption is that of invariance, which requires strategically equivalent methods of elicitation and logically identical descriptions of the options to yield the same preferences. Violations of invariance have now been documented in numerous domains, in hypothetical as well as real world situations, with both high and low stakes, and both with and without monetary incentives. As illustrated by Tversky and Kahneman (1986), violations of invariance themselves suffice to generate violations of cancellation and dominance. Some violations of transitivity have also been documented (Tversky, 1969), and are most likely to arise in decisions based on multiple criteria. They can also occur in collective behavior, as illustrated by well-known paradoxes in social choice (e.g., Arrow, 1963).

Certain assumptions of rational choice have had more normative appeal than others. Thus, while the assumption of invariance is indispensable for a normative account, the cancellation and transitivity conditions have been challenged by some theorists. The notion that humans abide by normative principles dies hard, especially amongst economists and philosophers (see Hogarth & Reder, 1986, for a good discussion.) As a consequence of this tension, several theories have been proposed that retain some of the more normatively appealing principles, like invariance, while relaxing others, such as cancellation and transitivity (for reviews, see Camerer, 1993; Machina, 1982; Schoemaker, 1982). Their apparent aim is to tailor a normative account to fit observed behavior. Naturally, as evidence continues to accumulate documenting the violation of even the most essential principles, decision theorists, like students of human reasoning, will have to accept the irreconcilability of the normative and the descriptive accounts.

In sum, the major psychological discovery about both reasoning and decision making is that normative theory and psychological facts pass each other by. People are not intuitive logicians, intuitive statisticians, or intuitive rational decision theorists. Instead, the precise character of their thoughts and decisions is the outcome of complex and unobservable mental processes, the nature of which researchers in both these areas of inquiry are trying to elucidate.

Some lessons from the study of reasoning and decision making

A significant lesson from the study of reasoning is that theories of mental processes should be computable, that is, sufficiently explicit that, in principle, they could be modeled in computer programs. Indeed, many researchers have implemented their theories in computer programs (e.g., Braine & O'Brien, 1991; Johnson-Laird & Byrne, 1991; Rips, 1983). The practice helps to ensure that theorists are not taking too much for granted and that their theories are not vague, incoherent, or, like mystical insights, only properly understood by their proponents. The effort to develop a computable theory concentrates the theorist's mind on the nature of underlying mental processes; it alerts the theorist to the design of mental architecture (Newell, 1990) and to the puzzle of how intellectual strategies might develop. Similarly, since programs should not be equated with theories, there can be a dialectical improvement in the theories: what a program does is not as important as the effects its development may have on the theorist's thinking.

A significant lesson from the study of decision making is the need for experiments to examine realistic problems. It is of limited interest to investigate text-book examples if they are so artificial and so remote from the exigencies of daily life that subjects are likely to adopt strategies that are otherwise alien to their everyday thinking. The result will be a burgeoning literature that is largely irrelevant to the real nature of thinking. In contrast, students of decision making have investigated, among others, the decisions of doctors about treatments, of gamblers in casinos, and of customers in shopping malls. Similarly, many of the laboratory studies, while hypothetical in nature, show an enhanced sensitivity to the verisimilitude of their tasks.

Another lesson from the study of decision making is the three-fold distinction that theorists draw among normative, descriptive and prescriptive accounts (e.g., Bell, Raiffa, & Tversky, 1988). The customary distinction is between the normative (how one ought to proceed) and the descriptive (how one in fact proceeds). But, if individuals are to be helped to improve their performance in daily life, it is unrealistic to hope that this may be achieved simply by teaching them decision theory. Recommendations need to go beyond normative and descriptive accounts and to advocate measures that actually help people make better decisions. Such prescriptive measures are likely not to fall neatly into either the normative or descriptive categories. If a decision problem is affected by the way in which it is framed, then a combination of the alternative frames into a single description may not overcome the effect: one frame may still be more salient than the other (cf. McNeil, Pauker, & Tversky, 1988). At that point, the best that decision makers can do is to examine their preferences from the different perspectives and, aware of the normative–descriptive tension, reason about the best way of reaching a decision. The development of effective prescriptions to overcome such difficulties calls for further thinking and analysis on the part of both lay people and researchers.

To a first approximation, these are the lessons that the study of reasoning and decision making have for one another: investigators of reasoning often use artificial materials or tasks remote from daily life, and seldom recognize the need for special prescriptive measures (but compare Bauer & Johnson-Laird, in press); investigators of decision making are often more concerned with what the mind is doing than with how it is doing it, that is, with specifying a computable account of the relevant mental processes (but compare Payne, Bettman, Coupey, & Johnson, 1992). We hope this special issue of *Cognition* will help workers in the two areas understand one another's research and share their insights. That must be the first step towards the integration of the two areas into a larger explanatory framework.

An introduction to the papers

The papers in this issue range over a variety of sorts of inferences and decisions. They express diverse points of view, propose different theories, and take different positions on the topic of human rationality. What they have in common, we believe, is a commitment to the idea that students of reasoning and decision making both stand to benefit from a closer interaction and dialogue with one another, and from a more interactive sharing of theories, methodologies, and findings.

Shafir, Simonson, and Tversky argue that a consideration of the reasons that enter into people's thinking about a decision problem may illuminate certain aspects of reflective choice that remain counterintuitive from the perspective of the classical theory.

Legrenzi, Girotto, and Johnson-Laird assume that reasoning and decision making both depend on the construction of mental models. They demonstrate that when individuals make deductive inferences or seek information in order to make decisions, they focus on what is explicitly represented in their models to the neglect of other possible information.

Smith, Shafir, and Osherson examine inductive inferences based on category membership and the heuristics that influence judgments of argument strength, that is, the probability that a conclusion is true given that the premises are true. They show that with unfamiliar predicates what matters most is the similarity between the premise and conclusion categories, whereas with familiar predicates probability judgments are based on both the similarity relations and the plausibility of the premises and conclusion.

Klayman and Brown consider what can be done to improve human judgment and reasoning. They show that one stratagem – changing the environment, that is, the way in which information is presented – can reduce error in a task based on medical diagnosis, moving subjects away from focusing on typical features to those that are genuinely diagnostic.

Pennington and Hastie analyze the reasoning of members of juries trying to reach a decision, and show how they rely on explanations that, in turn, are based on inferences that lead to a causal model of the events.

Evans, Over, and Manktelow take up the question of rationality. They distinguish between reasoning to achieve goals and reasoning as a logical process, and argue that the latter is not the basis for the former. They conclude that both decision theory and formal logic are inadequate models for assessing human competence.

Inevitably, much excellent work exists for which there was no room, but we have been fortunate that nearly everyone whom we invited has written an article for this special issue. We thank the authors for their papers and their patience, and the referees for their criticisms and suggestions. We also thank Jacques

Mehler, the editor of the journal, and Susana Franck, the editorial associate, for their help, advice, and encouragement.

References

Arrow, J. (1963). *Social choice and individual values*, 2nd edn. New York: Wiley.

Bauer, M.I., & Johnson-Laird, P.N. (in press). How diagrams can improve reasoning. *Psychological Science*.

Bell, D.E., Raiffa, H., & Tversky, A. (1988). Descriptive, normative, and prescriptive interactions in decision making. In D. Bell, H. Raiffa, & A. Tversky (Eds.), *Decision making: descriptive, normative, and prescriptive interactions.* Cambridge, UK: Cambridge University Press.

Beth, E.W., & Piaget, J. (1966) *Mathematical epistemology and psychology*. Dordrecht: Reidel.

Braine, M.D.S., & O'Brien, D.P.O. (1991). A theory of "if": a lexical entry, reasoning program, and pragmatic principles. *Psychological Review, 98,* 182–203.

Camerer, C.F. (1993). Recent tests of generalizations of expected utility theory. In W. Edwards (Ed.), *Utility theories: measurements and applications.* Hingham, MA: Kluwer.

Cherniak, C. (1986). *Minimal rationality.* Cambridge, MA: MIT Press.

Churchland, P.M. (1984). *Matter and consciousness.* Cambridge, MA: MIT Press.

Cohen, L.J. (1981). Can human irrationality be experimentally demonstrated? *Behavioral and Brain Sciences, 4,* 317–370.

Ericsson, K.A., & Simon, H.A. (1980). Verbal reports as data. *Psychological Review, 87,* 215–251.

Henle, M. (1962). The relation between logic and thinking. *Psychological Review, 69,* 366–378.

Hogarth, R.M., & Reder, M.W. (Eds.) (1986). The behavioral foundations of economic theory. *Journal of Business, 59* (4), Part 2.

Hughes, G.E., & Cresswell, M.J. (1968). *An introduction to modal logic.* London: Methuen.

Johnson-Laird, P.N., & Byrne, R.M.J. (1991). *Deduction.* Hillsdale, NJ: Erlbaum.

Machina, M.J. (1982). "Expected utility" analysis without the independence axiom. *Econometrica, 50* 277–323.

Macnamara, J. (1986). *A border dispute: the place of logic in psychology.* Cambridge, MA: Bradford Books/MIT Press.

McNeil, B.J., Pauker, S.G., & Tversky, A. (1988). On the framing of medical decisions. In D. Bell, H. Raiffa, & A. Tversky (Eds.), *Decision making: descriptive, normative, and prescriptive interactions.* Cambridge, UK: Cambridge University Press.

Newell, A. (1990). *Unified theories of cognition.* Cambridge, MA: Harvard University Press.

Nisbett, R.E., & Ross, L. (1980) *Human inference: strategies and shortcomings of social judgement.* Englewood Cliffs, NJ: Prentice Hall.

Nisbett, R.E., & Wilson, T.D. (1977). Telling more than we can know: verbal reports on mental processes. *Psychological Review, 84,* 231–259.

Payne, J.W., Bettman, J.R., Coupey, E., & Johnson, E.J. (1992). A constructive process view of decision making: multiple strategies in judgment and choice. *Acta Psychologica, 80,* 107–141.

Ramsey, F.P. (1990). Truth and probability. In Mellor, D.H. (Ed.), *Philosophical papers: F.P. Ramsey.* Cambridge, UK: Cambridge University Press. (Original work published 1926).

Rips, L.J. (1983). Cognitive processes in propositional reasoning. *Psychological Review, 90,* 38–71.

Schoemaker, P.J.H. (1982). The expected utility model: its variants, purposes, evidence, and limitations. *Journal of Economic Literature, 20,* 529–563.

Stich, S. (1983). *From folk psychology to cognitive science.* Cambridge, MA: MIT Press.

Tversky, A. (1969). Intransitivity of preferences. *Psychological Review, 76,* 31–48.

Tversky, A., & Kahneman, D. (1986). Rational choice and the framing of decisions. *Journal of Business, 59* (4), part 2, S251–S278.

von Neumann, J., & Morgenstern, O. (1947). *Theory of games and economic behavior* (2nd ed.). Princeton: Princeton University Press.

Wason, P.C., & Evans, J.St.B.T (1975) Dual processes in reasoning? *Cognition, 3,* 141–154.

2 Reason-based choice

Eldar Shafir
Department of Psychology, Princeton University

Itamar Simonson, and Amos Tversky
Department of Psychology, Graduate School of Business, Stanford University

Abstract

This paper considers the role of reasons and arguments in the making of decisions. It is proposed that, when faced with the need to choose, decision makers often seek and construct reasons in order to resolve the conflict and justify their choice, to themselves and to others. Experiments that explore and manipulate the role of reasons are reviewed, and other decision studies are interpreted from this perspective. The role of reasons in decision making is considered as it relates to uncertainty, conflict, context effects, and normative decision rules.

The result is that peculiar feeling of inward unrest known as *indecision*. Fortunately it is too familiar to need description, for to describe it would be impossible. As long as it lasts, with the various objects before the attention, we are said to *deliberate*; and when finally the original suggestion either prevails and makes the movement take place, or gets definitively quenched by its antagonists, we are said to *decide* . . . in favor of one or the other course. The reinforcing and inhibiting ideas meanwhile are termed the *reasons* or *motives* by which the decision is brought about.

William James (1890/1981)

My way is to divide half a sheet of paper by a line into two columns; writing over the one *Pro*, and over the other *Con*. Then, during three or four days' consideration, I put down under the different heads short hints of the different motives, that at different times occur to me for or against the measure. When I have thus got them all together in one view, I endeavor to estimate the respective weights . . . find at length where the balance lies . . . And, though the weight of reasons cannot be taken with the precision of algebraic quantities, yet, when each is thus considered, separately and

This research was supported by US Public Health Service Grant No. 1-R29-MH46885 from the National Institute of Mental Health, by Grant No. 89-0064 from the Air Force Office of Scientific Research and by Grant No. SES-9109535 from the National Science Foundation. The paper was partially prepared while the first author participated in a Summer Institute on Negotiation and Dispute Resolution at the Center for Advanced Study in the Behavioral Sciences, and while the second author was at the University of California, Berkeley. Funds for support of the Summer Institute were provided by the Andrew W. Mellon Foundation. We thank Robyn Dawes for helpful comments on an earlier draft.
*Corresponding author.

comparatively, and the whole matter lies before me, I think I can judge better, and am less liable
to make a rash step; and in fact I have found great advantage for this kind of equation, in what
may be called *moral* or *prudential algebra*.

Benjamin Franklin, 1772 (cited in Bigelow, 1887)

Introduction

The making of decisions, both big and small, is often difficult because of
uncertainty and conflict. We are usually uncertain about the exact consequences of
our actions, which may depend on the weather or the state of the economy, and
we often experience conflict about how much of one attribute (e.g., savings) to
trade off in favor of another (e.g., leisure). In order to explain how people resolve
such conflict, students of decision making have traditionally employed either
formal models or reason-based analyses. The formal modeling approach, which is
commonly used in economics, management science, and decision research,
typically associates a numerical value with each alternative, and characterizes
choice as the maximization of value. Such value-based accounts include normative
models, like expected utility theory (von Neumann & Morgenstern, 1947), as well
as descriptive models, such as prospect theory (Kahneman & Tversky, 1979). An
alternative tradition in the study of decision making, characteristic of scholarship
in history and the law, and typical of political and business discourse, employs an
informal, reason-based analysis. This approach identifies various reasons and
arguments that are purported to enter into and influence decision, and explains
choice in terms of the balance of reasons for and against the various alternatives.
Examples of reason-based analyses can be found in studies of historic presidential
decisions, such as those taken during the Cuban missile crisis (e.g., Allison,
1971), the Camp David accords (Telhami, 1990), or the Vietnam war (e.g.,
Berman, 1982; Betts & Gelb, 1979). Furthermore, reason-based analyses are
commonly used to interpret "case studies" in business and law schools. Although
the reasons invoked by researchers may not always correspond to those that
motivated the actual decision makers, it is generally agreed that an analysis in
terms of reasons may help explain decisions, especially in contexts where value-
based models can be difficult to apply.

Little contact has been made between the two traditions, which have typically
been applied to different domains. Reason-based analyses have been used
primarily to explain non-experimental data, particularly unique historic, legal and
political decisions. In contrast, value-based approaches have played a central role
in experimental studies of preference and in standard economic analyses. The two
approaches, of course, are not incompatible: reason-based accounts may often be
translated into formal models, and formal analyses can generally be paraphrased
as reason-based accounts. In the absence of a comprehensive theory of choice,

both formal models and reason-based analyses may contribute to the understanding of decision making.

Both approaches have obvious strengths and limitations. The formal, value-based models have the advantage of rigor, which facilitates the derivation of testable implications. However, value-based models are difficult to apply to complex, real world decisions, and they often fail to capture significant aspects of people's deliberations. An explanation of choice based on reasons, on the other hand, is essentially qualitative in nature and typically vague. Furthermore, almost anything can be counted as a "reason", so that every decision may be rationalized after the fact. To overcome this difficulty, one could ask people to report their reasons for decision. Unfortunately, the actual reasons that guide decision may or may not correspond to those reported by the subjects. As has been amply documented (e.g., Nisbett & Wilson, 1977), subjects are sometimes unaware of the precise factors that determine their choices, and generate spurious explanations when asked to account for their decisions. Indeed, doubts about the validity of introspective reports have led many students of decision making to focus exclusively on observed choices. Although verbal reports and introspective accounts can provide valuable information, we use "reasons" in the present article to describe factors or motives that affect decision, whether or not they can be articulated or recognized by the decision maker.

Despite its limitations, a reason-based conception of choice has several attractive features. First, a focus on reasons seems closer to the way we normally think and talk about choices. When facing a difficult choice (e.g., between schools, or jobs) we try to come up with reasons for and against each option – we do not normally attempt to estimate their overall values. Second, thinking of choice as guided by reasons provides a natural way to understand the conflict that characterizes the making of decisions. From the perspective of reason-based choice, conflict arises when the decision maker has good reasons for and against each option, or conflicting reasons for competing options. Unlike numerical values, which are easy to compare, conflicting reasons may be hard to reconcile. An analysis based on reasons can also accommodate framing effects (Tversky & Kahneman, 1986) and elicitation effects (Tversky, Sattath, & Slovic, 1988), which show that preferences are sensitive to the ways in which options are described (e.g., in terms of gains or losses), and to the methods through which preferences are elicited (e.g., pricing versus choice). These findings, which are puzzling from the perspective of value maximization, are easier to interpret if we assume that different frames and elicitation procedures highlight different aspects of the options and thus bring forth different reasons to guide decision. Finally, a conception of choice based on reasons may incorporate comparative considerations (such as relative advantages, or anticipated regret) that typically remain outside the purview of value maximization.

In this article, we explore the logic of reason-based choice, and test some specific hypotheses concerning the role of reasons in decision making. The article proceeds as follows. Section 1 considers the role of reasons in choice between equally attractive options. Section 2 explores differential reliance on reasons for and against the selection of options. Section 3 investigates the interaction between high and low conflict and people's tendency to seek other alternatives, whereas section 4 considers the relation between conflict and the addition of alternatives to the choice set. Section 5 contrasts the impact of a specific reason for choice with that of a disjunction of reasons. Section 6 explores the role that irrelevant reasons can play in the making of decisions. Concluding remarks are presented in section 7.

1. Choice between equally attractive options

How do decision makers resolve the conflict when faced with a choice between two equally attractive options? To investigate this question, Slovic (1975) first had subjects equate pairs of alternatives, and later asked them to make choices between the equally valued alternatives in each pair. One pair, for example, were gift packages consisting of a combination of cash and coupons. For each pair, one component of one alternative was missing, as shown below, and subjects were asked to determine the value of the missing component that would render the two alternatives equally attractive. (In the following example, the value volunteered by the subject may be, say, $10).

	Gift package A	*Gift package B*
Cash	–	$20
Coupon book worth	$32	$18

A week later, subjects were asked to choose between the two equated alternatives. They were also asked, independently, which dimension – cash or coupons – they considered more important. Value-based theories imply that the two alternatives – explicitly equated for value – are equally likely to be selected. In contrast, in the choice between gift packages above, 88% of the subjects who had equated these alternatives for value then proceeded to choose the alternative that was higher on the dimension that the subject considered more important.

As Slovic (1975, 1990) suggests, people seem to be following a choice mechanism that is easy to explain and justify: choosing according to the more important dimension provides a better reason for choice than, say, random selection, or selection of the right-hand option. Slovic (1975) replicated the above pattern in numerous domains, including choices between college applicants, auto tires, baseball players, and routes to work. (For additional data and a discussion of elicitation procedures, see Tversky et al., 1988.) All the results were consistent with the hypothesis that people do not choose between the equated alternatives at random. Instead, they resolve the conflict by selecting the alternative that is superior on the more important dimension, which seems to provide a compelling reason for choice.

2. Reasons pro and con

Consider having to choose one of two options or, alternatively, having to reject one of two options. Under the standard analysis of choice, the two tasks are interchangeable. In a binary choice situation it should not matter whether people are asked which option they prefer, or which they would reject. Because it is the options themselves that are assumed to matter, not the way in which they are described, if people prefer the first they will reject the second, and vice versa.

As suggested by Franklin's opening quote, our decision will depend partially on the weights we assign to the options' pros and cons. We propose that the positive features of options (their pros) will loom larger when choosing, whereas the negative features of options (their cons) will be weighted more heavily when rejecting. It is natural to select an option because of its positive features, and to reject an option because of its negative features. To the extent that people base their decisions on reasons for and against the options under consideration, they are likely to focus on reasons for choosing an option when deciding which to choose, and to focus on reasons for rejecting an option when deciding which to reject. This hypothesis leads to a straightforward prediction: consider two options, an *enriched* option, with more positive and more negative features, and an *impoverished* option, with fewer positive and fewer negative features. If positive features are weighted more heavily when choosing than when rejecting and negative features are weighted relatively more when rejecting than when choosing, then an enriched option could be both chosen and rejected when compared to an impoverished option. Let P_c and P_r denote, respectively, the percentage of subjects who choose and who reject a particular option. If choosing and rejecting are complementary, then the sum $P_c + P_r$ should equal 100. On the other hand, according to the above hypothesis, $P_c + P_r$ should be greater than 100 for the enriched option and less than 100 for the impoverished option. This pattern was observed by Shafir (1993). Consider, for example, the following problem which was presented to subjects in two versions that differed only in the bracketed questions. One half of the subjects received one version, the other half received the other. The enriched option appears last, although the order presented to subjects was counterbalanced.

Problem 1 ($n = 170$):

Imagine that you serve on the jury of an only-child sole-custody case following a relatively messy divorce. The facts of the case are complicated by ambiguous economic, social, and emotional considerations, and you decide to base your decision entirely on the following few observations. [To which parent would you award sole custody of the child?/Which parent would you deny sole custody of the child?]

	Award	*Deny*
Parent A: average income average health average working hours reasonable rapport with the child relatively stable social life	36%	45%
Parent B: above-average income very close relationship with the child extremely active social life lots of work-related travel minor health problems	64%	55%

Parent A, the impoverished option, is quite plain – with no striking positive or negative features. There are no particularly compelling reasons to award or deny this parent custody of the child. Parent B, the enriched option, on the other hand, has good reasons to be awarded custody (a very close relationship with the child and a good income), but also good reasons to be denied sole custody (health problems and extensive absences due to travel). To the right of the options are the percentages of subjects who chose to award and to deny custody to each of the parents. Parent B is the majority choice both for being awarded custody of the child and for being denied it. As predicted, $P_c + P_r$ for parent B ($64 + 55 = 119$) is significantly greater than 100, the value expected if choosing and rejecting were complementary ($z = 2.48$, $p < .02$). This pattern is explained by the observation that the enriched parent (parent B) provides more compelling reasons to be awarded as well as denied child custody.

The above pattern has been replicated in hypothetical choices between monetary gambles, college courses, and political candidates (Shafir, 1993). For another example, consider the following problem, presented to half the subjects in the "prefer" and to the other half in the "cancel" version.

Problem 2 (n = 172):

Prefer:
Imagine that you are planning a week vacation in a warm spot over spring break. You currently have two options that are reasonably priced. The travel

brochure gives only a limited amount of information about the two options. Given the information available, which vacation spot would you prefer?

Cancel:
Imagine that you are planning a week vacation in a warm spot over spring break. You currently have two options that are reasonably priced, but you can no longer retain your reservation in both. The travel brochure gives only a limited amount of information about the two options. Given the information available, which reservation do you decide to cancel?

		Prefer	*Cancel*
Spot A:	average weather average beaches medium-quality hotel medium-temperature water average nightlife	33%	52%
Spot B:	lots of sunshine gorgeous beaches and coral reefs ultra-modern hotel very cold water very strong winds no nightlife	67%	48%

The information about the two spots is typical of the kind of information we have available when deciding where to take our next vacation. Because it is difficult to estimate the overall value of each spot, we are likely to seek reasons on which to base our decision. Spot A, the impoverished option, seems unremarkable yet unobjectionable on all counts. On the other hand, there are obvious reasons – gorgeous beaches, an abundance of sunshine, and an ultra-modern hotel – for choosing spot B. Of course, there are also compelling reasons – cold water, winds, and a lack of nightlife – why spot B should be rejected. We suggest that the gorgeous beaches are likely to provide a more compelling reason when we choose than when we reject, and the lack of nightlife is likely to play a more central role when we reject than when we choose. Indeed, spot B's share of being preferred and rejected exceeds that of spot A ($P_c + P_r = 67 + 48 = 115$, $p < .05$). These results demonstrate that options are not simply ordered according to value, with the more attractive selected and the less attractive rejected. Instead, it appears that the relative importance of options' strengths and weaknesses varies with the nature of the task. As a result, we are significantly more likely to end up in spot B when we ask ourselves which we prefer than when we contemplate which to cancel (67% vs. 52%, $z = 2.83$, $p < .001$).

One of the most basic assumptions of the rational theory of choice is the principle of procedure invariance, which requires strategically equivalent methods of elication to yield identical preferences (see Tversky et al., 1988, for discussion). The choose–reject discrepancy represents a predictable failure of procedure invariance. This phenomenon is at variance with value maximization, but is easily understood from the point of view of reason-based choice: reasons for choosing are more compelling when we choose than when we reject, and reasons for rejecting matter more when we reject than when we choose.

3. Choice under conflict: seeking options

The need to choose often creates conflict: we are not sure how to trade off one attribute relative to another or, for that matter, which attributes matter to us most. It is a commonplace that we often attempt to resolve such conflict by seeking reasons for choosing one option over another. At times, the conflict between available alternatives is hard to resolve, which may lead us to seek additional options, or to maintain the status quo. Other times, the context is such that a comparison between alternatives generates compelling reasons to choose one option over another. Using reasons to resolve conflict has some non-obvious implications, which are addressed below. The present section focuses on people's decision to seek other alternatives; the next section explores some effects of adding options to the set under consideration.

In many contexts, we need to decide whether to opt for an available option or search for additional alternatives. Thus, a person who wishes to buy a used car may settle for a car that is currently available or continue searching for additional models. Seeking new alternatives usually requires additional time and effort, and may involve the risk of losing the previously available options. Conflict plays no role in the classical theory of choice. In this theory, each option x has a value $v(x)$ such that, for any offered set, the decision maker selects the option with the highest value. In particular, a person is expected to search for additional alternatives only if the expected value of searching exceeds that of the best option currently available. A reliance on reasons, on the other hand, entails that we should be more likely to opt for an available option when we have a convincing reason for its selection, and that we should be more likely to search further when a compelling reason for choice is not readily available.

To investigate this hypothesis, Tversky and Shafir (1992b) presented subjects with pairs of options, such as bets varying in probability and payoff, or student apartments varying in monthly rent and distance from campus, and had subjects choose one of the two options or, instead, request an additional option, at some cost. Subjects first reviewed the entire set of 12 options (gambles or apartments) to familiarize themselves with the available alternatives. In the study of choice between bets some subjects then received the following problem.

Conflict:

Imagine that you are offered a choice between the following two gambles:

(*x*) 65% chance to win $15
(*y*) 30% chance to win $35

You can either select one of these gambles or you can pay $1 to add one more gamble to the choice set. The added gamble will be selected at random from the list you reviewed.

Other subjects received a similar problem except that option *y* was replaced by option *x'*, to yield a choice between the following.

Dominance:

(*x*)   65% chance to win $15
(*x'*) 65% chance to win $14

Subjects were asked to indicate whether they wanted to add another gamble or select between the available alternatives. They then chose their preferred gamble from the resulting set (with or without the added option). Subjects were instructed that the gambles they chose would be played out and that their payoff would be proportional to the amount of money they earned minus the fee they paid for the added gambles.

A parallel design presented choices between hypothetical student apartments. Some subjects received the following problem.

Conflict:

Imagine that you face a choice between two apartments with the following characteristics:

(*x*) $290 a month, 25 minutes from campus
(*y*) $350 a month, 7 minutes from campus

Both have one bedroom and a kitchenette. You can choose now between the two apartments or you can continue to search for apartments (to be selected at random from the list you reviewed). In that case, there is some risk of losing one or both of the apartments you have found.

Other subjects received a similar problem except that option *y* was replaced by option *x'*, to yield a choice between the following.

Dominance:
(*x*) $290 a month, 25 minutes from campus
(*x'*) $330 a month, 25 minutes from campus

Note that in both pairs of problems the choice between *x* and *y* – the *conflict* condition – is non-trivial because the *x*s are better on one dimension and the *y*s are better on the other. In contrast, the choice between *x* and *x'* – the *dominance* condition – involves no conflict because the former strictly dominates the latter. Thus, while there is no obvious reason to choose one option over the other in the conflict condition, there is a decisive argument for preferring one of the two alternatives in the dominance condition.

On average, subjects requested an additional alternative 64% of the time in the conflict condition, and only 40% of the time in the dominance condition ($p <$ .05). Subjects' tendency to search for additional options, in other words, was greater when the choice among alternatives was harder to rationalize, than when there was a compelling reason and the decision was easy.

These data are inconsistent with the principle of value maximization. According to value maximization, a subject should search for additional alternatives if and only if the expected (subjective) value of searching exceeds that of the best alternative currently available. Because the best alternative offered in the dominance condition is also available in the conflict condition, value maximization implies that the percentage of subjects who seek an additional alternative cannot be greater in the conflict than in the dominance condition, contrary to the observed data.

It appears that the search for additional alternatives depends not only on the value of the best available option, as implied by value maximization, but also on the difficulty of choosing among the options under consideration. In situations of dominance, for example, there are clear and indisputable reasons for choosing one option over another (e.g., "This apartment is equally distant and I save $40!"). Having a compelling argument for choosing one of the options over the rest reduces the temptation to look for additional alternatives. When the choice involves conflict, on the other hand, reasons for choosing any one of the options are less immediately available and the decision is more difficult to justify (e.g., "Should I save $60 a month, or reside 18 minutes closer to campus?"). In the absence of compelling reasons for choice, there is a greater tendency to search for other alternatives.

4. Choice under conflict: adding options

An analysis in terms of reasons can help explain observed violations of the principle of independence of irrelevant alternatives, according to which the preference ordering between two options should not be altered by the introduction of additional alternatives. This principle follows from the standard assumption of value maximization, and has been routinely assumed in the analysis of consumer choice. Despite its intuitive appeal, there is a growing body of evidence that people's preferences depend on the context of choice, defined by the set of options under consideration. In particular, the addition and removal of options from the offered set can influence people's preferences among options that were available all along. Whereas in the previous section we considered people's tendency to seek alternatives in the context of a given set of options, in this section we illustrate phenomena that arise through the addition of options, and interpret them in terms of reasons for choice.

A major testable implication of value maximization is that a non-preferred option cannot become preferred when new options are added to the offered set. In particular, a decision maker who prefers y over the option to defer the choice should not prefer to defer the choice when both y and x are available. That the "market share" of an option cannot be increased by enlarging the offered set is known as the *regularity condition* (see Tversky & Simonson, in press). Contrary to regularity, numerous experimental results indicate that the tendency to defer choice can increase with the addition of alternatives. Consider, for instance, the degree of conflict that arises when a person is presented with one attractive option (which he or she prefers to deferring the choice), compared to two competing alternatives. Choosing one out of two competing alternatives can be difficult: the mere fact that an alternative is attractive may not in itself provide a compelling reason for its selection, because the other option may be equally attractive. The addition of an alternative may thus make the decision harder to justify, and increase the tendency to defer the decision.

A related phenomenon was aptly described by Thomas Schelling, who tells of an occasion in which he had decided to buy an encyclopedia for his children. At the bookstore, he was presented with two attractive encyclopedias and, finding it difficult to choose between the two, ended up buying neither – this, despite the fact that had only one encyclopedia been available he would have happily bought it. More generally, there are situations in which people prefer each of the available alternatives over the status quo but do not have a compelling reason for choosing among the alternatives and, as a result, defer the decision, perhaps indefinitely.

The phenomenon described by Schelling was demonstrated by Tversky and Shafir (1992b) in the following pair of problems, which were presented to two groups of students ($n = 124$ and 121, respectively).

High conflict:

Suppose you are considering buying a compact disk (CD) player, and have not yet decided what model to buy. You pass by a store that is having a 1-day clearance sale. They offer a popular SONY player for just $99, and a top-of-the-line AIWA player for just $169, both well below the list price. Do you?:

(*x*) buy the AIWA player.	27%
(*y*) buy the SONY player.	27%
(*z*) wait until you learn more about the various models.	46%

Low conflict:

Suppose you are considering buying a CD player, and have not yet decided what model to buy. You pass by a store that is having a 1-day clearance sale. They offer a popular SONY player for just $99, well below the list price. Do you?:

(*y*) buy the SONY player.	66%
(*z*) wait until you learn more about the various models.	34%

The results indicate that people are more likely to buy a CD player in the latter, *low-conflict*, condition than in the former, *high-conflict*, situation ($p < .05$). Both models – the AIWA and the SONY – seem attractive, both are well priced, and both are on sale. The decision maker needs to determine whether she is better off with a cheaper, popular model, or with a more expensive and sophisticated one. This conflict is apparently not easy to resolve, and compels many subjects to put off the purchase until they learn more about the various options. On the other hand, when the SONY alone is available, there are compelling arguments for its purchase: it is a popular player, it is very well priced, and it is on sale for 1 day only. In this situation, having good reasons to choose the offered option, a greater majority of subjects decide to opt for the CD player rather than delay the purchase.

The addition of a competing alternative in the preceding example increased the tendency to delay decision. Clearly, the level of conflict and its ease of resolution depend not only on the number of options available, but on how the options compare. Consider, for example, the following problem, in which the original AIWA player was replaced by an inferior model ($n = 62$).

Dominance:

Suppose you are considering buying a CD player, and have not yet decided what model to buy. You pass by a store that is having a 1-day clearance sale. They offer a popular SONY player for just $99, well below the list price, and an inferior AIWA player for the regular list price of $105. Do you?:

(*x'*)	buy the AIWA player.	3%
(*y*)	buy the SONY player.	73%
(*z*)	wait until you learn more about the various models.	24%

In this version, contrary to the previous *high-conflict* version, the AIWA player is dominated by the SONY: it is inferior in quality and costs more. Thus, the presence of the AIWA does not detract from the reasons for buying the SONY, it actually supplements them: the SONY is well priced, it is on sale for 1 day only, *and* it is clearly better than its competitor. As a result, the SONY is chosen more often than before the inferior AIWA was added. The ability of an asymmetrically dominated or relatively inferior alternative, when added to a set, to increase the attractiveness and choice probability of the dominating option is known as the asymmetric dominance effect (Huber, Payne, & Puto, 1982). Note that in both the *high-conflict* and the *dominance* problems subjects were presented with two CD players and an option to delay choice. Subjects' tendency to delay, however, is much greater when they lack clear reasons for buying either player, than when they have compelling reasons to buy one player and not the other ($p < .005$).

The above patterns violate the regularity condition, which is assumed to hold so long as the added alternatives do not provide new and relevant information. In the above scenario, one could argue that the added options (the superior player in one case and the inferior player in the other) conveyed information about the consumer's chances of finding a better deal. Recall that information considerations could not explain the search experiments of the previous section because there subjects reviewed all the potentially available options. Nevertheless, to test this interpretation further, Tversky and Shafir (1992b) devised a similar problem, involving real payoffs, in which the option to defer is not available. Students ($n = 80$) agreed to fill out a brief questionnaire for $1.50. Following the questionnaire, one half of the subjects were offered the opportunity to exchange the $1.50 (the default) for one of two prizes: a metal Zebra pen (henceforth, Zebra), or a pair of plastic Pilot pens (henceforth, Pilot). The other half of the subjects were only offered the opportunity to exchange the $1.50 for the Zebra. The prizes were shown to the subjects, who were also informed that each prize regularly costs a little over $2.00. Upon indicating their preference, subjects received their chosen option. The results were as follows. Seventy-five per cent of the subjects chose the Zebra over the payment when the Zebra was the only alternative, but only 47% chose the Zebra *or* the Pilot when both were available ($p < .05$). Faced with a tempting alternative, subjects had a compelling reason to forego the payment: the majority took advantage of the opportunity to obtain an attractive prize of greater value. The availability of competing alternatives of comparable value, on the other hand, did not present an immediate reason for choosing either alternative over the other, thus increasing the tendency to retain the default option. Similar effects in hypothetical medical decisions made by expert physicians are documented in Redelmeier and Shafir (1993).

In the above study the addition of a competing alternative was shown to increase the popularity of the default option. Recall that the popularity of an option may also be enhanced by the addition of an inferior alternative. Thus, in accord with the asymmetric dominance effect, the tendency to prefer *x* over *y* can be increased by adding a third alternative *z* that is clearly inferior to *x* but not to *y* (see Fig. 1). The phenomenon of asymmetric dominance was first demonstrated, by Huber, Payne, and Puto (1982), in choices between hypothetical options. Wedell (1991) reports similar findings using monetary gambles. The following example involving real choices is taken from Simonson and Tversky (1992). One group ($n = 106$) was offered a choice between $6 and an elegant Cross pen. The pen was selected by 36% of the subjects, and the remaining 64% chose the cash. A second group ($n = 115$) was given a choice among three options: $6 in cash, the same Cross pen, and a second pen that was distinctly less attractive. Only 2% of the subjects chose the less attractive pen, but its presence increased the percentage of subjects who chose the Cross pen from 36% to 46% ($p < .10$). This pattern again violates the regularity condition discussed earlier. Similar violations of regularity were observed in choices among other consumer goods. In one

Figure 1. *A schematic representation of asymmetric dominance. The tendency to prefer x over y can be increased by adding an alternative, z, that is clearly inferior to x but not to y.*

Figure 2. *A schematic representation of extremeness aversion. Option y is relatively more popular in the trinary choice, when both x and z are available, than in either one of the binary comparisons, when either x or z are removed.*

study, subjects received descriptions and pictures of microwave ovens taken from a "Best" catalogue. One group ($n = 60$) was then asked to choose between an Emerson priced at $110, and a Panasonic priced at $180. Both items were on sale, one third off the regular price. Here, 57% chose the Emerson and 43% chose the Panasonic. A second group ($n = 60$) was presented with these options along with a $200 Panasonic at a 10% discount. Only 13% of the subjects chose the more expensive Panasonic, but its presence increased the percentage of subjects who chose the less expensive Panasonic from 43% to 60% ($p < .05$).[1]

Simonson and Tversky (1992) have interpreted these observations in terms of "tradeoff contrast". They proposed that the tendency to prefer an alternative is enhanced or hindered depending on whether the tradeoffs within the set under consideration are favorable or unfavorable to that alternative. A second cluster of context effects, called *extremeness aversion*, which refers to the finding that, within an offered set, options with extreme values are relatively less attractive than options with intermediate values (Simonson, 1989). For example, consider two-dimensional options x, y, and z, such that y lies between x and z (see Fig. 2). Considerations of value maximization imply that the middle alternative, y, should be relatively less popular in the trinary choice than in either one of the binary comparisons (y compared to x, or y compared to z). Extremeness aversion, on the other hand, yields the opposite prediction because y has small advantages and disadvantages with respect to x and to z, whereas both x and z have more extreme advantages and disadvantages with respect to each other. This pattern was observed in several experiments. For example, subjects were shown five 35 mm cameras varying in quality and price. One group ($n = 106$) was then given a choice between two cameras: a Minolta X-370 priced at $170 and a Minolta 3000i priced at $240. A second group ($n = 115$) was given an additional option, the Minolta 7000i priced at $470. Subjects in the first group were split evenly between the two options, yet 57% of the subjects in the second group chose the middle option (Minolta 3000i), with the remaining divided about equally between the two extreme options. Thus, the introduction of an extreme option reduced the "market share" of the other extreme option, but not of the middle option. Note that this effect cannot be attributed to information conveyed by the offered set because respondents had reviewed the relevant options prior to making their choice.

We suggest that both tradeoff contrast and extremeness aversion can be understood in terms of reasons. Suppose a decision maker faces a choice between

---

[1]These effects of context on choice can naturally be used in sales tactics. For example, Williams-Sonoma, a mail-order business located in San Francisco, used to offer a bread-baking appliance priced at $279. They later added a second bread-baking appliance, similar to the first but somewhat larger, and priced at $429 – more than 50% higher than the original appliance. Not surprisingly, Williams-Sonoma did not sell many units of the new item. However, the sales of the less expensive appliance almost doubled. (To the best of our knowledge, Williams-Sonoma did not anticipate this effect.)

two alternatives, x and y, and suppose x is of higher quality whereas y is better priced. This produces conflict if the decision maker finds it difficult to determine whether the quality difference outweighs the price difference. Suppose now that the choice set also includes a third alternative, z, that is clearly inferior to y but not to x. The presence of z, we suggest, provides an argument for choosing y over x. To the extent that the initial choice between x and y is difficult, the presence of z may help the decision maker break the tie. In the pen study, for example, the addition of the relatively unattractive pen, whose monetary value is unclear but whose inferiority to the elegant Cross pen is apparent, provides a reason for choosing the Cross pen over the cash. Similarly, in the presence of options with extreme values on the relevant dimensions, the middle option can be seen as a compromise choice that is easier to defend than either extremes. Indeed, verbal protocols show that the accounts generated by subjects while making these choices involve considerations of asymmetric advantage and compromise; further-more, asymmetric dominance is enhanced when subjects anticipate having to justify their decisions to others (Simonson, 1989). It is noteworthy that the arguments leading to tradeoff contrast and extremeness aversion are comparative in nature; they are based on the positions of the options in the choice set, hence they cannot be readily translated into the values associated with single alter-natives.

Tversky and Simonson (in press) have proposed a formal model that explains the above findings in terms of a tournament-like process in which each option is compared against other available options in terms of their relative advantages and disadvantages. This model can be viewed as a formal analog of the preceding qualitative account based on reasons for choice. Which analysis – the formal or the qualitative – proves more useful is likely to depend, among other things, on the nature of the problem and on the purpose of the investigation.

5. Definite versus disjunctive reasons

People sometimes encounter situations of uncertainty in which they eventually opt for the same course of action, but for very different reasons, depending on how the uncertainty is resolved. Thus, a student who has taken an exam may decide to take a vacation, either to reward herself in case she passes or to console herself in case she fails. However, as illustrated below, the student may be reluctant to commit to a vacation while the outcome of the exam is pending. The following problem was presented by Tversky and Shafir (1992a) to 66 under-graduate students.

Disjunctive version:

Imagine that you have just taken a tough qualifying examination. It is the end of the fall quarter, you feel tired and run-down, and you are not sure that you passed the exam. In case you failed you have to take the exam again in a couple of months – after the Christmas holidays. You now have an opportunity to buy a very attractive 5-day Christmas vacation package in Hawaii at an exceptionally low price. The special offer expires tomorrow, while the exam grade will not be available until the following day. Would you?:

(a) buy the vacation package.	32%
(b) not buy the vacation package.	7%
(c) pay a $5 non-refundable fee in order to retain the rights to buy the vacation package at the same exceptional price the day after tomorrow – after you find out whether or not you passed the exam.	61%

The percentage of subjects who chose each option appears on the right. Two additional versions, called *pass* and *fail*, were presented to two different groups of 67 students each. These two versions differed only in the expression in brackets.

Pass/fail versions:

Imagine that you have just taken a tough qualifying examination. It is the end of the fall quarter, you feel tired and run-down, and you find out that you [passed the exam./failed the exam. You will have to take it again in a couple of months – after the Christmas holidays.] You now have an opportunity to buy a very attractive 5-day Christmas vacation package in Hawaii at an exceptionally low price. The special offer expires tomorrow. Would you?:

	Pass	*Fail*
(a) buy the vacation package.	54%	57%
(b) not buy the vacation package.	16%	12%
(c) pay a $5 non-refundable fee in order to retain the rights to buy the vacation package at the same exceptional price the day after tomorrow.	30%	31%

The data show that more than half of the students chose the vacation package when they knew that they passed the exam and an even larger percentage chose the vacation when they knew that they failed. However, when they did not know whether they had passed or failed, less than one third of the students chose the vacation and 61% were willing to pay $5 to postpone the decision until the following day, when the results of the exam would be known.[2] Once the outcome of the exam is known, the student has good – albeit different – reasons for taking the trip: having passed the exam, the vacation is presumably seen as a reward following a hard but successful semester; having failed the exam, the vacation becomes a consolation and time to recuperate before a re-examination. Not knowing the outcome of the exam, however, the student lacks a definite reason for going to Hawaii. Notice that the outcome of the exam will be known long before the vacation begins. Thus, the uncertainty characterizes the actual moment of decision, not the eventual vacation.

The indeterminacy of reasons for going to Hawaii discourages many students from buying the vacation, even when both outcomes – passing or failing the exam – ultimately favor this course of action. Tversky and Shafir (1992a) call the above pattern of decisions a *disjunction effect*. Evidently, a disjunction of different reasons (reward in case of success or consolation in case of failure) is often less compelling than either definite reason alone. A significant proportion of the students above were willing to pay, in effect, for information that was ultimately not going to affect their decision – they would choose to go to Hawaii in either case – but that promised to leave them with a more definite reason for making that choice. The willingness to pay for non-instrumental information is at variance with the classical model, in which the worth of information is determined only by its potential to influence decision.

People's preference for definite as opposed to disjunctive reasons has significant implications in cases where the option to defer decision is not available. Consider the following series of problems presented by Tversky and Shafir (1992a) to 98 students.

Win/lose version:

Imagine that you have just played a game of chance that gave you a 50% chance to win $200 and a 50% chance to lose $100. The coin was tossed and you have [won $200/lost $100]. You are now offered a second identical gamble: 50% chance to win $200 and 50% chance to lose $100. Would you?:

---

[2]An additional group of subjects ($n = 123$) were presented with both the fail and the pass versions, and asked whether or not they would buy the vacation package in each case. Two thirds of the subjects made the same choice in the two conditions, indicating that the data for the disjunctive version cannot be explained by the hypothesis that those who like the vacation in case they pass the exam do not like it in case they fail, and vice versa. Note that while only one third of the subjects made different decisions depending on the outcome of the exam, more than 60% of the subjects chose to wait when the outcome was not known.

	Won	*Lost*
(a) accept the second gamble.	69%	59%
(b) reject the second gamble.	31%	41%

The students were presented with the *win* version of the problem above, followed a week later by the *lose* version, and 10 days after that by the following version that is a disjunction of the previous two. The problems were embedded among other, similar problems so that the relation between the various versions was not transparent. Subjects were instructed to treat each decision separately.

Disjunctive version:

Imagine that you have just played a game of chance that gave you a 50% chance to win $200 and a 50% chance to lose $100. Imagine that the coin has already been tossed, but that you will not know whether you have won $200 or lost $100 until you make your decision concerning a second, identical gamble: 50% chance to win $200 and 50% chance to lose $100. Would you?:

(a) accept the second gamble.	36%
(b) reject the second gamble.	64%

The data show that a majority of subjects accepted the second gamble after having won the first gamble and a majority also accepted the second gamble after having lost the first gamble. However, the majority of subjects rejected the second gamble when the outcome of the first was not known. An examination of individual choices reveals that approximately 40% of the subjects accepted the second gamble both after a gain in the first and after a loss. Among these, however, 65% rejected the second gamble in the disjunctive condition, when the outcome of the first gamble was not known. Indeed, this response pattern (accepting in both conditions but rejecting in the disjunction) was the single most frequent pattern, exhibited by 27% of all subjects. This pattern, which violates Savage's (1954) sure-thing principle, cannot be attributed to unreliability (Tversky & Shafir, 1992a).

The students above were offered a gamble with a positive expected value, and an even chance of a non-trivial loss. Different reasons were likely to arise for accepting the second gamble depending on the outcome of the first. In the *win* condition, the decision maker is already up $200, so even a loss on the second gamble leaves him or her ahead overall, which makes this option quite attractive. In the *lose* condition, on the other hand, the decision maker is down $100. Playing the second gamble offers a chance to "get out of the red", which for many is more attractive than accepting a sure $100 loss. In the *disjunctive* condition, however, the decision maker does not know whether she is up $200 or down $100;

she does not know, in other words, whether her reason for playing the second gamble is that it is a no-loss proposition or, instead, that it provides a chance to escape a sure loss. In the absence of a definite reason, fewer subjects accept the second gamble.

This interpretation is further supported by the following modification of the above problem, in which both outcomes of the first gamble were increased by $400 so that the decision maker could not lose in either case.

> Imagine that you have just played a game of chance that gave you a 50% chance to win $600 and a 50% chance to win $300. Imagine that the coin has already been tossed, but that you will not know whether you have won $600 or $300 until you make your decision concerning a second gamble: 50% chance to win $200 and 50% chance to lose $100.

A total of 171 subjects were presented with this problem, equally divided into three groups. One group was told that they had won $300 on the first gamble, a second group was told that they had won $600 on the first gamble, and the third group was told that the outcome of the first gamble – $300 or $600 – was not known (the disjunctive version). In all cases, subjects had to decide whether to accept or to reject the second gamble which, as in the previous problem, consisted of an even chance to win $200 or lose $100. The percentage of subjects who accepted the second gamble in the $300, $600, and disjunctive versions, were 69%, 75%, and 73%, respectively. (Recall that the corresponding figures for the original problem were 59%, 69%, and 36%; essentially identical figures were obtained in a between-subjects replication of that problem.) In contrast to the original problem, the second gamble in this modified problem was equally popular in the disjunctive as in the non-disjunctive versions. Whereas in the original scenario the second gamble amounted to either a no-loss proposition or a chance to avoid a sure loss, in the modified scenario the second gamble amounts to a no-loss proposition regardless of the outcome of the first gamble. The increased popularity of the second gamble in the modified problem shows that it is not the disjunctive situation itself that discourages people from playing. Rather, it is the lack of a specific reason that seems to drive the effect: when the same reason applies regardless of outcome, the disjunction no longer reduces the tendency to accept the gamble.

As illustrated above, changes in the context of decision are likely to alter the reasons that subjects bring to mind and, consequently, their choices. Elsewhere (Shafir & Tversky, 1992) we describe a disjunction effect in the context of a one-shot prisoner's dilemma game, played on a computer for real payoffs. Subjects ($n = 80$) played a series of prisoner's dilemma games, without feedback, each against a different unknown player. In this setup, the rate of cooperation was 3% when subjects knew that the other player had defected, and 16% when they knew that the other had cooperated. However, when subjects did not know whether the other player had cooperated or defected (the standard version of the prisoner's dilemma game) the rate of cooperation rose to 37%. Thus, many subjects defected when they knew the other's choice – be it cooperation or defection – but cooperated when the other player's choice was not known. Shafir and Tversky (1992) attribute this pattern to the different perspectives that underlie subjects' behavior under uncertainty as opposed to when the uncertainty is resolved. In particular, we suggest that the reasons for competing are more compelling when the other player's decision is known and the payoff depends on the subject alone, than when the other's chosen strategy is uncertain, and the outcome of the game depends on the choices of both players.

The above "disjunctive" manipulation – which has no direct bearing from the point of view of value maximization – appears to influence the reasons for decision that people bring to mind. Another kind of manipulation that seems to alter people's reasons without bearing directly on options' values is described in what follows.

6. Non-valued features

Reasons for choice or rejection often refer to specific features of the options under consideration. The positive features of an option typically provide reasons for choosing that option and its negative features typically provide reasons for rejection. What happens when we add features that are neither attractive nor aversive? Can choice be influenced by features that have little or no value?

Simonson and his colleagues have conducted a number of studies on the effects of non-valued features, and tested the hypothesis that people are reluctant to choose alternatives that are supported by reasons that they do not find appealing. In one study, for example, Simonson, Nowlis, and Simonson (in press) predicted that people would be less likely to choose an alternative that was chosen by another person for a reason that does not apply to them. UC Berkeley business students ($n = 113$) were told that, because of budget cuts and in order to save paper and duplicating costs, a questionnaire that they will receive was designed for use by two respondents. Thus, when subjects had to enter a choice, they could see the choice made by the previous "respondent" and the reason given for it. The choices and reasons of the previous respondents were systematically manipulated. One problem, for example, offered a choice between attending the MBA programs at Northwestern and UCLA. In one version of the questionnaire, the previous respondent had selected Northwestern, and provided the (handwritten) reason, "I have many relatives in the Chicago area." Because this reason does not apply to most subjects, it was expected to reduce their likelihood of choosing Northwestern. In a second version, no reason was given for the choice of Northwestern. As expected, those exposed to an irrelevant reason were less likely to choose Northwestern than subjects who saw the other respondent's choice but not his or her reason (23% vs. 43%, $p < .05$). It should be noted that both Northwestern and UCLA are well known to most subjects (Northwestern currently has the highest ranked MBA program; the UCLA program is ranked high and belongs to the same UC system as Berkeley). Thus, it is unlikely that subjects made inferences about the quality of Northwestern based on the fact that another respondent chose it because he or she had relatives in Chicago.

In a related study, Simonson, Carmon, and O'Curry (in press) showed that endowing an option with a feature that was intended to be positive but, in fact, has no value for the decision maker can reduce the tendency to choose that option, even when subjects realize that they are not paying for the added feature. For example, an offer to purchase a collector's plate – that most did not want – if one buys a particular brand of cake mix was shown to lower the tendency to buy that particular brand relative to a second, comparable cake mix brand (from 31% to 14%, $p < .05$). Choosing brands that offer worthless bonuses was judged (in a related study) as more difficult to justify and as more susceptible to criticism. An analysis of verbal protocols showed that a majority of those who failed to select the endowed option explicitly mentioned not needing the added feature. It should be noted that sale promotions, such as the one involving the collector's plate offer above, are currently employed by a wide range of companies and there is no evidence that they lead to any inferences about the quality of the promoted product (e.g., Blattberg & Neslin, 1990).

The above manipulations all added "positive", albeit weak or irrelevant, features, which should not diminish an option's value; yet, they apparently provide a reason against choosing the option, especially when other options are otherwise equally attractive. Evidently, the addition of a potentially attractive feature that proves useless can provide a reason to reject the option in favor of a competing alternative that has no "wasted" features.

7. Concluding remarks

People's choices may occasionally stem from affective judgments that preclude a thorough evaluation of the options (cf. Zajonc, 1980). In such cases, an analysis of the reasons for choice may prove unwarranted and, when attempted by the decision maker, may actually result in a different, and possibly inferior, decision (Wilson & Schooler, 1991). Other choices, furthermore, may follow standard operating procedures that involve minimal reflective effort. Many decisions, nonetheless, result from a careful evaluation of options, in which people attempt to arrive at what they believe is the best choice. Having discarded the less attractive options and faced with a choice that is hard to resolve, people often search for a compelling rationale for choosing one alternative over another. In this paper, we presented an analysis of the role of reasons in decision making, and considered ways in which an analysis based on reasons may contribute to the standard quantitative approach based on the maximization of value. A number of hypotheses that derive from this perspective were investigated in experimental settings.

The reasons that enter into the making of decisions are likely to be intricate and diverse. In the preceding sections we have attempted to identify a few general principles that govern the role of reasons in decision making, and thus some of the fundamental ways in which thinking about reasons is likely to contribute to our understanding of the making of decisions. A reliance on the more important dimensions – those likely to provide more compelling reasons for choice – was shown in section 1 to predict preferences between previously equated options. The notions of compatibility and salience were summoned in section 2 to account for the differential weighting of reasons in a choice versus rejection task. Reasons, it appears, lend themselves to certain framing manipulations that are harder to explain from the perspective of value maximization. In section 3, manipulating the precise relationships between competing alternatives was shown to enhance or reduce conflict, yielding decisions that were easier or more difficult to rationalize and justify. Providing a context that presents compelling reasons for choosing an option apparently increases people's tendency to opt for that option, whereas comparing alternatives that render the aforementioned reasons less compelling tends to increase people's tendency to maintain the status quo or search for other alternatives. The ability of the context of decision to generate reasons that affect choice was further discussed in section 4, where the addition and removal of competing alternatives was interpreted as generating arguments for choice based on comparative considerations of relative advantages and compromise. The relative weakness of disjunctive reasons was discussed in section 5. There, a number of studies contrasted people's willingness to reach a decision based on a definite reason for choice, with their reluctance to arrive at a decision in the presence of uncertainty about which reason is actually relevant to the case at hand. Section 6 briefly reviewed choice situations in which the addition of purported reasons for choosing an option, which subjects did not find compelling, was seen to diminish their tendency to opt for that option, even though its value had not diminished.

The nature of the reasons that guide decision, and the ways in which they interact, await further investigation. There is evidence to suggest that a wide variety of arguments play a role in decision making. We often search for a convincing rationale for the decisions that we make, whether for inter-personal purposes, so that we can explain to others the reasons for our decision, or for intra-personal motives, so that we may feel confident of having made the "right" choice. Attitudes toward risk and loss can sometimes be rationalized on the basis of common myths or clichés, and choices are sometimes made on the basis of moral or prudential principles that are used to override specific cost–benefit calculations (cf. Prelec & Herrnstein, 1991). Formal decision rules, moreover, may sometimes act as arguments in people's deliberations. Thus, when choosing between options x and z, we may realize that, sometime earlier, we had preferred x over y and y over z and that, therefore, by transitivity, we should now choose x over z. Montgomery (1983) has argued that people look for dominance structures in decision problems because they provide a compelling reason for choice. Similarly, Tversky and Shafir (1992a) have shown that detecting the applicability of the sure-thing principle to a decision situation leads people to act in accord with this principle's compelling rationale. Indeed, it has been repeatedly observed that the axioms of rational choice which are often violated in non-transparent situations are generally satisfied when their application is transparent (e.g., Tversky & Kahneman, 1986). These results suggest that the axioms of rational choice act as compelling arguments, or reasons, for making a particular decision when their applicability has been detected, not as universal laws that constrain people's choices.

In contrast to the classical theory that assumes stable values and preferences, it appears that people often do not have well-established values, and that preferences are actually constructed – not merely revealed – during their elicitation (cf. Payne, Bettman, & Johnson, 1992). A reason-based approach lends itself well to such a constructive interpretation. Decisions, according to this analysis, are often reached by focusing on reasons that justify the selection of one option over another. Different frames, contexts, and elicitation procedures highlight different aspects of the options and bring forth different reasons and considerations that influence decision.

The reliance on reasons to explain experimental findings has been the hallmark of social psychological analyses. Accounts of dissonance (Wicklund & Brehm, 1976) and self-perception (Bem, 1972), for example, focus on the reasons that people muster in an attempt to explain their counter-attitudinal behaviors. Similarly, attribution theory (Heider, 1980) centers around the reasons that people attribute to others' behavior. These studies, however, have primarily focused on postdecisional rationalization rather than predecisional conflict. Although the two processes are closely related, there are nevertheless some important differences. Much of the work in social psychology has investigated how people's decisions affect the way they think. The present paper, in contrast, has considered how the reasons that enter into people's thinking about a problem influence their decision. A number of researchers have recently begun to explore related issues. Billig (1987), for example, has adopted a rhetorical approach to understanding social psychological issues, according to which "our inner deliberations are silent arguments conducted within a single self" (p. 5). Related "explanation-based" models of decision making have been applied by Pennington and Hastie (1988, 1992) to account for judicial decisions, and the importance of social accountability in choice has been addressed by Tetlock (1992). From a philosophical perspective, a recent essay by Schick (1991) analyzes various decisions from the point of view of practical reason. An influential earlier work is Toulmin's (1950) study of the role of arguments in ethical reasoning.

In this article, we have attempted to explore some of the ways in which reasons and arguments enter into people's decisions. A reason-based analysis may come closer to capturing part of the psychology that underlies decision and thus may help shed light on a number of phenomena that remain counterintuitive from the perspective of the classical theory. It is instructive to note that many of the experimental studies described in this paper were motivated by intuitions stemming from a qualitative analysis based on reasons, not from a value-based perspective, even if they can later be interpreted in that fashion. We do not propose that accounts based on reasons replace value-based models of choice. Rather, we suggest that an analysis of reasons may illuminate some aspects of reflective choice, and generate new hypotheses for further study.

References

Allison, G.T. (1971). *Essence of decision: explaining the Cuban missile crisis*. Boston: Little Brown.

Bem, D.J. (1972). Self-perception theory. In L. Berkowitz (Ed.), *Advances in experimental social psychology* (Vol. 6). New York: Academic Press.

Berman, L. (1982). *Planning a tragedy*. New York: Norton.

Betts, R., & Gelb, L. (1979). *The irony of Vietnam: the system worked*. Washington, DC: Brookings Institution.

Bigelow, J. (Ed.) (1887). *The complete works of Benjamin Franklin* (Vol. 4). New York: Putnam.

Billig, M. (1987). *Arguing and thinking: a rhetorical approach to social psychology*. New York: Cambridge University Press.

Blattberg, R.C., & Neslin, S.A. (1990). *Sales promotion: concepts, methods, and strategies*. Englewood Cliffs, NJ: Prentice-Hall.

Heider, F. (1980). *The psychology of interpersonal relations*. New York: Wiley.

Huber, J., Payne, J.W., and Puto, C. (1982). Adding asymmetrically dominated alternatives: violations of regularity and the similarity hypothesis. *Journal of Consumer Research, 9*, 90–98.

James, W. (1981). *The principles of psychology* (Vol. 2). Cambridge, MA: Harvard University Press.

Kahneman, D., & Tversky, A. (1979). Prospect theory: an analysis of decision under risk. *Econometrica, 47*, 263–291.

Montgomery, H. (1983). Decision rules and the search for a dominance structure: towards a process model of decision making. In P. Humphreys, O. Svenson, & A. Vari (Eds.), *Analyzing and aiding decision processes*. Amsterdam: North-Holland.

Nisbett, R.E., & Wilson, T.D. (1977). Telling more than we can know: verbal reports on mental processes. *Psychological Review, 84*, 231–259.

Payne, J.W., Bettman, J.R., & Johnson, E.J. (1992). Behavioral decision research: a constructive process perspective. *Annual Review of Psychology, 43*, 87–131.

Pennington, N., & Hastie, R. (1988). Explanation-based decision making: effects of memory structure on judgment. *Journal of Experimental Psychology: Learning, Memory, and Cognition, 14*, 521–533.

Pennington, N., & Hastie, R. (1992). Explaining the evidence: tests of the story model for juror decision making. *Journal of Personality and Social Psychology, 62*, 189–206.

Prelec, D., & Herrnstein, R.J. (1991). Preferences or principles: alternative guidelines for choice. In R.J. Zeckhauser (Ed.), *Strategy and choice*. Cambridge, MA: MIT Press.

Redelmeier, D., & Shafir, E. (1993). Medical decisions over multiple alternatives. Working paper, University of Toronto.

Savage, L.J. (1954). *The foundations of statistics*. New York: Wiley.

Schick, F. (1991). *Understanding action: an essay on reasons*. New York: Cambridge University Press.

Shafer, G. (1986). Savage revisited. *Statistical Science*, *1*, 463–485.

Shafir, E. (1993). Choosing versus rejecting: why some options are both better and worse than others. *Memory & Cognition*, *21*, 546–556.

Shafir, E., & Tversky, A. (1992). Thinking through uncertainty: nonconsequential reasoning and choice. *Cognitive Psychology*, *24*, 449–474.

Simonson, I. (1989). Choice based on reasons: the case of attraction and compromise effects. *Journal of Consumer Research*, *16*, 158–174.

Simonson, I., Carmon, Z., & O'Curry, S. (in press). Experimental evidence on the negative effect of unique product features and sales promotions on brand choice. *Marketing Science*.

Simonson, I., Nowlis, S., & Simonson, Y. (in press). The effect of irrelevant preference arguments on consumer choice. *Journal of Consumer Psychology*.

Simonson, I., & Tversky, A. (1992). Choice in context: tradeoff contrast and extremeness aversion. *Journal of Marketing Research*, *29*, 281–295.

Slovic, P. (1975). Choice between equally valued alternatives. *Journal of Experimental Psychology: Human Perception and Performance*, *1*, 280–287.

Slovic, P. (1990). Choice. In D. Osherson & E. Smith (Eds.), *An invitation to cognitive science* (Vol. 3). Cambridge, MA: MIT Press.

Telhami, S. (1990). *Power and leadership in international bargaining: the path to the Camp David accords*. New York: Columbia University Press.

Tetlock, P.E. (1992). The impact of accountability on judgment and choice: toward a social contingency model. In M.P. Zanna (Ed.), *Advances in experimental social psychology* (Vol. 25). New York: Academic Press.

Toulmin, S. (1950). *The place of reason in ethics*. New York: Cambridge University Press.

Tversky, A., & Kahneman, D. (1986). Rational choice and the framing of decisions. *Journal of Business*, *59*, 251–278.

Tversky, A., Sattath, S., & Slovic, P. (1988). Contingent weighting in judgment and choice. *Psychological Review*, *95*, 371–384.

Tversky, A., & Shafir, E. (1992a). The disjunction effect in choice under uncertainty. *Psychological Science*, *3*, 305–309.

Tversky, A., & Shafir, E. (1992b). Choice under conflict: the dynamics of deferred decision. *Psychological Science*, *3*, 358–361.

Tversky, A., & Simonson, I. (in press). Context-dependent preferences. *Management Science*.

von Neumann, J., & Morgenstern, O. (1947). *Theory of games and economic behavior*. Princeton, NJ: Princeton University Press.

Wedell, D.H. (1991). Distinguishing among models of contextually induced preference reversals. *Journal of Experimental Psychology: Learning, Memory, and Cognition*, *17*, 767–778.

Wicklund, R.A., & Brehm, J.W. (1976). *Perspectives on cognitive dissonance*. Hillsdale, NJ: Erlbaum.

Wilson, T.D., & Schooler, J.W. (1991). Thinking too much: introspection can reduce the quality of preferences and decisions. *Journal of Personality and Social Psychology*, *60*, 181–192.

Zajonc, B. (1980). Preferences without inferences. *American Psychologist*, *35*, 151–175.

3 Focussing in reasoning and decision making

P. Legrenzi, and V. Girotto
Dipartimento di Psicologia, Università degli Studi di Trieste

P.N. Johnson-Laird
Department of Psychology, Princeton University

Abstract

Our principal hypothesis is that reasoning and decision making are alike in that they both depend on the construction of mental models, and so they should both give rise to similar phenomena. In this paper, we consider one such phenomenon, which we refer to as "focussing": individuals are likely to restrict their thoughts to what is explicitly represented in their models. We show that focussing occurs in four domains. First, individuals fail to draw inferences in the modus tollens form: if p then q, not-q, therefore not-p, because they focus on their initial models of the conditional, which make explicit only the case where the antecedent (p) and consequent (q) occur. Second, in Wason's selection task, they similarly tend to select only those cards that are explicitly represented in their initial models of the conditional rule. Third, their requests for information in order to enable them to make a decision about whether or not to carry out a certain action are focussed on the action to the exclusion of alternatives to it. In each of these cases, we show how the focussing bias can be reduced by certain experimental manipulations. Finally, in counterfactual reasoning, focussing underlies individuals' attempts to imagine an alternative scenario that avoids an unfortunate ending to a story.

Introduction

The classical theory of decision making, whatever its status as a specification of rationality, does not begin to explain the mental processes underlying decisions (e.g., Slovic, 1990). On the one hand, the theory is radically incomplete: it has nothing to say about when one should decide to make a decision, or how one should determine the range of options, or how one should assess the utilities of various outcomes. On the other hand, the theory conflicts with the evidence on

Preparation of this paper was supported by a grant from CNR.

how people reach decisions in daily life: their conspicuous failure to maximize expected utility has led some theorists to worry about human rationality (cf. Lindley, 1985) and others, notably Simon (1959), to argue for a different criterion for human decisions.

An obvious feature of many decisions in daily life is their dependence on reasoning. Consider, for example, buying a new car. The first decision, of course, is to decide that one needs a new car. It is then necessary to determine the range of relevant options, both by trying to specify what one wants and by assessing which cars approximate to these desiderata. Finally, a decision amongst the options must be made. The process is complex, and this summary does not do justice to the adventitious and opportunistic factors that come into play – a particular feature of a car, for example, may not seem desirable until it has been demonstrated to the prospective purchaser. Different cars may have different but conflicting advantages, and it is no easy matter to map them onto a single dimension of utility. A number of component skills, however, can be discerned beneath the variety of approaches that individuals bring to the task of decision making. The key components are as follows:

- Seeking information
- Making hypotheses
- Making inferences
- Weighing advantages and disadvantages
- Applying criteria to make a decision

Hence, at a still deeper level of analysis, various sorts of inferential abilities come into play.

If individuals reason in order to make decisions, then phenomena that occur in reasoning should occur in making judgements and decisions. Logicians distinguish between deductive and inductive reasoning. Human reasoners, however, are seldom interested in deductive validity for its own sake. They aim for conclusions that are true and useful; they often lack sufficient information to reach a valid conclusion, and so are forced to go beyond the information given and to make an induction. In our view, however, the mental machinery underlying both deduction and induction is remarkably similar, and depends not on formal rules of inference but on the construction of mental models (Johnson-Laird, 1993). If so, then the predictions of the model theory should also apply to making decisions. Our aim in this paper is to explore one consequence of this idea – a phenomenon that we refer to as the "focussing effect", which is an inevitable consequence of the use of models in reasoning.

When individuals construct models, they make explicit as little information as possible in order to minimize the load on working memory. They construct as few explicit models as possible, and they inevitably focus on that information which is explicit in their models and concomitantly fail to consider other alternatives. Theories based on formal rules cannot make this prediction because they have no machinery for formulating the equivalent of a conclusion based on an initial model of the premises: such conclusions are often invalid, and so they cannot be derived from rules that lead only to valid conclusions. In contrast, the model theory implies that people are inferential *satisficers*: if they come up with a conclusion that fits the available facts, they will tend not to examine other possibilities, with the potentially disastrous consequence of overlooking the correct conclusion. Many of the cognitive errors that have led to real-life disasters have exactly this form. For example, the operators at Three Mile Island explained the high temperature of a relief valve in terms of a leak, and overlooked the possibility that it was stuck open; the master of the English Channel ferry, *The Herald of Free Enterprise*, inferred that the bow doors had been closed, and overlooked the possibility that they had been left open; the engineers at Chernobyl found an erroneous explanation for the initial explosion and over-looked the possibility that the reactor had been destroyed.

The paper begins with an outline of theories of reasoning based on formal rules, and it follows with an account of the contrasting model theory. It then examines focussing in four domains. The first is deduction in the form known as modus tollens, e.g.:

If the plane is on course, then the radar should show only water
The radar is showing a land mass
Therefore, the plane is not on course

Inferences of this form can be difficult, and indeed the failure to draw this particular conclusion may have contributed to the disaster that befell the ill-fated Flight 007 of Korean Airlines. The cockpit recording shows that crew established the two premises, but instead of drawing the conclusion they changed the topic of conversation (see Overton, 1990). We argue that the difficulty of modus tollens is caused in part by focussing, and we report a new experimental study that shows how a simple manipulation helps subjects to defocus. The second domain is a well-known problem in deductive reasoning, Wason's selection task, and we show how focussing leads to errors in its performance. The third domain is decision making. We introduce a new procedure for studying how individuals make decisions. Subjects have to make a simple riskless decision, and their task is to request information, which is provided by the experimenter, until they are able to make the decision. The sequence of questions that they ask reveals the degree of focussing. We report an experiment using this procedure, which shows that the context of decision can play a crucial role in reducing the focussing effect. The fourth domain is counterfactual reasoning, and we report a study that demonstrates the potency of focussing in the construction of counterfactual scenarios.

What is common to all these cases is the strong tendency for individuals to focus on those entities that are explicitly represented in their models (in contravention to the rational requirements of reasoning and decision making), and our attempts to promote the conditions in which alternative possibilities can be made more salient so that focussing disappears or weakens.

FORMAL RULE THEORIES OF REASONING

When people reason deductively, they start with some information – either evidence of the senses or a verbal description – and they assess whether a given conclusion follows validly from this information. In real life there is often no given conclusion, and so they generate a conclusion for themselves. Logic alone is insufficient to characterize intelligent reasoning in this case, because any set of premises yields an infinite number of valid conclusions. Most of them are banal, such as the conjunction of a premise with itself, and no sane individual, apart from a logician, would dream of drawing such a conclusion. Hence, human reasoners are guided by more than logic. The evidence suggests that they tend to maintain the information conveyed by the premises, to re-express it more parsimoniously, and to establish something not directly asserted in a premise. If nothing meets these constraints, they declare that there is no valid conclusion.

Most cognitive scientists assume that deductive reasoning depends on mental rules of inference that are akin to those of the formal method of "natural deduction" (e.g., Braine, 1978; Braine & O'Brien, 1991; Macnamara, 1986; Osherson, 1974–6; Pollock, 1989; Reiter, 1973; Rips, 1983; Sperber & Wilson, 1986). Each connective, such as *if*, *and*, and *or*, has its own formal rules of inference. Deduction accordingly consists in recovering the logical form of premises, and then using the formal rules to try to find a derivation of the conclusion from the premises. If no derivation of the conclusion can be found, then reasoners will respond that the inference is invalid.

For example, given the premises:

If there is a circle then there is a triangle
There is a circle

the valid conclusion:

Therefore, there is a triangle

is easy to deduce, because the mind is equipped with an inferential rule corresponding to modus ponens:

If p then q

p

Therefore, q

In contrast, the following premises:

If there is a circle then there is a triangle
There isn't a triangle

often fail to elicit the valid deduction:

Therefore, there isn't a circle

Many intelligent individuals say that nothing follows in this case. The difficulty arises, according to rule theories, because the mind is not equipped with a rule corresponding to this modus tollens inference, and so reasoners must engage in a chain of deductions to arrive at the conclusion. In general, formal rule theories predict that the difficulty of a deduction depends on two factors: the length of the formal derivation, and the unavailability (or difficulty of use) of the relevant rules. Theories differ in their detailed accounts of the difficulty of modus tollens: it introduces negation or an inconsistency, it depends on a reductio ad absurdum, or it depends on some other chain of deductions. There is a consensus, however, on the absence of modus tollens from the mental repertoire of inferential rules (cf. Braine & O'Brien, 1991; Rips, 1983).

THE MENTAL MODEL THEORY OF REASONING

The theory of mental models presents a different view of reasoning (Johnson-Laird, 1983; Johnson-Laird & Byrne, 1991). The mind does not contain any formal rules of inference akin to a system of "natural deduction". Instead, people reason from their understanding of a situation, and so their starting point is a set of mental models – often, a single model – constructed from perceiving the world or from comprehending discourse. They formulate a conclusion based on the set of models. And they evaluate the conclusion by searching for alternative models that might refute it. We will outline the theory in terms of these stages, and then illustrate them in terms of the modus ponens and modus tollens inferences that we described earlier.

The first stage corresponds, we assume, to the normal processes of perception and comprehension based on the evidence of the senses, discourse, or imagination, and on any relevant general knowledge. The resulting mental models have a structure corresponding, not to the linguistic structure of discourse or to the syntax of a mental language, but to the structure of the states of affairs, whether perceived, or conceived, that the models represent. A model may be experienced as an image: images are the perceptual correlates of models from a particular point of view. However, many models contain elements, such as negation, that cannot be visualized (see Johnson-Laird & Byrne, 1991, p. 130). What matters is not the subjective experience of the model, which may lie outside conscious awareness, but the structure of the model: sets of entities are represented by sets of mental tokens, the properties of entities are represented by properties of the tokens, and the relations between entities are represented by the relations between the tokens. A model makes *explicit* those objects, properties, and relations that are relevant to potential actions; that is, it makes them available to inference and decision making without the need for further processing. Models, however, make as little as possible explicit because of the limited capacity of working memory. Since their structure corresponds to the structure of situations, models differ from other proposed forms of mental representation, such as semantic networks (e.g., Quillian, 1968) or the propositional representations used for formal rules (e.g., Kintsch, 1974; Braine, 1978). The difference will become clear later when we consider connectives and quantifiers.

The second stage is to formulate a putative conclusion. We assume that it corresponds to the normal process of verbal description. Because conclusions are based on models of the given information, they will not throw semantic information away by adding disjunctive alternatives. The main task is thus to draw a parsimonious conclusion which, if possible, expresses a relation that is not explicit in the premises. If there is no such conclusion, then people say that there is no valid conclusion. Formal theories have neglected the formulation of conclusions, and, like many automated systems of theorem proving, have often assumed that a conclusion is given for evaluation (e.g., Rips, 1983). The model theory, however, has led to a novel algorithm for generating parsimonious conclusions (see Johnson-Laird & Byrne, 1991, p. 183).

The third and critical stage for inference is to evaluate the putative conclusion. The theory assumes that it depends on checking whether alternative models of the situation falsify the conclusion. With simple deductions, human reasoners may be able to anticipate the alternative models, but with complex deductions they can seldom do so, and so they must search for alternative models. Unfortunately, they are not equipped with a comprehensive and systematic search procedure. If there is no alternative model falsifying the conclusion, then it is deductively valid; that is, it must be true given that the premises are true. If there is such a model, then the conclusion is invalid. Prudent reasoners should return to the second stage and try to formulate a new conclusion that satisfies all the models which they have so far constructed. And if they succeed, they should search for further counter-examples, and so on, until they exhaust all possible models (or themselves). If it is uncertain whether there is an alternative model that falsifies a conclusion, then the conclusion can be drawn on a tentative or probabilistic basis (e.g., Johnson-Laird, 1983; Kahneman & Tversky, 1982). The distinction between deduction and induction is accordingly located primarily in the comprehension and search stages: inductions go beyond the given information because they introduce additional information into models, whereas valid deductions do not; deductions depend on exhaustive searches, whereas inductions do not.

To illustrate how the model theory works, we will reconsider the modus ponens and modus tollens deductions. An initial understanding of a conditional, such as:

If there is a circle then there is a triangle

yields two alternative models. One is an explicit model of the possible state of affairs in which the antecedent holds, and the other is an implicit model in which the antecedent does not hold:

$$\bigcirc \qquad \triangle$$
$$. \quad . \quad .$$

The implicit model, which is denoted by the three dots, is a place-holder that has no initial content and thus minimizes the load on working memory. If necessary, this model may be fleshed out later with an explicit content, but conditional inferences in daily life can often be made from this initial set of models (see Johnson-Laird, Byrne, & Schaeken, 1992). They are consistent with either a one-way conditional, which allows that there may be a triangle without a square, or with a bi-conditional, which makes no such allowance, that is, "if, and only if, there is a circle then there is a triangle". The one-way conditional is made more explicit in the following models:

$$[\bigcirc] \qquad \triangle$$
$$. \quad . \quad .$$

where the square brackets indicate that an element is exhaustively represented; that is, it cannot occur in any model created by fleshing out the implicit model. The consequent is not exhausted, and so it can occur in other models. (Strictly speaking, exhaustion is a relative notion, but we will ignore this qualification here.) The biconditional interpretation calls for both antecedent and consequent to be exhausted:

$$[\bigcirc] \qquad [\triangle]$$
$$. \quad . \quad .$$

and in this case reasoners may be more likely to flesh out the implicit model initially (see below). The premise for modus ponens:

    There is a circle

eliminates the implicit model from any of these sets, and so the conclusion is immediately forthcoming from the remaining explicit model:

    There is a triangle

    In contrast, the modus tollens premise:

    There is not a triangle

eliminates the explicit model to leave only the implicit model, from which – as many subjects say (e.g., Evans, 1982) – nothing seems to follow. The deduction can be made only by fleshing out the models of the one-way conditional, for example:

$$\begin{array}{cc} \bigcirc & \triangle \\ \neg\bigcirc & \triangle \\ \neg\bigcirc & \neg\triangle \end{array}$$

or the bi-conditional:

$$\begin{array}{cc} \bigcirc & \triangle \\ \neg\bigcirc & \neg\triangle \end{array}$$

where "$\neg$" represents negation. The premise, "There is not a triangle", eliminates any model containing a triangle to leave only the model:

$$\begin{array}{cc} \neg\bigcirc & \neg\triangle \end{array}$$

This model yields the conclusion:

    There is not a circle

which is valid because no model of the premises falsifies it.

    The evidence for the model theory of deduction has been presented elsewhere (e.g., Johnson-Laird & Byrne, 1991; Johnson-Laird et al., 1992), and so here we will only summarize it. It shows that the *content* of premises with the same logical form can have a decisive effect on what conclusions people draw. The late Jean Piaget discovered this effect, and introduced a clause in small print – the "horizontal décalage", essentially a redescription of the phenomenon – to try to sweep it away (e.g., Inhelder & Piaget, 1958). Yet the phenomenon is inimical to formal theories of inference. The evidence also shows that when people reason they are concerned about meaning and truth. They are influenced by what they believe to be true, which affects both the conclusions that they formulate for themselves and their evaluation of given conclusions. When they draw their own conclusions, they maintain the semantic information from the premises, and treat as improper any conclusions that throw it away by adding disjunctive alternatives. We have carried out experiments on all the main domains of deduction, including inferences based on propositional connectives such as *if* and *or*, inferences based on relations such as *on the right of*, and *in the same place as*, inferences based on quantifiers such as *none*, *any*, and *only*, and meta-logical inferences based on assertions about what is true and what is false. Where the model and rule theories make opposite predictions, the results confirm the model theory and run counter to the formal rule theory. Without exception, all the experiments corroborate the main predictions of the model theory: easy deductions call for one explicit model only; difficult deductions call for more than one explicit model; and erroneous conclusions are usually the result of constructing only one of the possible models of the premises. In the remainder of this paper, we will examine some consequences of focussing on the explicit elements in models.

AN EXPERIMENT ON FOCUSSING IN DEDUCTIVE REASONING

Modus ponens can be drawn with a focus on the initial models of the conditional premise; modus tollens calls for the fleshing out of alternative models. Hence, performance of modus tollens should be improved by any manipulation that forces reasoners to cease focussing on the initial models and to make explicit the models where the consequent is false. A recent experiment carried out in collaboration with our colleagues has examined this prediction when subjects have to draw their own conclusions from modus ponens and modus tollens premises (see Girotto, Mazzocco, & Tasso, 1992).

The experimental manipulation was simple. The premises of the inferences were presented either in their traditional order of the conditional premise followed by the categorical premise, or else in an inverted order with the categorical premise followed by the conditional premise. When a conditional premise, such as "If there is a circle at the top of the card then there is a triangle at the bottom of the card", is presented in the traditional order of modus tollens, then the interpretation of the categorical premise, "There is a square at the bottom of the card", has to occur while working memory is already pre-occupied with the models of the conditional. Hence, it is difficult for reasoners to flesh out their models of the conditional, and they are likely merely to eliminate the explicit model of the conditional and to replace the implicit model with one representing the categorical premise ("There is a square at the bottom of the card"). It then seems that no conclusion follows.

In contrast, when the categorical premise, "There is a square at the bottom of the card", occurs first for modus tollens, the subjects represent this contingency right from the start. When they then begin to interpret the conditional, "If there is a circle at the top of a card then there is a triangle at the bottom of the card", they can immediately discard the model in which the antecedent and the consequent hold, and thereby free up the processing capacity of working memory. It is now easier to flesh out the implicit model of the conditional to include the explicit combination of the square with the negated antecedent, which yields the conclusion:

There is not a circle at the top of the card

The inverted order with the categorical premise first may help in another way. It may lead individuals to switch round the order of the elements in their models of the conditional, so that the representation of the consequent precedes the representation of the antecedent in working memory. The modus tollens deduction in this case no longer calls for reasoners to work backwards from the most recent item to enter working memory to a previous item: they can work in the same direction as the information entered working memory from the denial of the consequent to the denial of the antecedent (cf. the so-called "figural effect" in syllogistic reasoning as described in Johnson-Laird & Byrne, 1991).

The theory accordingly predicts that performance with modus tollens should be improved in the inverted order of presentation. The effect of the order of premises on modus ponens should be negligible because the inference can be drawn from the initial models of the conditional. If the model theory is correct, then switching round the order of premises should improve modus tollens. However, if formal rule theories are correct, then modus tollens is difficult because it requires a longer and more difficult derivation, and switching round the order of the premises should have no effect on performance. It does not eliminate the negation, or the more complex derivation. It has no effect on logical form.

Method

Design and materials

The experimental design was based on four independent groups of subjects: each group carried out one form of inference (modus ponens or modus tollens) in either the traditional order of premises (conditional followed by categorical) or the inverted order (categorical followed by conditional). The experimental materials had a neutral content designed to insulate them from the subjects' beliefs or prejudices: they concerned geometrical shapes at the top and at the bottom of a series of cards. A five-page booklet was given to the subjects. The first page stated the general task instructions. The second page described a pack of cards, each carrying two geometrical shapes: one at the top, and another at the bottom. The page also included an example of a card (with a trapezium at the top and a diamond at the bottom). The following pages presented the problem. The modus tollens version of the problem in the traditional order was as follows (in a translation from the original Italian):

> Alberto put some of the cards in a box, on the basis of the following rule:
>
> > If there is a circle at the top of the card, then there is a square at the bottom.
>
> Vittorio, who doesn't know what Alberto has done, has taken one of the cards from the box, but he can see only the bottom part, where there is a triangle. Is it possible to draw a conclusion about the upper part (the concealed part) of the card taken from the box by Vittorio? If so, what is the conclusion?

In the inverted order, the problem was the same except that the information about Vittorio's card came first:

> Vittorio has taken one of the cards from a box, but he can see only the bottom part, where there is a triangle. Vittorio doesn't know that Alberto put some of the cards in the box, on the basis of the following rule:
>
> > If there is a circle at the top of the card, then there is a square at the bottom
>
> Is it possible to draw a conclusion about the upper part (the concealed part) of the card taken by Vittorio? If so, what is the conclusion?

The two conditions presenting the modus ponens problem were similar: in the traditional order, the conditional was stated before the description of Vittorio's card; and in the inverted order, it was given after the description of Vittorio's card. Readers will note that rather than an explicit negation in the modus tollens premises, the materials used a categorical assertion that is inconsistent with the consequent of the conditional. This avoided the problem of counterbalancing the position of the negation. As we will see shortly, it had no critical effect on performance.

Subjects

We tested 92 18–19-year-old students of a high school (in which the major courses concerned scientific matters) of a north Italian town. They were randomly assigned to one of four conditions: modus ponens in the traditional order ($n = 17$) and in the inverted order ($n = 18$), and modus tollens in the traditional order ($n = 28$) and the inverted order ($n = 29$).

Results and discussion

The percentages of subjects who drew the correct conclusions were as follows:

modus ponens in the traditional order: 88% of subjects
modus ponens in the inverted order: 89% of subjects
modus tollens in the traditional order: 40% of subjects
modus tollens in the inverted order: 69% of subjects

There was a significant improvement in modus tollens when the categorical premise occurred first (rank-sum analysis of variance for contingency tables, $z = 2.1$, $p < .025$), but there was no effect of the order of premises on modus ponens. Hence, it is possible to reduce the focussing effect in the way predicted by the model theory.

Rule theories have no obvious explanation for these results. They could explain them only by introducing some pragmatic principles that would produce different interpretations of the premises as a function of their order of presentation. Subsequently, different inferential rules would be applied to these representations to derive a conclusion (cf. Braine & O'Brien, 1991). Such an explanation, however, is post hoc, whereas the model theory's prediction motivated the experiment in the first place.

Further experiments carried out by Girotto and his colleagues have shown that the same phenomena occur when the modus tollens problems contain categorical premises that are explicitly negative (e.g. "There is not a square"), when the subjects are asked to evaluate given conclusions (e.g., "Is it possible to find a circle on the top, concealed, part of the card?"), and when the inference is presented directly without the context of the two individuals, Alberto and Vittorio. A simple switch in the order of premises can help subjects to defocus, that is, to flesh out their models with explicit information about alternative possibilities.

FOCUSSING IN THE SELECTION TASK

One factor lying behind the success of the model theory's predictions is that reasoners can consider only the information that they have explicitly represented in their models. This factor, we believe, underlies failure in Wason's selection task. In the original version of the task (Wason, 1966; Wason & Johnson-Laird, 1972), four cards are put in front of a subject, bearing on their uppermost faces a single symbol: A, B, 2, and 3; and the subjects know that every card has a letter on one side and a number on the other side. Their task is to select just those cards that they need to turn over in order to determine whether the following conditional rule is true or false:

If a card has an A on one side then it has a 2 on the other side

The majority of subjects select the A card, or the A and the 2 cards. Surprisingly, they fail to select the card corresponding to the case where the consequent is false: the 3 card. Yet, the combination of an A with a 3 falsifies the rule.

The selection task has generated a large literature, which is not easy to integrate, and one investigator, Evans (1989), has even wondered whether it tells us anything about deduction. He argues that subjects make those selections that merely match the cards mentioned in the rule. Hence, when the rule is negative:

If there is an A then there is *not* a 2

the subjects correctly select the 2 card (which falsifies the consequent). However, deontic conditional rules, such as:

If a person is drinking beer then the person must be over 18

also tend to elicit the correct selection of the cards corresponding to the true antecedent and the false consequent (e.g., Griggs, 1983; Wason, 1983). Several investigators have therefore argued that content-specific rules of inference underlie reasoning in the selection task (e.g., Cheng & Holyoak, 1985).

The model theory explains the selection task in a different way (Johnson-Laird & Byrne, 1991, p. 79):

(1) The subjects consider only those cards that are explicitly represented in their models of the rule, that is, they focus on these cards.
(2) They select from these cards those for which the hidden value could have a bearing on the rule, that is, those that are represented exhaustively (with square brackets in our diagrams of models).

Hence, any manipulation that leads to the fleshing out of the models of the conditional with explicit representations of the false consequent will tend to yield insight into the task. An insightful selection may even depend on an explicit representation of what is impossible given the truth of the conditional, that is, A and not-2.

The conditional, "If there is an A on one side, then there is a 2 on the other side", yields models of a one-way conditional, or of a bi-conditional, containing only the cards mentioned in the rule:

  [A]   2
  .   .   .

or:

  [A]   [2]
  .   .   .

and so people tend to select the A card, or the A and the 2 card. The model theory is thus compatible with Evans's matching bias, on the assumption that negation leads to fleshing out the models with the state of affairs that is denied (Wason, 1965). Likewise, experience with the rule about beer drinking helps to flesh out the models with more explicit information:

  [drinking beer]   over 18
  ¬ drinking beer   [¬ over 18]
          .   .   .

and so subjects will now tend to select the card corresponding to the negated consequent.

In summary, the cause of errors in the selection task is similar to their cause in modus tollens: reasoners focus on what is explicitly represented in their initial models, and so they overlook alternative possibilities. The advantages of this explanation are three-fold. First, it explains why the matching bias disappears with other connectives, such as disjunctions. It does not occur because the initial interpretations of these connectives, unlike those of conditionals, do not contain wholly implicit models. Second, it explains why the matching bias disappears as a result of many different experimental manipulations. Some of these manipulations concern the use of a realistic or deontic content; others have nothing to do with content, such as the use of a linguistically simpler rule, rules concerning single objects, and so on (see Johnson-Laird & Byrne, 1991, pp. 80–81). Third, the explanation's purview is much wider than that of other theories, which fail to explain the full range of situations in which insight occurs. Such theories include those based on pragmatic reasoning schemas (Cheng & Holyoak, 1985), social contracts (Cosmides, 1989), or "matching" bias as a linguistically determined judgement of relevance (Evans, 1989, p. 33).

Critics may argue: if any manipulation that improves performance is assumed to flesh out mental models, how could the theory ever be disproved? In fact, it is vulnerable to tests in two ways. On the one hand, as we have seen, it predicts that matching should not occur with connectives that do not initially yield implicit models. On the other hand, it predicts, for example, that the initial representation of a premise of the form, "There is a circle only if there is a triangle", is more likely to contain a model of the negated consequent:

$$[\bigcirc] \qquad \triangle$$
$$\neg\bigcirc \qquad [\neg\triangle]$$

$$\cdot \qquad \cdot$$

Hence, the theory predicts that the "only if" form of the conditional should improve performance in the selection task. So far, we have obtained evidence for this effect only where the content of the conditional concerned deontic matters (see Girotto, Mazzocco, & Cherubini, 1992). What is true is that the model theory does not predict which particular realistic contents will lead to insight into the task, but neither does any other theory. There are likely to be considerable individual differences. Indeed, some individuals perform correctly with abstract materials, and other individuals fail to perform correctly even with deontic materials. A causal explanation of these differences is not in the offing. However, the model theory has the advantage of both generality and parsimony: any manipulation that reduces the subjects' focus on an initial incomplete representation of the conditional should improve performance. Focussing is a matter of a general theory of reasoning, and it applies to a variety of domains, including the following phenomenon where responses cannot literally match a linguistic constituent of a conditional.

The phenomenon known as "pseudo-diagnosticity" was demonstrated by Doherty, Mynatt, Tweney, and Schiavo (1979). Their subjects had to determine whether a certain clay pot had come from Coral Island or Shell Island. They were told the features of the particular pot; for example, it had curved handles. They could gain information about the percentages of pots from one island with each of these features or their binary opposites; for example, they could learn that 21% of pots from Coral Island had curved handles, and 79% had straight handles. There were 12 potentially available statistics, but subjects were allowed to select only 6 of them. Few subjects appreciated the need to examine the statistics for both islands. If they formed the hypothesis, say, that the pot came from Coral Island, then they tended to assess how many of the pot's features were present in pots from Coral Island, and they ignored the critical information about the same features in pots from Shell Island. A similar observation was made by Beyth-Marom and Fischhoff (1983). They presented their subjects with the following scenario: "You have met Mr. Maxwell at a party to which only university professors and business executives were invited. The only thing you know about Mr. Maxwell is that he is a member of the Bear's Club." At this point, one group of subjects had to judge the probability that Mr. Maxwell was a university professor, and another group of subjects had to judge whether it was more probable that he was a university professor than a business executive. The subjects were then asked which of several items of information they would prefer to know in order to make the decision. Most subjects in both groups rated as relevant the information about the proportion of professors at the party who were members of the Bear's Club. In contrast, the proportion of executives at the party who were members of the Bear's Club was judged to be relevant by 78% of the subjects in the second group, but only 54% of the subjects in the first group. The standard interpretation of pseudo-diagnosticity is in terms of attentional bias and a failure to consider alternative possibilities (e.g., Baron, 1988, p. 247). Subjects consider the cases that have both the symptom (membership of the Bear's Club) and the positive category (membership of the set of professors); they ignore the other contingencies (see also Smedslund, 1963; Nisbett and Ross, 1980, p. 92; Evans, 1989, p. 62).

The account of pseudo-diagnosticity in terms of an attentional bias is correct in our view, but we would go further: the underlying mechanism is once again a consequence of models that represent only certain information in an explicit way. A conjecture relating two events, such as a symptom and a disease, corresponds to a conditional. Hence, subjects who are evaluating such a conjecture are likely to represent it by models similar to those of the corresponding conditional:

If ⟨symptom⟩ then ⟨disease⟩

They therefore construct an initial set of models that makes explicit only one model – the model in which the symptom and disease co-occur. Their subsequent search for information is guided by this explicit model. It is the focus of their efforts, and so they concentrate on information about the presence of the symptom and the presence of the disease. They will be prey to the fallacy *post hoc ergo propter hoc*; that is, they will judge that the disease is caused by the symptom because the two co-occur, and they will fail to consider cases where the symptom is present but the disease is absent. Individuals may be able to defocus. For example, the task of judging whether Mr. Maxwell is more likely to be a professor than a business executive calls for a comparison, and so the subjects will construct two contrasting models and consider information about both conditional probabilities to be relevant. The task of defocussing in a diagnostic context accordingly resembles its counterpart in the selection task. The same account in terms of mental models applies to both sets of phenomena.

AN EXPERIMENT ON FOCUSSING IN DECISION MAKING

"Utility theory ... provides at best only part of a normative standard of decision making. The rest of the standard has to do with a thorough search for

alternative actions, goals, and evidence about consequences and their probabilities" (Baron, 1988, p. 289). What focussing implies, however, is that in many
circumstances individuals will fail to make a thorough search for alternatives. In
particular, if they are faced with the choice of either carrying out a certain action
or not carrying it out, then, according to the theory, they will initially construct a
model of the action and an alternative model in which it does not occur. The
latter will either be implicit or else merely a model in which the action is negated.
Hence, individuals will be focussed on the action and search for more information
about it in order to reach the decision. They will neglect to search for information
about alternative actions, and so contravene the rational standard for decision
making. Empirical evidence exists that people fail to consider alternative options
and their costs when they are unstated (i.e., people seem to ignore the
opportunity cost principle, Friedman & Neumann, 1980). In the case of the
selection task, there are various manipulations that can help subjects to defocus;
for example, the content of the rule can be changed so as to make information
about alternatives more available. In the decision task, we can similarly predict
that focussing should be reduced by any manipulation that makes alternatives to
the action more available.

We tested this prediction in an experiment in which we used a new approach to
understanding the mental processes underlying decision making. The subjects'
task was to make a simple riskless decision, for example, whether or not to go to
see a certain movie, but they could request any information that they needed in
order to make the decision, and the experimenter provided it to them (from one
of two pre-established descriptions). The subjects continued to request information until they were able to announce their decision. In the control group, the
decision was presented without any background context, and so the subjects
should be highly focussed; that is, they should tend to request information about
the action and to ignore its alternatives. In the context group, the decision
occurred within a particular context: the subjects were asked to imagine that they
were visiting, say, Rome for the first time, and that the experimenter was an
expert on the city's tourist attractions. They were then given the task of deciding
whether or not to go to a particular event. The context should make alternatives
more available, and so the subjects in this group should be less focussed on the
action in their requests for information to help them make the decision.

Method

Design

We tested two separate groups of subjects: a control group and a context
group, and each subject made five decisions in a different random order about

whether or not to go to a movie, to attend a sporting event, to visit a painting exhibition, to have dinner at a particular restaurant, and to attend an auction.

Materials and procedure

On each trial, the instructions for the control group were of the following form: "You have to decide whether or not (to go to see a certain film). We will give you any information you want until you can make the decision." The instructions made clear that the decision applied to the subjects' current action rather than to some indefinite future action. For the context group, they were of the following form:

> "Imagine that you are visiting Rome for the first time, but only for one day; and imagine that I have lived in Rome for a long time and have an excellent knowledge of the tourist attractions of the town. Your task is decide whether or not (to go to see a certain film). I will give you any information you want until you can make the decision."

Each trial of the context group referred to a different well-known tourist city chosen at random from Paris, Athens, Madrid, Tokyo, Rio, and Rome.

For both the control and the context group, we prepared two different descriptions for each event, for example, two types of film (French vs. American, two movie-makers, two actors, two judgements by the critics), two types of restaurant (Chinese vs. Mexican, two ranges of price, two locations), two types of sport event (tennis vs. soccer), and so on. One of the two descriptions was selected at random for each subject. The experimenter used this description as a basic for answering the subjects' requests for information. Each trial continued until the subject made a decision. Finally, the experimenter asked the subjects to give the reasons why they had made their particular decision. The entire experimental session was tape-recorded, and the main data that we analyzed were the subjects' questions and final decisions.

Subjects

We tested 16 undergraduates at University College, London, in the experiment, which lasted for about 30 minutes.

Results and discussion

Overall, the subjects asked a mean of 2.55 questions in order to reach a decision. They made a mean of 2.25 positive decisions (out of the five trials) in the

Table 1.   *The mean number of questions focussed on the action and the mean number of questions about alternatives for the control group and the context group*

	Questions about the actions	Questions about alternatives
The control group	2.8	0
The context group	2.1	0.25

control group, and a mean of 2.0 positive decisions in the context group. Table 1 presents the mean number of questions focussing on the action and the mean number of questions about alternatives to it for both of the two groups. As the table shows, there is a highly significant focussing effect (which occurs for all subjects, $p = .05$[16]). However, there was a significant effect of the contextual variable. None of the 8 subjects in the control group ever asked any questions about alternatives to the focussed action, whereas 7 out of the 8 subjects in the context group asked at least one question about alternatives to it (Fisher–Yates exact test, $p < .003$). These questions were typically of the form: "What else is there for me to do in Rome?" Asking about alternatives was correlated with deciding *not* to take the relevant action: the 7 subjects in the context group asked a total of 10 questions about alternatives to the action, but only one of these questions was associated with a positive decision.

When individuals have to choose between going to a certain movie and not going to see it, they tend to focus on the movie in their requests for information to help them to make the decision. We observe the same phenomenon in daily life. There is a natural tendency to focus when a single option is offered for a decision and no obvious alternatives are available. This result is contrary to any theory which assumes that decision makers explicitly consider alternative courses of action. In particular, it is contrary to the classical theory of decision making to which most economists still adhere. Focussing is important to our understanding of how the mind departs from rational principles: if one knows nothing about the alternatives to a particular course of action, one can neither assess their utilities nor compare them with the utility of the action. Hence, one cannot make a rational decision. Of course, *not* taking an action may have consequences (and thus a utility) regardless of the alternative that is actually pursued, but with a few obvious exceptions, such as not taking the antidote to a poison, a negative decision is seldom evaluated as such. The choice between, say, going to the cinema or not going to the cinema is represented by two disjunctive models. The first model is explicit and exhaustive, and so the other model, which corresponds to *not* going to the cinema, can be implicit:

[c]

. . .

where 'c' denotes a model of going to the cinema. The task for the decision maker therefore appears to be to gather information about c.

The effect of context is to change the nature of the decision, and thus the sort of strategy that subjects are likely to use to make it (Payne, Bettman, Coupey, & Johnson, 1992). Without the tourist context, subjects are likely to compare the movie to some idealized instance. With the tourist context, they are likely to compare it with some other activity. Hence, the two decisions are not psychologically equivalent. The context enables individuals to defocus: it makes alternatives available for fleshing out the implicit model. The subjects can compare the attributes of alternatives. Hence, our results corroborate Payne et al.'s account of the contingent and constructive use of strategies in decision making.

One unexpected finding was the close association between asking about alternatives to the focussed action and reaching a negative decision. One reason may be that subjects who ask for and receive information about alternatives are thereby led to a negative decision. Another reason may be that subjects who are in the process of rejecting a course of action are thereby led to ask about alternatives. There may even be some other underlying factors that bias subjects to ask about alternatives and to reach negative decisions. These potential explanations are not mutually exclusive, but we suspect that the first of them is likely to be the main factor, because subjects reach negative decisions without asking about alternatives, whereas all but one instance of asking about alternatives led to a negative decision. The matter cannot be resolved without further experimentation.

FOCUSSING IN COUNTERFACTUAL REASONING

When people understand discourse, they construct a model of the situation described in the discourse (e.g., Garnham, 1987; Johnson-Laird, 1983). Recent research has shown that events that concern the central character in a narrative are particularly salient: "readers take the character's perspective; they follow the character's thoughts, activating mental images of the same things that the character is thinking about" (Bower & Morrow, 1990, p. 47). Hence, as Morrow, Bower, and Greenspan (1989) have shown, when subjects read the following sentence in a narrative:

John is in the cafeteria and he's thinking of going to the library

they are faster and more accurate in locating items in the library than in locating items in the cafeteria. There seems to be a natural tendency to focus on what is explicit in a model based on discourse, and particularly those elements relevant to the protagonist's actions.

This phenomenon should have consequences for thinking about counterfactual alternatives to the events in a narrative (e.g., Kahneman & Varey, 1990; Miller, Turnbull, & McFarland, 1990). When readers are forced to envisage such alternatives in order, say, to undo the tragic outcome of a story, they should be focussed on what is most explicit in their models of the story. They should think of alternatives to these events rather than invoking scenarios that are independent of their focus. Consider, for instance, the following synopsis of a story:

> A bank employee, Mr. Bianchi, was going home after work, but his progress toward home was delayed by a series of misfortunes (the manoeuvres of a lorry, the passage of a flock of sheep, and a tree trunk lying across the road) and by an intentional decision of his own (to enter a bar to drink a beer). When he arrived home, he found his wife on the floor. He realized that she had suffered a heart attack and that she was dying. He tried to help her, but his efforts were in vain.

What are subjects likely to envisage in order to avoid the story's unfortunate outcome? They might imagine that an ambulance containing a mobile coronary-care unit happened to stop outside Mr. Bianchi's garden at just the right moment, or that his wife called him at work and he was able to arrange for a helicopter to fly her to hospital. These possibilities seem far-fetched because they are not alternatives to any of the explicit events in the narrative. And so subjects should tend not to think of them. They should instead generate counterfactual scenarios that modify explicit elements in their models of the narrative. In particular, the subjects should base their models on the protagonist's actions, and so they should tend to modify precisely these elements, for example, the decision of Mr. Bianchi to enter the bar.

This prediction has been confirmed in an experimental study carried out by Girotto, Legrenzi, and Rizzo (1991). The subjects had to imagine four different alternatives to the story about Mr. Bianchi in which his wife did not die, and to list these alternatives in their order of importance. More than 70% of the subjects' alternatives concerned explicit elements of the story. Each alternative scenario was classified as either active or passive depending on the role played by the protagonist. An active alternative was one in which the protagonist acted or made a decision; for example, "Mr. Bianchi decided not to drink the beer", "Mr. Bianchi helped to remove the tree trunk". A passive alternative was one in which Mr. Bianchi played no such role; for example, "the bar was closed"; "the trunk did not fall". Although modifications could have been of either sort for the bar event, most of the subjects' changes (70%) were of the active sort. For the other events of the story, even those outside the protagonist's control, about 30% of the changes were of the active sort. Indeed, Mr. Bianchi's decision to enter the bar was the event most often selected for change (25% of all responses) whatever its position in the story and whether it was presented as normal ("Mr. Bianchi, as usual, decided to enter the bar . . .") or abnormal ("Mr. Bianchi, exceptionally for his habits, decided to enter the bar . . ."). Hence, the event that was most available for change was the protagonist's intentional action, regardless of the sequence of the events in the story (*pace* Wells, Taylor, & Turtle, 1987), and of its degree of normalcy (*pace* Kahneman & Miller, 1986). Even when the subjects introduced alternatives from outside the story, these alternatives tended to involve the protagonist.

There is undoubtedly a focus on the protagonist in generating alternative scenarios (see also Kahneman & Miller, 1986), but there is also an additional factor, which may be peculiar to the counterfactual task: the degree to which an event is under the protagonist's control, which may be particularly salient in the model of the story constructed from the protagonist's point of view. It follows that one action by the protagonist will evoke a counterfactual alternative more readily than another action if the former is interpreted as more under the protagonist's control than the latter. This hypothesis was corroborated by Girotto et al. (1991) using a story in which all the episodes were actions performed by the protagonist. An event corresponding to a fully controllable action (entering the bar to drink a beer) was the first event to be changed by 76% of the subjects, in comparison to two other actions forced upon the protagonist by his physical state (deciding to go back to the office for a pair of glasses because his first pair broke, and deciding to stop the car because of an asthma attack).

In sum, as in the case of the construction of a mental model based on a narrative, subjects focus on information relevant to the protagonist when they make inferences about counterfactual states of affairs.

GENERAL DISCUSSION

Focussing is not a new idea in the psychology of thinking. Bruner, Goodnow, and Austin (1956) introduced it in their study of concept attainment: they posited a strategy based on choosing potential instances of an unknown concept by focussing on an initial given positive instance of the concept. This tendency to concentrate on positive instances was also observed in Wason's (1960) studies of hypothesis testing. He gave his subjects an initial triplet of numbers – 2, 4, 6 – and then asked them to find the rule underlying such triplets. They tended to test their hypotheses using positive instances of them. This tendency has been called "confirmation bias", and has been found in inductive reasoning and in other domains such as social judgement (Nisbett & Ross, 1980). Klayman and Ha (1987) reinterpreted the bias as a more general "positive test" strategy, that is, a tendency to test a hypothesis by checking positive instances of it, which is compatible with the desire to confirm the hypothesis or with the desire to disconfirm it. Evans (1989, p. 42) explains the phenomenon, and the matching-bias data from studies of conditionals, as a consequence of a "positivity" bias. He argues that, unlike Klayman and Ha's heuristic, this bias is not a deliberate heuristic, but arises from "preconscious heuristic processes which determine the locus of the subjects' attention". In our view, all these different heuristics are manifestations of the same underlying mechanism: an inevitable focus on the explicit elements of models.

The focussing mechanism derives from a general theory of reasoning rather than from a hypothesis about some specific experimental results. The general model-based theory is both parsimonious and explicit. However, its explicitness has a cost because it reveals the incompleteness of the theory. One major determinant of what is explicit in mental models is the verbal description of a problem, and another major determinant is the "availability" of knowledge (Tversky & Kahneman, 1973). Yet the theory does not predict the precise circumstances in which an individual will, or will not, flesh out models of a problem explicitly. Hence, it does not explain the circumstances in which individuals are satisfied with a representation of the problem that is only partially explicit. Nevertheless, such partial representations are precisely what lead to the focussing hypothesis, which is a consequence of the construction of models that make explicit only certain items. The hypothesis, in turn, has led us to successful predictions about four different areas: the modus tollens deduction, the selection task, the search for information in riskless decisions, and the construction of counterfactual scenarios. We will review these findings before we consider the general implications of the model theory.

When subjects reason from modus tollens premises of the form *if p then q*, *not-q*, they often respond that nothing follows from the premises. This error can be explained by a focus on the initial explicit model of the conditional, and a failure to represent the alternative possibilities where the antecedent is false. When the premises are presented in the opposite order, then, as the model theory predicts, the initial representation of the categorical premise immediately elimi-nates the explicit model of the conditional and thereby helps the subjects to flesh out the implicit model, and so the inference is easier.

In the original form of the selection task, subjects are asked to select those cards that could show whether the following sort of conditional rule is true or false:

If there is an A on one side of a card, then there is a 2 on the other side

They tend to select either the A card alone, or the A and the 2 card. The focussing hypothesis explains the phenomenon in terms of what is made explicit in the models of the conditional. Hence, any manipulations that lead subjects to flesh out these models should enhance performance, and indeed a variety of such manipulations has been found to produce this effect.

A decision is sometimes defined as a conscious choice between at least two possible courses of action (e.g., Castles, Murray, & Potter, 1971, cited by Fox, 1990). Paradoxically, when subjects have to decide whether or not to carry out a certain action, the effect of focussing is to reduce the decision to a choice between one and a half alternatives. The models of the decision contain explicit information about the action, but not necessarily any explicit information about *not* taking the action. The subjects are thus focussed on the action itself, and they seek information only about its attributes in order to help them to make the decision. Subjects are able to defocus, however, when the scenario for the decision makes alternatives to the action more available. They seek information about these alternatives in accordance with the normative standards for decision making.

When subjects have to envisage an alternative counterfactual scenario that avoids an unfortunate outcome, they are once again focussed on the events explicitly represented in their models of the narrative. Such models, however, tend to represent events from the point of view of the protagonist: the protagonist's actions are particularly salient, and especially those that are likely to be represented as under his or her control. The extent to which this latter factor is local to the particular counterfactual task calls for further empirical investigation.

Focussing should lead to predictable requests for certain sorts of information in making decisions between two explicit alternatives. For example, suppose individuals have to choose between two alternative vacation resorts:

Resort A has good beaches, plenty of sunshine, and is easy to get to
Resort B has good beaches, cheap food, and comfortable hotels

What further information are individuals likely to request in order to choose between the two resorts? The focussing hypothesis implies that they will seek to build models that flesh out the missing attributes. They know, for example, that resort A has plenty of sunshine, but they know nothing about the weather at resort B, and so they will seek information about this attribute. We can further predict that once the specified attributes have been fleshed out in this way, the subjects will be able to make a decision provided that one resort has all the positive attributes of the other, and some additional positive attributes. In summary, the initial specification of the decision acts as a focus for both the information that subjects seek and their ultimate decision, and consequently they will tend to overlook other attributes, such as hostility to tourists, a dictatorial government, or rampant food poisoning, that are not included in the original specification. Yet, these attributes might well influence their decisions in other instances. We note that one factor in the early success of Ross Perot in his bid for the US Presidency appears to have been the attractiveness of those attributes that he revealed in his television appearances. Those who supported him appeared to have focussed on these attributes, and to have neglected those others – such as most matters of policy – that he chose not to reveal.

Focussing may well account for a number of so-called "framing" effects in decision making and their analogues in deductive reasoning. The same decision can be framed in different ways that will lead individuals to build different models of the choices. In a study by Tversky and Kahneman (1981), a choice between two different programs for combatting a disease was framed in terms of lives saved:

Program A will save 200 lives (out of 600)
Program B has a 1/3 probability of saving 600 lives and a 2/3 probability of saving no one

and the majority of subjects preferred program A. However, when the same choice was framed in terms of numbers who die:

Program A will lead to 400 deaths (out of 600)
Program B has a 1/3 probability of no one dying and a 2/3 probability of 600 deaths

the majority of subjects preferred program B. Tversky and Kahneman explain this phenomenon in terms of the respective reference points of the two ways of framing the problem, and the shape of the function relating gains and losses to subjective value: a loss hurts more than a gain pleases. The reference point for the first problem is 600 lives lost, and so the choices lie on the concave part of the function for gains, whereas the reference point for the second problem is 0 lives lost, and so the choices lie on the convex part of the function for losses. It may be, however, that part of the difference is merely in the models that subjects build for the respective versions of option A: in the first problem, a model that makes explicit 200 lives saved, and, in the second problem, a model that makes explicit 400 deaths. A is accordingly attractive in the first problem, but unattractive in the second problem.

The framing of problems in deductive reasoning similarly influences performance. According to the model theory, the assertion:

All the authors are boxers

is represented by a single model of the following sort:

```
[a]    b
[a]    b
 .   .   .
```

where each line in this diagram represents a different individual in the same model, an "a" represents an author, and a "b" represents a boxer. The square brackets indicate that a set has been exhaustively represented in the model; that is, members of the set of authors cannot occur elsewhere in the model; and the three dots allow for other sorts of individual yet to be made explicit. The number of individuals remains arbitrary, but it is likely to be small. The assertion:

> Only the boxers are authors

has the same truth conditions as the previous assertion, but, according to the theory, it makes explicit right from the start that anyone who is *not* a boxer is also *not* an author. Hence, its initial model is of the following sort:

```
   b      [a]
   b      [a]
[¬b]      ¬a
 .   .   .
```

and so the models of the two assertions are equivalent in content, though the equivalence is not immediately apparent. Deductions based on what is explicit in a model should be easier than those that depend on fleshing out implicit information. It follows that the premises:

> All athletes are boxers
> Mark is an athlete

should readily yield the conclusion:

> Mark is a boxer

whereas the premises:

> All athletes are boxers
> Mark is not a boxer

should less readily yield the conclusion:

> Mark is not an athlete

For the corresponding problems based on "only", there should be no difference between the premises:

> Only boxers are athletes
> Mark is an athlete

and:

> Only boxers are athletes
> Mark is not a boxer

because the models contain explicit negative information right from the start. The results from an experiment corroborated this hypothesis (see Johnson-Laird & Byrne, 1989). Hence, the framing of a problem can lead to models that differ in what they make explicit about the situation, and this difference in turn can affect the conclusions that reasoners draw.

When individuals make a choice between two alternatives, then choosing one alternative is logically equivalent to rejecting the other. Yet, as Shafir (1991) has shown, the two tasks of choosing and rejecting may not be psychologically equivalent. When subjects have to select an option, they focus on the positive attributes of the alternatives; but when they have to reject an option, they focus on the negative attributes of the alternatives. Shafir was accordingly able to offer choices where one and the same alternative had both many positive attributes and many negative attributes in comparison to the other alternative. The result was that subjects tended both to choose this alternative in the choice task and to reject it in the rejection task. We can predict that there should be a similar effect on seeking and evaluating information about the options. In the context of choosing an option, subjects will pay more attention to positive attributes, whereas in the context of rejecting an option, they will pay more attention to negative attributes.

The application of the model theory to the study of decision making should permit one to make predictions on the basis of what is known about the use of mental models in deductive reasoning, and so we can predict that model-based phenomena other than those of focussing should occur in making decisions. In this final section of the paper we will consider the possibility. The single most robust phenomenon in deductive reasoning is that deductions that call for more than one model are harder than those that call for only one model. We have observed this phenomenon in studies of propositional, relational, syllogistic, and multiply quantified reasoning (for a review, see Johnson-Laird & Byrne, 1991). Deductive performance can be tested to the point where it breaks down merely by increasing the number of disjunctive models that have to be constructed (see the study of "double disjunctions" in Johnson-Laird et al., 1992). We can expect that decisions will likewise grow more difficult as a function of the number of options.

Indeed, like deduction, there can be a breakdown in rationality as soon as there are two explicit alternatives to choose from – as shown by the so-called "disjunctive effect" in decision making (see Tversky & Shafir, 1992, and the paper in this issue by Shafir, Simonson, & Tversky). An everyday example of this phenomenon occurred during the early stages of the recent US Presidential campaign: at one point, the opinion polls revealed that Bush would lose to a Democrat, but that he would beat each individual Democratic candidate. In general, as Shafir and Tversky (1992) have shown experimentally, subjects may choose a particular option when a certain event occurs, and when it does not occur. Yet, when the outcome is unknown, they do not choose it. In our terms, the need to hold in mind the disjunctive alternatives makes the inferential task difficult: subjects are unable or reluctant to derive the consequences of each alternative and to assess what they have in common. Part of this difficulty, as Shafir and Tversky argue, may be that the reasons for the choice are quite different for the alternative outcomes, for example, choosing a Hawaiian vacation as a reward for passing an exam as opposed to as a consolation for failing the exam. In attempting to make the decision when the outcome is unknown, there is no simple reason for choosing the vacation. The disjunctive alternatives appear to conflict.

We can predict at least one other disjunctive effect in decision making: if the information available about a particular option is disjunctive in form, then the resulting conflict or load on working memory will make it harder to infer a reason for choosing this option in comparison to an option for which categorical information is available. The harder it is to infer a reason for a choice, the less attractive that choice is likely to be.

CONCLUSION

Focussing is a widespread phenomenon in reasoning and decision making. Certain experimental manipulations, however, enable subjects to defocus: they flesh out their models of alternative possibilities, and use these models in making deductions and decisions. Neither of these effects – focussing and defocussing – is predicted by the respective classical theories of the two domains, that is, theories of reasoning based on formal rules of inference, and theories of decision making based on the maximization of expected utilities. Both phenomena, however, are predicted by the theory that reasoning depends on the construction of mental models or scenarios of the relevant situations.

References

Baron, J. (1988). *Thinking and deciding*. Cambridge, UK: Cambridge University Press.
Beyth-Marom, R., & Fischhoff, B. (1983). Diagnosticity and pseudodiagnosticity. *Journal of Personality and Social Psychology, 45*, 1185–1197.

Bower, G.H., & Morrow, D.G. (1990). Mental models in narrative comprehension. *Science, 247*, 44–48.

Braine, M.D.S. (1978). On the relation between the natural logic of reasoning and standard logic. *Psychological Review, 85*, 1–21.

Braine, M.D.S., & O'Brien, D.P.O. (1991). A theory of "if": A lexical entry, reasoning program, and pragmatic principles. *Psychological Review, 98*, 182–203.

Bruner, J.S., Goodnow, G., & Austin, G. (1956). *A study of thinking.* New York: Wiley.

Castles, F.G., Murray, D.I., & Potter, D.C. (Eds.) (1971). *Decisions, organizations and society.* Harmondsworth, UK: Penguin.

Cheng, P.W., & Holyoak, K.J. (1985). Pragmatic reasoning schemas. *Cognitive Psychology, 17*, 391–416.

Cosmides, L. (1989). The logic of social exchange: Has natural selection shaped how humans reason? Studies with the Wason selection task. *Cognition, 31*, 187–276.

Doherty, M.E., Mynatt, C.R., Tweney, R.D., & Schiavo, M.D. (1979). Pseudodiagnosticity. *Acta Psychologica, 43*, 11–21.

Evans, J.St.B.T. (1982). *The psychology of deductive reasoning.* London: Routledge & Kegan Paul.

Evans, J.St.B.T. (1989). *Bias in human reasoning.* Hillsdale, NJ: Erlbaum.

Fox, J. (1990). Automating assistance for safety critical decisions. In D.E. Broadbent, A. Baddeley, & J.T. Reason (Eds.), *Human factors in hazardous situations* (pp. 107–119). Oxford: Clarendon Press. (*Philosophical Transactions of the Royal Society of London B, 327*, 555–567.)

Friedman, L.A., & Neumann, B.R. (1980). The effects of opportunity costs on project investment decisions: A replication and extension. *Journal of Accounting Research, 18*, 407–419.

Garnham, A. (1987). *Mental models as representations of discourse and text.* Chichester: Ellis Horwood.

Girotto, V., Legrenzi, P., & Rizzo, A. (1991). Event controllability in counterfactual thinking. *Acta Psychologica, 78*, 111–133.

Girotto, V., Mazzocco, A., & Cherubini, P. (1992). Judgements of deontic relevance in reasoning: A reply to Jackson and Griggs. *Quarterly Journal of Experimental Psychology, 45A*, 547–574.

Girotto, V., Mazzocco, A., & Tasso, A. (1992). The effect of premise order effect on conditional reasoning: A test of the mental model theory. Unpublished manuscript, Department of Psychology, University of Trieste.

Griggs, R.A. (1983). The role of problem content in the selection task and in the THOG problem. In J.St.B.T. Evans (Ed.), *Thinking and reasoning: Psychological approaches.* London: Routledge & Kegan Paul.

Inhelder, B., & Piaget, J. (1958). *The growth of logical thinking from childhood to adolescence.* London: Routledge & Kegan Paul.

Johnson-Laird, P.N. (1983). *Mental models.* Cambridge, UK: Cambridge University Press.

Johnson-Laird, P.N. (1993). *Human and machine thinking.* Hillsdale, NJ: Erlbaum.

Johnson-Laird, P.N., & Byrne, R.M.J. (1989). *Only* reasoning. *Journal of Memory and Language, 28*, 313–330.

Johnson-Laird, P.N., & Byrne, R.M.J. (1991). *Deduction.* Hillsdale, NJ: Erlbaum.

Johnson-Laird, P.N., Byrne, R.M.J., & Schaeken, W. (1992). Propositional reasoning by model. *Psychological Review, 99*, 418–439.

Kahneman, D., & Miller, D.T. (1986). Norm theory: Comparing reality to its alternatives. *Psychological Review, 93*, 136–153.

Kahneman, D., & Tversky, A. (1982) The simulation heuristic. In D. Kahneman, P. Slovic, & A. Tversky (Eds.), *Judgment under uncertainty: Heuristics and biases* (pp. 201–208). Cambridge, UK: Cambridge University Press.

Kahneman, D., & Varey, C.A. (1990). Propensities and counterfactuals: The loser that almost won. *Journal of Personality and Social Psychology, 59*, 1101–1110.

Kintsch, W. (1974). *The representation of meaning in memory.* Hillsdale, NJ: Erlbaum.

Klayman, J., & Ha, Y.-W. (1987). Confirmation, disconfirmation and information in hypothesis testing. *Psychological Review, 94*, 211–228.

Lindley, D.V. (1985). *Making decisions*, 2nd edn. Chichester: Wiley.

Macnamara, J. (1986). *A border dispute: The place of logic in psychology.* Cambridge, MA: MIT Press.

Miller, D.T., Turnbull, W., & McFarland, C. (1990). Counterfactual thinking and social perception: Thinking about what might have been. In P. Zanna (Ed.), *Advances in experimental social psychology* (Vol. 23, pp. 305–331). Orlando, FL: Academic Press.

Morrow, D.G., Bower, G.H., & Greenspan, S.L. (1989). Updating situation models during narrative comprehension. *Journal of Memory and Language, 28,* 292–312.

Nisbett, R., & Ross, L. (1980). *Human inference: Strategies and shortcomings of social judgement.* Englewood Cliffs, NJ: Prentice-Hall.

Osherson, D.N. (1974–6). *Logical abilities in children* (Vols. 1–4). Hillsdale, NJ: Erlbaum.

Overton, W.F. (1990). Competence and procedures: Constraints on the development of logical reasoning. In W.F. Overton (Ed.), *Reasoning, necessity and logic: Developmental perspectives.* Hillsdale, NJ: Erlbaum.

Payne, J.W., Bettman, J.R., Coupey, E., & Johnson, E.J. (1992). A constructive process view of decision making: Multiple strategies in judgment and choice. *Acta Psychologica, 80,* 107–141.

Pollock, J. (1989). *How to build a person: A prolegomenon.* Cambridge, MA: MIT/Bradford Books.

Quillian, M.R. (1968). Semantic memory. In M. Minsky (Ed.), *Semantic information processing.* Cambridge, MA: MIT Press.

Reiter, R. (1973). A semantically guided deductive system for automatic theorem-proving. *Proceedings of the Third International Joint Conference on Artificial Intelligence,* 41–46.

Rips, L.J. (1983). Cognitive processes in propositional reasoning. *Psychological Review, 90,* 38–71.

Shafir, E. (1991). Choosing versus rejecting: Why some options are both better and worse than others. Unpublished manuscript, Department of Psychology, Princeton University.

Shafir, E., & Tversky, A. (1992). Thinking through uncertainty: Nonconsequential reasoning and choice. *Cognitive Psychology, 24,* 449–474.

Simon, H.A. (1959). Theories of decision making in economics and behavioral science. *American Economic Review, 49,* 253–283.

Slovic, P. (1990). Choice. In D.N. Osherson, & E.E. Smith (Eds.), *An invitation to cognitive science. Vol. 3: Thinking* (pp. 89–116). Cambridge, MA.: MIT Press.

Smedslund, J. (1963). The concept of correlation in adults. *Scandinavian Journal of Psychology, 4,* 165–173.

Sperber, D., & Wilson, D. (1986). *Relevance: Communication and cognition.* Oxford: Basil Blackwell.

Tversky, A., & Kahneman, D. (1973). Availability: A heuristic for judging frequency and probability. *Cognitive Psychology, 5,* 207–232.

Tversky, A., & Kahneman, D. (1981). The framing of decisions and the psychology of choice. *Science, 211,* 453–458.

Tversky, A., & Shafir, E. (1992). The disjunction effect in choice under uncertainty. *Psychological Science, 3,* 305–309.

Wason, P.C. (1960). On the failure to eliminate hypotheses in a conceptual task. *Quarterly Journal of Experimental Psychology, 12,* 129–140.

Wason, P.C. (1965). The context of plausible denial. *Journal of Verbal Learning and Verbal Behavior, 4,* 7–11.

Wason, P.C. (1966). Reasoning. In B.M. Foss (Ed.), *New horizons in psychology.* Harmondsworth, UK: Penguin.

Wason, P.C. (1983). Realism and rationality in the selection task. In J.St.B.T. Evans (Ed.), *Thinking and reasoning: Psychological approaches.* London: Routledge & Kegan Paul.

Wason, P.C., & Johnson-Laird, P.N. (1972). *Psychology of reasoning: Structure and content.* London: Batsford; Cambridge, MA: Harvard University Press.

Wells, G.L., Taylor, B.R., & Turtle, J.W. (1987). The undoing of scenarios. *Journal of Personality and Social Psychology, 53,* 421–430.

4 Similarity, plausibility, and judgments of probability

Edward E. Smith
Department of Psychology, University of Michigan, Ann Arbor

Eldar Shafir
Department of Psychology, Princeton University

Daniel Osherson
IDIAP, Martigny, Valais, Switzerland

Abstract

Judging the strength of an argument may underlie many reasoning and decision-making tasks. In this article, we focus on "category-based" arguments, in which the premises and conclusion are of the form All members of C have property P, *where C is a natural category. An example is "Dobermanns have sesamoid bones. Therefore, German shepherds have sesamoid bones." The strength of such an argument is reflected in the judged probability that the conclusion is true given that the premises are true. The processes that mediate such probability judgments depend on whether the predicate is "blank" – an unfamiliar property that does not enter the reasoning process (e.g., "have sesamoid bones") – or "non-blank" – a relatively familiar property that is easier to reason from (e.g., "can bite through wire"). With blank predicates, probability judgments are based on similarity relations between the premise and conclusion categories. With non-blank predicates, probability judgements are based on both similarity relations and the plausibility of premises and conclusion.*

Introduction

Reasoning and decision making in the face of uncertainty often require one to estimate the probabilities of uncertain events. In a series of influential studies,

The research reported in this article was supported by Air Force Contract No. AFOSR-92-0265 to Smith, US Public Health Service Grant No. 1-R29-MH46885 to Shafir, and Swiss National Science Foundation Contract No. 21-32399.91 to Osherson. We thank Douglas Medin for helpful comments on an earlier version of the manuscript.

Kahneman and Tversky (e.g., 1973, Tversky & Kahneman, 1983) demonstrated that lay people base their intuitive estimates of probability on decision heuristics, which, though often useful, sometimes yield normatively incorrect judgments. One such heuristic estimates the probability that individual i has property P in terms of how representative i is of P. Many empirical studies of this heuristic have involved a paradigm in which subjects are presented with a description of a hypothetical person, and asked to estimate the probability that the person is an instance of a target category; for example, "Linda is 31, liberal, and outspoken. What is the probability that she is a social worker?" In cases like this, the representativeness of the individual reduces to the typicality of the instance in the target-category – roughly, how good an example the instance is of the category – and the critical finding is that probability judgments are an increasing function of typicality (Shafir, Smith, & Osherson, 1990).

The Kahneman–Tversky paradigm bears on contexts in which one needs to estimate the probability that an object belongs to a particular category. There is, however, another natural paradigm in which instances and categories are used to support probability judgments. In this paradigm, subjects are informed that some members of a category have a particular property, and then have to estimate the probability that other members have the property as well; for example, "A majority of surgeons oppose socialized medicine. What is the probability that a majority of internists do so as well?" These inferences are said to be "category based". Presumably, subjects are treating surgeons and internists as subsets of the category of physicians, and this categorization plays a role in the inference process. Like the judgments studied by Kahneman and Tversky, category-based judgments occur frequently in everyday life, and seem to be based on heuristics rather than normative principles (Osherson, Smith, Wilkie, Lopez, & Shafir, 1990). Such judgments are the concern of this paper.

Distinctions

To structure our report, we need to introduce some terminology and distinctions. Note first that any probability question can be characterized as an argument, in which the known propositions are the *premises* of the argument and the proposition whose probability is in question is the *conclusion* of the argument. To illustrate, the preceding example amounts to the following argument (where the statement above the line is the premise, and the one below the line is the conclusion):

(1) A majority of surgeons oppose socialized medicine
     ———————————————————————————————————————
     A majority of internists oppose socialized medicine

In providing further examples, it is useful to switch to biological categories like birds and mammals, because there seems to be more consensus among people about the subsets of such categories than about the subsets of social categories. Two further examples of category-based arguments are:

(2) Robins have sesamoid bones
     Ducks have sesamoid bones
     _____

     All birds have sesamoid bones

(3) Robins have sesamoid bones
     Ducks have sesamoid bones
     _____

     Sparrows have sesamoid bones

In both cases, a subject might be asked to estimate the probability that the conclusion is true given that the premises are true.

Arguments like (2) are distinguished by the fact that the conclusion category, BIRD, properly includes the premise categories, ROBIN and DUCK; such arguments are said to be "general" (from here on in, we use capitals to indicate categories). In arguments like (3), in contrast, all categories are at the same hierarchical level; these arguments are said to be "specific". In this paper, we focus on specific arguments, though there will be some mention of general arguments.[1]

Another distinction concerns properties or predicates. *Having sesamoid bones* is a recognizable biological property, but not one that most people are familiar with, or can readily reason about. Such predicates are called "blank". They are to be distinguished from non-blank predicates like *can fly faster than 20 miles an hour*; we are familiar with, and can reason about, such a predicate. A rough test of whether a predicate is blank or not is whether it applies equally to all categories in a domain, or instead characterizes some categories better than others. *Having sesamoid bones*, for instance, seems no more likely of one bird species than another, whereas *can fly faster than 20 miles per hour* clearly characterizes some birds (e.g., hawks and eagles) better than others (e.g., chickens and ducks). This distinction between blank and non-blank predicates is a major concern of the present paper. To preview our results, we will show that: with blank predicates, judgments of probability are based mostly on similarity and typicality relations between premise and conclusion categories, just as they are in

---

[1]Specific arguments can also be distinguished by the fact that any natural category (e.g., BIRD) that properly includes any of the premise categories or the conclusion category properly includes the others as well. Arguments that are neither specific nor general are referred to as "mixed". For discussion of mixed arguments, see Osherson et al. (1990).

the representativeness heuristic; with non-blank predicates, however, probability judgments are based not only on similarity relations, but also on the plausibility of the premises and conclusion.

With this as background we can state our agenda. In the next section we consider category-based arguments with blank predicates. We will be brief here because much of the relevant research has appeared elsewhere (see Osherson et al., 1990; Osherson, Stern, Wilkie, Stob, & Smith, 1991; Smith, Lopez, & Osherson, 1992). In the third section we turn our attention to non-blank predicates. We present a model of how people reason about such predicates when judging the strength of arguments, along with some relevant data. Concluding remarks occupy the fourth and final section.

Category-based arguments with blank predicates

Factors that affect probability judgment

We are interested in factors that affect probability judgments about specific arguments. To uncover these factors, we presented 40 University of Michigan undergraduates with a series of 24 arguments, and asked them to estimate the probability of each conclusion on the assumption that the respective premises were true. Certain pairs of arguments offered contrasts that differed on only one factor, and these contrasts provide evidence for a number of phenomena. Four such phenomena are considered below.

One contrasting pair of arguments consisted of:

(4a) Tigers use serotonin as a neurotransmitter
      Cougars use serotonin as a neurotransmitter   [.86]
      ───
      Bobcats use serotonin as a neurotransmitter

(4b) Tigers use serotonin as a neurotransmitter
      Cougars use serotonin as a neurotransmitter   [.39]
      ───
      Giraffes use serotonin as a neurotransmitter

The numbers in brackets indicate the average conditional probability that subjects assigned to that particular argument (i.e., the probability they assigned to the conclusion being true, given that the premises were true). The two arguments in (4) differ with respect to the similarity of the premise categories to the conclusion category, this similarity being greater in (4a) than (4b); clearly,

Table 1. *Some phenomena involving specific arguments*

Phenomenon	Stronger argument	Weaker argument
1. Premise–conclusion similarity	TIGER, COUGAR/BOBCAT	TIGER, COUGAR/GIRAFFE
2. Premise–conclusion asymmetry	LION/BAT	BAT/LION
3. Premise typicality (after Rips, 1975)	HORSE/GOAT	PIG/GOAT
4. Premise diversity	CHIMPANZEE, FOX/POLAR BEAR	WOLF, FOX/POLAR BEAR

subjects favored conclusions that were more similar to the premises. We refer to this effect as the "premise–conclusion similarity" phenomenon.

Table 1 lists three phenomena involving specific arguments that emerged from this study plus a fourth phenomenon that is due to Rips (1975). The first column of the table names the phenomenon. The second and third columns give the premise and conclusion categories used in the contrasting pair of arguments that define the phenomena. Column 2 lists arguments judged more probable (the "stronger" arguments), and Column 3 the less probable (or "weaker") arguments. The arguments are presented in the format "premise category . . ./ conclusion category", with the blank predicate being suppressed. The difference between the stronger and weaker argument is statistically significant in most cases by a sign test.

After premise–conclusion similarity, the next phenomenon listed in Table 1 is asymmetry. It is defined only for single-premise arguments, and reveals that such arguments need not be symmetric. In particular, a single-premise argument will be judged more probable when the more typical category is in the premise than in the conclusion. For example, lions having a particular property makes it more probable that bats do, than vice versa. This asymmetry phenomenon is closely related to a phenomenon reported by Rips (1975), which we term the "typicality" phenomenon. It is listed as the third phenomenon in Table 1; it says that, other things being equal, arguments with more typical premise categories (e.g., HORSE) are judged more probable than those with less typical premise categories (e.g., PIG), even when the similarity between premise and conclusion categories is kept constant. The fourth phenomenon in the table is "premise diversity". This phenomenon shows that, other things being equal, the more diverse, or dissimilar, the premise categories, the more probable the argument is judged. Chimpanzees and foxes sharing a common property makes it more probable that polar bears have it, than does the fact that wolves and foxes share the same property. Note that more diverse premise categories may not be more typical, or more similar, to the conclusion category; for example, in the preceding example, the occurrence of chimpanzees increases diversity but not typicality or similarity to the conclusion. In what follows, we focus on the four phenomena of Table 1.

The similarity coverage model

To explain the preceding phenomena, among others, Osherson et al. (1990) advanced the *similarity coverage* model. This is a model of argument strength, where "strength" refers to the extent to which belief in an argument's premises causes the reasoner to believe in the argument's conclusion. When an argument's predicate is blank, its strength is captured by the judged probability of the conclusion given the premises, since prior belief in the conclusion plays no role. In such cases, a model of argument strength can also serve as a model of conditional probability judgment. Although the similarity coverage model applies both to general and to specific arguments of this kind, we focus on the latter in what follows.

The model

According to the model, the judged probability of an argument depends on two variables:

(i) The similarity of the premise categories to the conclusion category.
(ii) The extent to which the premise categories "cover" the lowest-level category that includes the premise and conclusion categories.

The first, or "similarity", term is straightforward; the only wrinkle is that when there are multiple premises, similarity is determined by a maximum rule. For argument (3), for example, the similarity term consists of the maximum similarity of robins or ducks on the one hand, to sparrows on the other. One piece of evidence for the maximum rule is that argument (3) does not change much in strength if the premise about ducks is removed. More generally, the maximum rule captures the intuition that, when judging the probability that a conclusion category has a particular property, we pay most of our attention to the most similar premise category.

The second, or "coverage", term of the model requires more unpacking. Note first that it presupposes that subjects judging a specific argument generate a more general category, namely, the lowest-level category that includes the premise and conclusion categories. We refer to this category as the "inclusive" category. For argument (4a), the inclusive category might be FELINE; for argument (4b), the inclusive category might be MAMMAL. The introduction of an inclusive category captures the intuition that when informed, for example, that tigers and cougars have a property, the subject considers the possibility that all felines have the property and, therefore, that bobcats do. The judgment of a specific argument thus includes the generation of a general argument. The strength of this general argument is evaluated by computing the extent to which its premises, for example, tigers and cougars, "cover" the inclusive category, for example, FELINE.

We now need to explicate the notion of "coverage". Intuitively, members of a general category cover that category to the extent that, on average, they are similar to other members. As an aid to intuition, Fig. 1 contains a two-dimensional representation – obtained by multidimensional scaling – of the similarities between various instances of the concept FRUIT (Tversky & Hutchinson, 1986). Similarity here is reflected by closeness in the space. If we restrict our attention to the coverage provided by single members, typical members like APPLE or PLUM cover the space better than atypical members like COCONUT or OLIVE; that is, the average metric distance of APPLE or PLUM to all other instances in Fig. 1 is less than that of COCONUT or OLIVE to all other instances in Fig. 1. The fact that a typical member provides relatively good coverage of a category gives us insight into why single-premise arguments with typical premise categories tend to be judged stronger than arguments with atypical premise categories, as revealed in the asymmetry and typicality phenomena. If we consider the coverage provided by multiple members of a category, however,

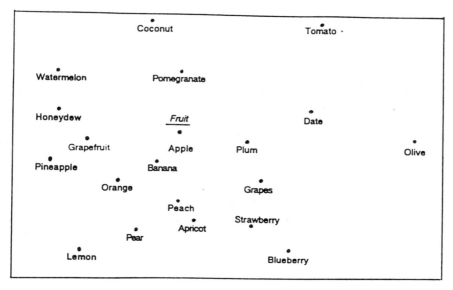

Figure 1.   *A two-dimensional space for representing the similarity relations among 20 instances of fruit. From Tversky and Hutchinson (1986).*

more than typicality is involved. Intuitively, APPLE, PLUM, and ORANGE cover the space in Fig. 1 less well than do COCONUT, GRAPEFRUIT, and BLUEBERRY, even though the former are generally more typical than the latter. This difference in coverage arises because whatever category member is close to APPLE is also close to PLUM and ORANGE, so PLUM and ORANGE add little by way of coverage; in contrast, there are some members that are close to GRAPEFRUIT or BLUEBERRY but not to COCONUT, so GRAPEFRUIT and BLUEBERRY are adding coverage. This gives us insight into the diversity phenomenon.

Thus, a subset of a general category covers that category to the extent that, for any member of the latter you think of, at least one member of the former is similar to it. This statement leads naturally to an algebraic definition of coverage. Let $P_1 \ldots P_m/C$ be a general argument with premise categories CAT $(P_1) \ldots$ CAT(P_m) and conclusion category CAT(C). Furthermore, let $c_1 \ldots c_n$ be instances of CAT(C) that a person judging the argument considers (perhaps unconsciously). And let SIM(CAT(P_i), c_j) be the similarity between premise-category P_i and conclusion-category instance c_j. Then the coverage of an argument, which we will denote by COV(CAT$(P_1) \ldots$ CAT(P_m); CAT(C)), is defined as the average of:

$$\text{MAX}[\text{SIM}(\text{CAT}(P_1), c_1), \ldots, \text{SIM}(\text{CAT}(P_m), c_1)]$$
$$\text{MAX}[\text{SIM}(\text{CAT}(P_1), c_2), \ldots, \text{SIM}(\text{CAT}(P_m), c_2)]$$
$$\cdot$$
$$\cdot$$
$$\cdot$$
$$\text{MAX}[\text{SIM}(\text{CAT}(P_1), c_n), \ldots, \text{SIM}(\text{CAT}(P_m), c_n)]$$

Coverage, then, is the average maximum similarity between (sampled) conclusion-category instances and premise categories. Returning to argument (4a), for which FELINE is presumably the inclusive category, the coverage term of the argument would be given by COV(TIGER, COUGAR; FELINE), and might include terms like:

MAX[SIM(TIGER, LEOPARD), SIM(COUGAR, LEOPARD)]; and
MAX[SIM(TIGER, HOUSECAT), SIM(COUGAR, HOUSECAT)]

Note that in the special case of single-premise arguments, such as TIGER/ COUGAR, there is no maximum to consider. Hence, COV(CAT(P); CAT(C)) is simply the average similarity of the premise category to instances of the conclusion category. Coverage therefore reduces to the typicality of the premise category in the conclusion category (this fits with our geometric representation in Fig. 1).

Combining the similarity and coverage terms, our final model of argument strength is given by:

$$(\alpha)\ \text{MAX}[\text{SIM}(\text{CAT}(P_1), \text{CAT}(C)), \ldots, \text{SIM}(\text{CAT}(P_m), \text{CAT}(C))]$$
$$+ (1 - \alpha)\ \text{COV}[(\text{CAT}(P_1)), \ldots, \text{CAT}(P_m); \text{INCLUSIVE CATEGORY}]$$

The positive constant $\alpha (0 \leqslant \alpha \leqslant 1)$ indicates the weight given to the similarity term: the weight given to coverage is simply $1 - \alpha$.[2]

Applications of the model

The similarity coverage model readily explains the four phenomena described earlier. The first phenomenon was premise–conclusion similarity, and we illustrated it by showing that an argument with premise categories TIGER and COUGAR and conclusion category BOBCAT is judged more probable than an argument with the same premise categories but conclusion category GIRAFFE. Assume that the inclusive category for the former argument is FELINE and that for the latter argument is MAMMAL. Then, according to the model, the strengths of the two arguments are given by:

(a) $(\alpha)\ \text{MAX}[\text{SIM}(\text{TIGER}, \text{BOBCAT}), \text{SIM}(\text{COUGAR}, \text{BOBCAT})]$
$+ (1 - \alpha)\ \text{COV}[\text{TIGER}, \text{COUGAR}; \text{FELINE}];$ and

(b) $(\alpha)\ \text{MAX}[\text{SIM}(\text{TIGER}, \text{GIRAFFE}), \text{SIM}(\text{COUGAR}, \text{GIRAFFE})]$
$+ (1 - \alpha)\ \text{COV}[\text{TIGER}, \text{COUGAR}; \text{MAMMAL}]$

The similarity term is clearly greater for (a) than (b). The coverage term is also greater for (a) than (b), because tigers and cougars are more similar on average to other cats than to other mammals. This explains why argument (4a) is judged the stronger.

Consider next the typicality phenomenon, which we illustrated by the argument HORSE/GOAT being judged more probable than the argument PIG/GOAT. Because Rips (1975) selected these items so that the similarity between premise and conclusion categories was held constant, we can focus on just the coverage term. Since MAMMAL is presumably the inclusive category for both arguments, for the model to predict the result of interest, the coverage of (HORSE; MAMMAL) must exceed that of (PIG; MAMMAL). Because coverage for single-premise arguments reduces to typicality, and because HORSE is in fact a more typical MAMMAL than is PIG, the result is accounted for. By a comparable line of reasoning, the asymmetry phenomenon is accounted for.

The last phenomenon to consider is that of premise diversity, which we

---

[2] In Osherson et al.'s (1990) analysis, coverage and α are defined for each particular individual. In the present treatment they are assumed to be the same for all individuals under consideration for ease of exposition.

illustrated by showing that CHIMPANZEE, FOX/POLAR BEAR is judged stronger than WOLF, FOX/POLAR BEAR. The items were selected so that the premise categories that differ between the arguments, CHIMPANZEE and WOLF, were roughly equally similar to the conclusion category. Hence, the similarity terms for the two arguments are roughly the same, and again we can focus on the coverage terms. Assuming that the inclusive category for both arguments is MAMMAL, coverage for the stronger or more probable argument might include terms such as:

MAX[SIM(CHIMPANZEE, SQUIRREL), SIM(FOX, SQUIRREL)]; and
MAX[SIM(CHIMPANZEE, MONKEY), SIM(FOX, MONKEY)]

Coverage for the weaker argument might include terms such as:

MAX[SIM(WOLF, SQUIRREL), SIM(FOX, SQUIRREL)]; and
MAX[SIM(WOLF, MONKEY), SIM(FOX, MONKEY)]

When the sampled conclusion instance is SQUIRREL, there should be little difference between the two arguments; that is, it is doubtful that WOLF is appreciably more similar to SQUIRREL than FOX is. However, when the sampled instance is MONKEY, the maximum similarity will be greater in the more diverse argument because CHIMPANZEE is more similar to MONKEY than WOLF is. More generally, only for the diverse argument will there be some conclusion instances that are covered by the second premise but not the first. Considerations like these account for the premise diversity phenomenon.

The preceding applications of the similarity coverage model comprise only a small part of the empirical support for the model. Osherson et al. (1990) present other phenomena that are predicted by the model. This same paper also presents the results of several experiments which show that the similarity coverage model provides a quantitative account of strength or probability judgments to specific and general arguments. Smith et al. (1992) provide additional experiments and quantitative tests of the model, and Osherson et al. (1991) show that a variant of the model quantitatively predicts strength or probability judgments on an individual subject basis.

Both the similarity and coverage terms of the model reflect similarity relations. This makes the model a close relative to the representativeness heuristic of Kahneman and Tversky (1973), which often reduces to similarity and typicality (Shafir et al., 1990). Things change substantially, however, when the predicates in our paradigm are accorded a more familiar content.

Category-based arguments with non-blank predicates

Counter-examples to the phenomena

Some of the phenomena that we have studied with blank predicates are extremely robust. The similarity and typicality phenomena, for example, have been obtained with preschool children (Lopez, Gunthil, Gelman, & Smith, 1992; see also Carey, 1985, and Gelman & Markman, 1987), and with a wide variety of categories, including artifacts, number categories, and social categories (Armstrong, 1991; Rothbart & Lewis, 1988; Sloman & Wisniewski, 1992). The robustness of the similarity phenomenon would seem to result from its close relation to the principle of stimulus generalization (similar stimuli occasion similar responses). It is thus of considerable interest that counter-examples to the phenomena can be generated by changing the predicates from blank ones to more familiar ones.

Consider the following pair of arguments (where "poodles" refers to "toy poodles"):

(5a) Dobermanns can bite through wire
  _____
  German shepherds can bite through wire

(5b) Poodles can bite through wire
  _____
  German shepherds can bite through wire

Note first that the predicate, *can bite through wire*, is non-blank. We are relatively familiar with its contents, and we can reason about it. Also, it clearly meets the criterion for non-blankness that we mentioned earlier: it applies differentially to various members of a domain (it applies more to Dobermanns than to poodles, for example). What is of particular importance is that, for most people, argument (5b) is stronger than argument (5a). The intuition behind this judgment seems to be that, "If even poodles can do it, surely German shepherds can". But this judgment violates the similarity phenomenon, since poodles seem less similar to German shepherds than do Dobermanns.

In a like manner, arguments (6a) and (6b) offer a counter-example to the typicality phenomenon:

(6a) Collies can bite through wire
  _____
  German shepherds can bite through wire

(6b) Poodles can bite through wire
_____
German shepherds can bite through wire

Informal judgments favor the second argument as the stronger one, even though collies are more typical dogs than poodles are. Arguments (7a) and (7b) provide a counter-example to the asymmetry phenomenon described earlier:

(7a) Collies can bite through wire
_____
Poodles can bite through wire

(7b) Poodles can bite through wire
_____
Collies can bite through wire

Again, informal judgments find the second argument as stronger ("If poodles can do it, likely collies can too"), even though the more typical category appears in the premise of argument (7a), not in that of (7b). In like manner, one could produce counter-examples to the premise diversity phenomenon.

What lies behind these counter-examples? As we will see, it is not that similarity relations cease to play a role when non-blank predicates are used. Rather, similarity is being overshadowed by another factor in these examples – the plausibility of the premise – where a less plausible premise, once accepted as true, seems to induce greater belief in the corresponding conclusion than does a more plausible premise. What we now need to do is to explicate the notion of plausibility.

The gap model

Basic ideas

The intuitions that lie behind our model for non-blank predicates are captured by the following hypothetical monologue of a subject judging arguments (5b) and (5a), respectively:

"Hmm. Poodles can bite through wire. I thought that to bite through wire, an animal had to have powerful jaws. But poodles are kind of weak. I guess an animal doesn't have to be that powerful to bite through wire. Then a German shepherd is almost certainly powerful enough to do it."

"Hmm. Dobermanns can bite through wire. That fits with what I thought, to bite through wire an animal has to have powerful jaws. I'm not sure whether or not a German shepherd is powerful enough to do it."

The key ideas are:

(1) The non-blank predicate potentiates a subset of the premise category's attributes (e.g., powerfulness, size). From here on, these are the only relevant attributes. The non-blank predicate is associated with one or more of these attributes (e.g., powerfulness) and with values on them.

(2) The premise category (e.g., POODLE) is evaluated to see if its values on the relevant attributes are at least as great as those that characterize the predicate. The predicate's values are used as criteria that the category must pass.

(3) If the premise category's values are less than those of the predicate (e.g., POODLE's powerfulness level is less than the criterion set up by the predicate), the latter are scaled down; otherwise, the predicate's values are left unchanged (as in the Dobermann example). In this way, the plausibility of the premise plays a role.

(4) To the extent that the predicate's values are scaled down, the conclusion category's values are more likely to be at least as great as those of the predicate, and hence the conclusion is likely to be judged more probable. In this way, the premise indirectly affects the plausibility of the conclusion.

These processes differ from those underlying the similarity coverage model in that they require a decomposition of the predicate into its constituent attributes and values. In the similarity coverage model, a predicate is essentially treated as a whole (presumably because it is blank).

Probability of statements

We now embody the foregoing intuitive account into an explicit model that seems to offer the simplest possible realization of the key ideas. The model can be viewed as having two functions, which correspond to estimating the probability of an individual statement and estimating the probability of a conclusion of an argument given its premises. In what follows, we illustrate how the model works by relying on the poodle and Dobermann examples. (For a more extended discussion of the model, see Osherson, Smith, Myers, Shafir, & Stob, in press.)

Let us assume that the categories and predicate of interest have the attribute value structure given in Table 2. The values of attributes are assumed to correspond to real numbers (this amounts to beliefs being represented by real vectors in an appropriate attribute space). Note that the final column in the table gives the values of 9 and 9, which represents the powerfulness and size level required of an animal to be able to bite through wire. Presumably, these values,

Table 2.   A. *Hypothetical attributes and values associated with three categories and one predicate figuring in arguments (5)–(7)*

	Poodles	Dobermanns	German shepherds	Can bite through wire
Powerfulness	3	7	6	9
Size	2	6	7	9

B. *Hypothetical similarity ratings*

Poodles, German shepherds = .3
Dobermanns, German shepherds = .6

unlike the others in the table, are not part of a pre-existing representation. Rather, by some knowledge-based processes, people are able to compute such attribute-value representations for predicates "on-the-fly". In essence, people may treat the predicate as an *ad hoc category* (ANIMALS THAT BITE THROUGH WIRE), and use whatever knowledge generation processes they typically use when constructing such makeshift categories (Barsalou, 1983).

Consider how the model determines the probability of a statement. For a statement to be probable, the values of the category should be at least as great as the corresponding values of the predicate. This idea may be quantified with the "cut-off" operator $\dot{-}$, defined over real numbers by:

$$x \dot{-} y = \text{Max}\{0, x - y\}$$

(Thus $5 \dot{-} 3 = 2$ and $3 \dot{-} 5 = 0$.) Now suppose there are n relevant attributes. Letting C designate the vector for the category's values and P the vector for the predicate's values, the probability of a category-property statement is estimated to be:

$$\frac{1}{1 + \sum_{i=1}^{n} (P_i \dot{-} C_i)} \tag{1}$$

where P_i and C_i are the values at the ith coordinate (attribute) of the vectors P and C. To illustrate, according to Eq. (1) and Table 2, the probability that German shepherds can bite through wire is:

$$\frac{1}{1 + [(9 \dot{-} 6) + (9 \dot{-} 7)]} = 0.17 \tag{2}$$

Equation (1) will always yield a number in $[0, 1]$. Probability 1 is attained if $C_i \geq P_i$ for all attributes, that is, if the category's values satisfy all the criteria set by the predicate (the surplus of C_i over P_i plays no role in the calculation). Since the fundamental entity, $P_i \dot{-} C_i$, may be conceived as the "gap" between the predicate's and category's value on attribute *i*, the present theory is called the "gap model". These gaps are what lie behind the plausibility (or implausibility) of a statement.[3]

Conditional probability of statements

Now that we know how the gap model assigns a probability to an individual statement, we can consider how the model assigns a probability to a conclusion of an argument given its premises. Assigning such a conditional probability requires a number of steps. These include an initial modification of the argument's predicate due to the impact of the premises, and subsequent estimation of the conclusion's probability. The following example illustrates how these steps are implemented in the model.[4]

Argument (5b) may be abbreviated as:

(5b) (POODLE, WIRE)

 (GERMAN SHEPHERD, WIRE)

where each category is assumed to be represented by its values. In the first step, the subject assesses the impact of the premise by comparing the category's critical values to those of the predicate. On the attribute of powerfulness, the relevant gap is WIRE $\div$ POODLE = $(9 \div 3)$ (see Table 2). This signifies that poodles do not have the powerfulness needed to bite through wire. However, (POODLES, WIRE) is a premise, and hence assumed to be true. Therefore animals like poodles need not have a powerfulness of 9 to bite through wire. The subject is thus led to lower the powerfulness value for WIRE when evaluating the conclusion. In doing this, he or she considers not only the gap between WIRE and POODLE, but also the similarity between poodles and German shepherds. The similarity between the two kinds of dogs approximates the perceived relevance of the premise to the conclusion, and thus affects the extent to which the conclusion predicate is changed. Hence, the powerfulness value for WIRE is lowered by:

$$(\text{WIRE}_1 \div \text{POODLE}_1) \times \text{similarity (POODLE, GERMAN SHEPHERD)} \tag{3}$$

[3]A potential problem with Eq. (1) is that any addition of an attribute to the category and predicate tends to lower the probability of statements, since probability declines with the sum of the gaps. This aspect can be changed by taking an average of the gaps. To keep things simple, though, we will leave Eq. (1) as is.

[4]For an argument with a non-blank predicate, the judged probability of its conclusion given its premises is not a pure measure of the argument's strength. This is because the probability judgment may reflect one's prior belief in the argument's conclusion as well as the extent to which belief in the premises causes one to believe in the conclusion. For this reason, in both our examples and our experiments, we usually compare arguments that have the identical conclusion.

where the subscript 1 indicates that we are dealing with the first attribute. Hypothetical similarity values are provided in the bottom half of Table 2. Plugging the relevant numbers into Eq. (3) gives:

$$(9 \div 3) \times 0.3 = 1.8 \tag{4}$$

Thus the powerfulness value of WIRE is lowered by 1.8, so the modified value is $9 - 1.8$ or 7.2.

By a similar logic, the second attribute in Table 2, size, also gives rise to a gap, $WIRE_2 \div POODLE_2$. As a consequence, WIRE's size value is lowered by:

$$(9 \div 2) \times 0.3 = 2.1 \tag{5}$$

The modified value for WIRE's size is therefore $9 - 2.1$ or 6.9.

The premise (POODLE, WIRE) has thus modified the WIRE representation from its original values of (9, 9) to the new values of (7.2, 6.9). It remains only to consider the last step of the process, and calculate the probability of the conclusion. This step was explicated in our description of how one estimates the probability of individual statements. To implement this step, we need to insert into Eq. (1) the two gaps that involve GERMAN SHEPHERD and the modified WIRE – namely $7.2 \div 6$ and $6.9 \div 7$:

$$\frac{1}{1 + 1.2 + 0} = 0.45 \tag{6}$$

Observe that the latter probability exceeds the unconditional probability that German shepherds can bite through wire, calculated earlier to be 0.17 (see Eq. (2)). The difference is due to the impact of the premise (POODLE, WIRE), which changes the subject's interpretation of WIRE, bringing it into greater conformity with the values of POODLE.

It is instructive to go through comparable calculations for argument (5a), which may be abbreviated as:

(5a) (DOBERMANN, WIRE)
_____

(GERMAN SHEPHERD, WIRE)

In assessing the impact of the premise, the gap for powerfulness is $(9 \div 7)$ (see Table 2). Given that Dobermanns are 0.6 similar to German shepherds (see Table 2), the powerfulness value of WIRE is lowered by

$$(9 \div 7) \times 0.6 = 1.2 \tag{7}$$

This makes the modified powerfulness value of WIRE $9 - 1.2$, or 7.8. The gap for size is $(9 \div 6)$ (see Table 2). Hence the size value of WIRE lowered by:

$$(9 \div 6) \times 0.6 = 1.8 \tag{8}$$

making the size value of WIRE $9 - 1.8$, or 7.2. The values for the modified WIRE representation are therefore (7.8, 7.2), and the two gaps involving GERMAN SHEPHERD and the modified WIRE are consequently $7.8 \div 6$ and $7.2 \div 7$. Inserting these gaps into Eq. (1) gives the probability of the argument's conclusion as

$$\frac{1}{1 + 1.8 + 0.2} = 0.33 \tag{9}$$

Again the conditional probability exceeds the unconditional probability that German shepherds can bite through wire (0.17). The conditional probability obtained with DOBERMANN as premise category, 0.33, is less than that obtained with POODLE as premise category, 0.45. This fits our informal finding that argument (5a) is judged less probable than (5b).

This convergence of theory and data is merely demonstrational, since the critical parameters in Table 2 were generated for purposes of illustration. Indeed, small changes in the values of some entries in Table 2 would lead to the DOBERMANN argument being predicted to be stronger than the POODLE one (e.g., increasing the similarity between Dobermann and German shepherds could change the prediction). This implies that, when interpreting data with respect to the gap model, we cannot always expect the effect of premise gaps to overwhelm that of premise–conclusion similarity; that is, when premise gaps favor one argument but premise–conclusion similarity favors another, which argument emerges as stronger depends on the specific parameter values. Intuitively, gaps capture what has been learned from the premise, similarity reflects the relevance of this to the conclusion, and the final impact depends on the magnitudes of both factors.

The fact that the similarity between premise and conclusion plays a key role in the gap model provides an important link to the similarity coverage model. In both models, something about the premise predicate is generalized to the conclusion category to the extent the premise and conclusion categories are similar. However, in the similarity coverage model, the predicate – assumed to be blank – is left intact, whereas in the gap model the predicate's values are modified before it plays a role in the evaluation of the conclusion.[5]

---

[5]Another difference between the two models concerns how similarity between categories is computed. In applications of the similarity coverage model, we have assumed that each category is intrinsically associated with a large set of attributes, and that similarity between categories is computed over all these attributes (Osherson et al., 1991). In applications of the gap model, we have typically assumed that only attributes potentiated by the predicate matter, and hence that similarity between categories considers only two or three attributes (Osherson et al., in press). In essence, a non-blank predicate picks out certain *criteria* and similarity is computed only with respect to these criteria (Medin, Goldstone, & Gentner, 1993).

Multiple premises

The gap model can be extended to deal with arguments containing more than a single premise. The basic idea is embodied in a "maximization" principle. Specifically, when evaluating the gap for each attribute, every premise category is considered and the category with maximal impact is selected for use, where "impact" is defined as the product of gap and similarity. To illustrate, suppose argument (5a) were enriched to include a premise about collies in addition to that about Dobermanns. In calculating the gap on the powerfulness attribute, COLLIE will lead to a larger gap than DOBERMANN, assuming that collies are judged less powerful than Dobermanns; assuming further that collies and Dobermanns are roughly equally similar to German shepherds (the conclusion category), COLLIE would then have greater impact than DOBERMANN. Hence, by the maximization principle, only the gap due to COLLIE would be used to modify the powerfulness value of WIRE. The maximization principle can be stated more generally for arguments with any number of predicates. A similar proposal, couched in a connectionist architecture, has been made by Sloman (1993).[6]

This completes our description of the gap model. Its most important psychological claims are worth highlighting:

(1) The mental representations of categories and predicates can in part be summarized by attribute value structures (by real vectors in an appropriate attribute space).

(2) A category–predicate statement is judged probable to the extent that the values evoked by the predicate are contained in the category.

(3) An argument's premises increase the probability of its conclusion by lowering the values presumed necessary for possession of the predicate.

(4) The impact of a premise depends on (a) the gap between its predicate and category values, and (b) the similarity of its category to that of the conclusion.

(5) The impact of multiple premises is governed by the maximization principle.

Some qualitative results

To provide an empirical test of the gap model, we asked subjects to judge the probabilities of various one-premise arguments. The arguments were selected so

[6]The maximization principle introduces a kind of coverage notion into the gap model. Thus, when a second premise is added to an argument, it is unlikely to ever have substantially greater maximal impact than the initial premise if its category has similar values to the initial premise category. Hence, adding a more diverse premise category can lead to more of a modification in the predicate. Note that this notion of coverage differs from that in the similarity coverage model in that it concerns a space of features rather than a space of objects.

that there would be substantial variation in premise plausibility (which reflects premise gaps) and premise–conclusion similarity.[7]

Procedure

Five different categories of animals were used: house-cats, lions, camels, hippos, and elephants. House-cats and lions seem relatively similar to one another, as do hippos and elephants; all other couplings yield less similar pairs. (These intuitions were supported by subjects' similarity ratings.) Two different predicates were used: *have skins that are more resistant to penetration than most synthetic fibers* and *have a visual system that fully adapts to darkness in less than 5 minutes*. Each predicate was used with each category. We expected the first, or SKIN, predicate to result in a more plausible proposition when attributed to larger animals, such as hippos and elephants, than to smaller ones, such as house-cats; we expected the second, or VISUAL, predicate to result in a more plausible proposition when attributed to felines than to the other mammals. (These expectations were also supported by subjects' ratings.)

For each predicate, there are 20 possible one-premise arguments: each of the 5 categories could appear in the conclusion, with any of the 4 remaining categories appearing in the premise. The 20 arguments involving the VISUAL predicate were presented before the 20 involving the SKIN predicate. Within each of these 2 blocks, the 20 arguments appeared in random order.

On each trial, the subject was first presented the conclusion of the argument, and asked to rate on an 11-point scale how likely it was that the statement was true (where 0 indicated the statement was definitely not true and 10 indicated the statement was definitely true). Then the premise was presented, and subjects were instructed to consider it true. Subjects then reported how likely it was that the original claim (the conclusion) was true given the new information. After completing their probability ratings, subjects rated the similarity of all pairs of animals on an 11-point scale (where 0 indicated minimal similarity, and 10 maximum similarity). The subjects were 20 University of Michigan undergraduates who were paid for their participation.

Results

Table 3 gives the probability estimates for the SKIN predicate. These estimates were derived by first averaging over the 20 subjects, and then dividing each average by 10 to yield a number between 0 and 1. The first column of the table presents the data for cases in which a conclusion was presented alone. The next four columns indicate how the probabilities changed when each possible premise was added. To illustrate, consider the first row of Table 3, which contains the data for arguments in which house-cats served as the conclusion. The .40 in the first

[7]We are indebted to Kevin Biolsi for his assistance in all aspects of the following experiments.

Table 3.   *Probability estimates for arguments with predicate,* Have skins that are more resistant to penetration than most synthetic fibers

Conclusion alone	With premise			
House-cats .40	Lions .59	Camels .47	Hippos .41	Elephants .38
Lions .55	House-cats .80	Camels .61	Hippos .53	Elephants .53
Camels .60	House-cats .77	Lions .73	Hippos .60	Elephants .60
Hippos .79	House-cats .93	Lions .78	Camels .82	Elephants .85
Elephants .80	House-cats .80	Lions .80	Camels .86	Hippos .87

Pairwise similarity ratings

	House-cats	Lions	Camels	Hippos	Elephants
House-cats	–	8.10	2.85	1.55	1.45
Lions		–	5.45	3.20	3.95
Camels			–	3.00	3.75
Hippos				–	7.35
Elephants					–

column means that the probability attributed to the statement HOUSE-CAT SKIN when it appeared alone was .40. Adding the premise of LION SKIN boosted the probability of the HOUSE-CAT SKIN conclusion to .59; adding the premise CAMEL SKIN boosted the probability of the conclusion to .47; and so on. The bottom of the table contains the average pairwise similarity ratings for the five animals; these ratings will be needed in interpreting the probability estimates.[8]

Some points of interest can be gleaned from looking just at the first column of the top of the table – just at the probabilities attributed to the conclusions when they appeared alone. The SKIN property is non-blank, since the probability with which it is attributed to the five mammals ranges from .40 to .80. Because each of these statements also serves as a premise (in an argument with a different conclusion), there is also a substantial variation in premise plausibility. In particular, the premise involving house-cats is the least plausible, whereas the premises involving hippos and elephants are the most plausible. (Within each row, the premises are increasingly plausible as one moves from left to right.)

The more implausible a premise, the larger the premise gaps. The clearest evidence for the effect of gaps *per se* on judgments would come from cases where premise implausibility varies but premise–conclusion similarity remains relatively

[8]Ideally, we should have obtained two sets of similarity ratings for these animals, one in the context of the SKIN predicate and the other in the context of the VISUAL predicate (see footnote 5).

constant. The row corresponding to camels at the top of Table 3 comes the closest to offering such a case, as there is relatively little variation in similarity ratings involving camels (see the bottom of Table 3). The probabilities assigned to arguments with CAMEL SKIN as their conclusion in fact monotonically decrease as the premise becomes more plausible; this is clear-cut evidence for a gap mechanism. In two of the other rows of Table 3 – those which have house-cats or lions in their conclusion – premise implausibility is positively correlated with premise–conclusion similarity; that is, in these two rows, as one moves across the premises from left to right, the premise becomes both more plausible and less similar to the conclusion. In these cases the gap model unequivocally predicts that probabilities should decline in moving from left to right, and this prediction is supported in both rows of interest. In the remaining two rows – those corresponding to hippos and elephants – premise implausibility and premise–conclusion similarity point in opposite directions (as the former decreases, the latter increases). In such cases the gap model makes no clear prediction (since the critical commodity in the model is the product of gap and similarity). For the row corresponding to elephants, similarity seems to dominate, as the estimated probabilities consistently increase with premise–conclusion similarity. For the row corresponding to hippos, the largest estimated probability goes with the most implausible premise, but aside from that the estimated probabilities track similarity.

The preceding observations received statistical support in a stepwise regression analysis. The dependent measure was the change in the probability of a conclusion occasioned by the addition of a premise (this eliminated the influence that prior belief in a conclusion has on the conditional probability judgments). Premise–conclusion similarity entered the regression model first, and the only other factor in the final model was the interaction between similarity and plausibility. The coefficient for the similarity factor was .74 ($p < .01$), and that for the interaction factor was $-.09$ ($p < .05$); the multiple correlation was $R = .70$ ($F(3, 16) = 5.22$, $p = .01$). The form of the interaction was that the effect of implausibility was greater for more similar premise–conclusion pairs; exactly this kind of interaction is predicted by the gap model because implausibility (gap) is multiplied by similarity.

Table 4 presents the comparable data for the VISUAL predicate. There is substantial variation in the probability of the predicate being attributed to the various animals, from .42 to .79, which means there is substantial variation in premise plausibility. (Again, within each row, the premises increase in plausibility as one moves from left to right, but now the felines are associated with high plausibility whereas the hippos and elephants are associated with low plausibility.)

As before, first we consider the results for arguments that have camels in their conclusions, this being the closest we can come to a case where premise–conclusion similarity remains constant. Although there is not much variation in

Table 4.   *Probability estimates for arguments with predicate,* Have a visual system that fully adapts to darkness in less than 5 minutes

Conclusion alone	With premise			
Hippos	Elephants	Camels	Lions	House-cats
.42	.63	.47	.42	.43
Elephants	Hippos	Camels	Lions	House-cats
.47	.69	.54	.52	.41
Camels	Hippos	Elephants	Lions	House-cats
.53	.55	.58	.56	.51
Lions	Hippos	Elephants	Camels	House-cats
.74	.66	.71	.76	.86
House-cats	Hippos	Elephants	Camels	Lions
.79	.74	.81	.75	.93

the judgments in the relevant row, there is at least some indication of a decline in probability estimates as the premise becomes more plausible. Moving to the first two rows of Table 4, those for hippos and elephants, we have cases in which both premise implausibility and similarity decline as one moves across the premises. Probability estimates systematically decline as one moves from left to right, as predicted by the gap model. In the last rows, which contain the data for lions and house-cats, plausibility and similarity point in opposite directions. In both of these cases, similarity seems to dominate. Thus, overall, premise–conclusion similarity seems to be playing a somewhat greater role in these data than in the data for the SKIN predicate considered previously.

A stepwise regression analysis again provides statistical support for our qualitative observations. Using increments in probability estimates as the dependent measure, the first factor to enter the model was premise–conclusion similarity, and the other factor in the final model was the interaction between similarity and plausibility. The coefficient for similarity was .52 ($p < .01$), that for the interaction was $-.04$ ($p < .01$), and the multiple correlation was .89 ($F(2, 17) = 32.92$, $p < .01$). Again, the form of the interaction was that predicted by the gap model, the effect of implausibility being greater when premise–conclusion similarity is greater. One last result is worth noting because it supports our observation that premise–conclusion similarity played a greater role with the VISUAL than the SKIN predicate. The simple correlation between similarity and probability estimates was .83 for the data obtained with the VISUAL predicate, versus .57 for the SKIN data. This difference in correlation is significant ($p < .05$).

Why did the similarity factor dominate the plausibility factor more with the VISUAL predicate than the SKIN predicate? Two possible answers are worth considering. One possibility is that whether premise–conclusion similarity dominates implausibility (or vice versa) depends on the specific values of the relevant attributes and the specific values of the pairwise similarities (see p. 83). Thus, the particular values for our five animals on the relevant attributes of SKIN (e.g., size) may have been such as to produce a dominance of implausibility, whereas those on the attributes of VISUAL (e.g., nocturnal) may have produced a dominance of similarity. Alternatively, the SKIN and VISUAL predicates may differ in important qualitative respects. For example, the SKIN predicate seems to involve a *continuous* variation on an attribute like size – animals with very impenetrable skins tend to be large (elephant), those with medium impenetrable skin tend to be of medium size (lion), and those with relatively penetrable skin tend to be small (house-cat). In contrast, the VISUAL predicate may involve more of a *threshold* variation on some underlining attribute – either an animal has enough of this attribute to fully adapt to darkness in less than 5 minutes or it does not. If such a qualitative difference in predicates was the case, the gap model would likely provide a better account of the predicate associated with continuous variation because this is the kind of variation assumed in the model.

Some quantitative results

Having provided some qualitative support for the gap model, we now consider quantitative evidence. We are interested in the model's ability to make predictions about subjects' probability judgments for various arguments. This issue has been investigated in an experiment by Osherson, Smith, Myers, Shafir, and Stob (in press), and in what follows we describe some of their major findings.

Procedure

The materials included the 5 categories and 2 predicates used in the previous experiment, along with a new set of 5 categories and 2 predicates. The 5 new categories of animals were bears, beavers, squirrels, monkeys, and gorillas; the 2 new predicates were *have three distinct layers of fat tissue surrounding vital organs* (hereafter, abbreviated as FAT) and *have over 80% of their brain surface devoted to neocortex* (hereafter, NEOCORTEX). We will refer to the new material as "Set 2", and to the ones taken from Experiment 1 as "Set 1". Note that, as is the case with Set 1, Set 2 provides variations in similarity (e.g., bears are similar to beavers, and monkeys to gorillas), and in the applicability of the predicate to the category (e.g., FAT applies better to bears than to monkeys, whereas NEO-CORTEX shows the reverse pattern).

More arguments were used in this study than the previous one. The arguments were constructed from the materials within a set in the same manner as in the previous study (i.e., a premise or conclusion of an argument consisted of a pairing of one of the categories with a predicate). For each predicate, there were : (i) 5 zero-premise arguments, that is, 5 cases where only a conclusion appeared; (ii) 20 one-premise arguments; (iii) 30 two-premise arguments; (iv) 20 three-premise arguments; and (v) 5 four-premise arguments. Hence, there were 80 arguments per predicate (which exhausts all the possibilities with 5 categories), for a total of 160 different arguments for each set.

Each subject made probability judgments about 160 arguments, presented in random order. Half the subjects worked with arguments constructed from Set 1, and the other half worked with arguments from Set 2. The phrasing of the probability question differed from that in the previous study. Now the entire argument was presented at once, and subjects were simply asked, "What is the probability that [the conclusion is true] given that [the premises are true]?" The "given that" clause did not appear for zero-premise arguments. The subjects were 30 University of Michigan undergraduates who were paid for their participation.

Results

To fit the gap model to an individual subject's data we need to know the attribute values of the relevant categories and predicates for that subject. These values were estimated by the following four-step procedure.

(1) The 160 arguments evaluated by a given subject were divided into two sets of 80 corresponding to the predicate appearing therein. Each set of 80 arguments was treated separately; this essentially divided each subject into two halves, and in what follows we refer to these 60 data sets (2 for each of our 30 subjects) as "half-subjects."

(2) The 80 arguments of a given half-subject were again partitioned into two sets. One set was used to fix the parameters of the gap model (as described below); these are the "fixing" arguments. The other set was used to test the predictions of the model once its parameters were fixed; these are the "testing" arguments. Different kinds of partitions were used, but we will focus on those in which either 20, 30, or 50 randomly selected arguments were used as the fixing arguments, and the remaining 60, 50, or 30 arguments served as the testing arguments.

(3) We assumed that each category and predicate could be represented by just two attributes. This means that the 5 categories and 1 predicate appearing in the 80 arguments of a half-subject are each associated with 2 values, for 12 values in all. These 12 values were the parameters to be determined. For each half-subject, a procedure was employed to find values of the 12 free parameters that maximize the gap model's fit to the fixing arguments. To illustrate, consider the partition in which the fixing set contained 20 fixing arguments. Choice of the 12 parameters caused the gap model to assign probabilities to each of the 20 fixing arguments. These predicted probabilities were then compared to those produced by a given subject for the 20 arguments, and the correlation between the predicted and

observed probabilities provided a measure of goodness to fit. The set of 12 parameters that maximized this correlation was retained for use in the next step.

(4) Once the best set of 12 parameters – associated with a given half-subject and a given partition of arguments – was obtained, the gap model with those parameters was applied to the testing arguments of the partition in question. The probabilities generated by the model were compared to the corresponding probabilities generated by the subject, with the correlation between predicted and observed probabilities providing a measure of goodness of fit of the model. Note that there are *no* free parameters in this last step.

Table 5 provides the results of our model fitting. The first column specifies how many fixing arguments were used, and the second gives the median correlation obtained in step (4) over all 60 half-subjects. Even with only 20 fixing arguments, the correlation between predicted and observed probability estimates is .72. The correlation rises with more fixing arguments. A question of some interest is, to what extent are these good fits dependent on similarity playing a role? To answer this question, we considered a variant of the gap model that contained no similarity factor, and fit this variant to the data using our four-step procedure. The results of these fits are in parentheses in Table 5. In all cases, the fit of the model to data is significantly poorer when similarity no longer plays a role. This is further evidence that similarity is an important element in modelling judgments about non-blank predicates, just as it was in modelling judgments about blank predicates.

An alternative procedure for fitting the model involves first obtaining subjects' estimates of values for the relevant attributes; then the model can be fit to data with no free parameters. We have done some preliminary work with this procedure. After making probability judgments as in the preceding experiment, subjects were presented with a list of 30 attributes that had been preselected to be appropriate to the categories and predicates of interest. They rated the extent to which each attribute characterizes each category or predicate. Using these estimated values to predict the subjects' probability judgments, we found correlations between predicted and obtained probability that generally range

Table 5. *Median correlations between predicted and ob-*
served probability estimates for different parti-
tions of fixing and testing arguments (numbers in
parentheses are for a variant of the gap model in
which similarity plays no role)

Number of arguments used for fixing	Median correlation
20	.72 (.60)
30	.77 (.70)
50	.84 (.77)

between .40 and .50. This is substantially lower than the correlations reported in Table 5. Higher correlations may be obtained with the present procedure by allowing the relevant attributes to vary with the arguments, rather than using a single list of attributes for all arguments (in which case, some attributes may not be relevant for many of the arguments). Additional studies are envisioned in which we employ more sensitive techniques for determining what attributes figure in subjects' judgments of particular arguments.

Concluding comments

Summary

Estimating the likelihood of a proposition on the basis of previous information can be thought of as assigning a probability to the conclusion of an argument based on its premises. We have explored two kinds of psychological factors that influence such probability assignment. First, in the context of blank predicates, we showed that argument strength depends on similarity relations between premise and conclusion categories. These relations were captured in the similarity coverage model, which explains a number of robust qualitative effects, including the premise–conclusion similarity and premise typicality phenomena. Counter-examples to these phenomena, however, were shown to arise in the context of predicates that are non-blank. Unlike the case with blank predicates, in which little is known about the predicate, subjects presented with non-blank predicates are likely to reason about the nature of the predicate and its plausibility *vis-à-vis* the category. Indeed, argument strength with non-blank predicates was shown to be a function of the premises' and conclusion's plausibility, in addition to category similarity. As reflected in the gap model, the perceived implausibility of premises captures how much has been learned from the fact that they are supposedly true, and the similarity between premise and conclusion categories reflects the relevance of what has been learned to the argument's conclusion.

In moving from blank to non-blank predicates, the reasoner's reliance on similarity decreases. Indeed, for some non-blank predicates, similarity seems to play no role at all. To illustrate, consider the following arguments:

(8a) A rhino can break this kind of scale
    ───────────────────────────────────
    An elephant can break this kind of scale

(8b) A refrigerator can break this kind of scale
    ───────────────────────────────────────
    An elephant can break this kind of scale

Both arguments seem equally strong despite the fact that premise–conclusion similarity is far greater in the first than the second case (presumably premise plausibility is comparable in the two arguments). In these cases, there is little or no uncertainty about which attributes are critical (i.e., weight seems to underly the predicate), and consequently there seems to be no need to consider the similarity between premise and conclusion categories (Douglas Medin, personal communication). More generally, it appears that: a high degree of confidence about the critical attribute, as in the preceding example, leads to an almost total reliance on premise plausibility; a lack of confidence about the critical attributes, as with blank predicates, leads to an almost exclusive reliance on similarity; and a limited degree of confidence about the critical attributes, as with most of the non-blank predicates considered in this paper, leads to a reliance on both plausibility and similarity. In this manner, we can see the connection between the gap model and the similarity coverage model.

Possible extensions

In what follows, we briefly note three possible extensions of our analysis of non-blank predicates.

Thus far, we have assumed that similarities are never negative. Some category pairs, however, may be perceived as more different than they are similar, which suggests they may be perceived as negatively similar (this suggestion is compatible with Tversky's, 1977, contrast model of similarity). Negative similarities seem especially possible when the predicates are non-blank. A non-blank predicate may be associated with only one or two attributes, and if two categories have values at the extremes of these attributes they may be perceived as contraries. To the extent that similarity is assumed to reflect the relevance of premise to conclusion, it may be that a similarity score around zero entails little or no relevance, whereas high positive and high negative similarities both reflect great relevance, but of opposite sorts. Thus, assuming we believe that mice and squirrels have similar eating preferences whereas mice and lions have very different preferences, we may think that the fact that mice love onions increases the chances that squirrels love them, but also increases the chances that lions do *not*. The introduction of negative similarities to the gap model has a number of interesting implications that we have only begun to explore.

A second extension of the gap model stems from its prediction that the addition of a premise can *never* lower the probability of a conclusion. That is, given the model's particular cut-off operator and its notion of critical values, an additional premise can only increase the strength of a conclusion (when non-negative gaps occur and when similarity is relatively high), or leave it unchanged (when the gaps are negligible or when similarity is relatively low). However, as demonstrated by Osherson et al. (1990), premises may sometimes lower conclusion probability when blank predicates are used, and this seems all the more likely with non-blank predicates. One way to remedy this potential problem is to introduce into the gap model coverage principles like those used in the similarity coverage model, since an additional premise may change the inclusive category (currently, the gap model makes no use of category structure). Another way to account for decreasing belief with increasing premises is to change the particular fashion in which attribute values are compared (i.e., replace the cut-off operator); and still another possible change is the introduction of negative similarities, as described above. If any of these changes were implemented, the model would be able to predict an occasional lowering of belief in an argument's conclusion with additional premises.

A third elaboration of our model stems from an extension of our paradigm. Up to this point we have used arguments in which the categories vary but the predicate remains fixed. It is equally possible to entertain arguments in which the category is fixed but the predicates vary, and strength variations in such arguments may also be captured by the gap model. Consider, for example, arguments (9a) and (9b):

(9a) Geese can attain flight speeds of 110 miles per hour

Geese can develop a "lift" in excess of twice their body weight by agitating their wings

(9b) Geese can develop a "lift" in excess of twice their body weight by agitating their wings

---

Geese can attain flight speeds of 110 miles per hour

Intuitively, (9a) seems stronger than (9b). This fits with the key ideas behind the gap model; the proposition about flight speeds seems more implausible than that about "lift", and an argument is judged stronger when the more implausible proposition is in the premise rather than the conclusion. However, whereas the fixed-predicate type of argument naturally leads us to a gap-induced modification of the shared predicate (which is then transferred to the conclusion), the current, fixed-category argument seems likely to involve modification of the shared category. That is, while in our previous discussion people were assumed to adjust a predicate's critical values in light of the categories that are seen to possess the predicate, the envisioned extension of the gap model would incorporate changes in the values of the category in light of the predicates that it is said to possess.

Finally, arguments that involve both varied categories and predicates would require a model that incorporates both kinds of adjustment processes.

A final comment

Reasoning and decision making require the constant estimation and readjustment of the probabilities of propositions. Our subjective probability estimates, based on what we have come to know and believe so far, affect the ways in which we reason about future outcomes, and the decisions that we make. The discovery of facts previously considered implausible lead us to adjust our views in more substantial ways than facts that we do not find surprising. The ways in which we adjust our views depend largely on our categorization schemes, and on the similarities that we perceive between the categories under consideration. Further work in the cognitive and decision sciences should help clarify the ways in which plausibility and similarity affect inductive inference and judgments of probability.

References

Armstrong, S.L. (1991). Category and property specificity in category based induction. Poster presented at Psychonomic Society, San Francisco.

Barsalou, L. (1983). Ad hoc categories. *Memory & Cognition, 11,* 211–227.

Carey, S. (1985). *Conceptual change in childhood.* Cambridge, MA: MIT Press.

Gelman, S.A. & Markman, E. (1987). Young children's induction from natural kinds: The role of categories and appearances. *Child Development, 58,* 1532–1541.

Kahneman, D., & Tversky, A. (1973). On the psychology of prediction. *Psychological Review, 80,* 237–251.

Lopez, A., Gunthil, G., Gelman, S.A., & Smith, E.E. (1992). The development of category based induction. *Child Development, 63,* 1070–1090.

Medin, D.L., Goldstone, K., & Gentner, D. (1993). Respects for similarity. *Psychological Review, 100,* 254–278.

Osherson, D.N., Smith, E.E., Wilkie, O., Lopez, A., & Shafir, E. (1990). Category based induction. *Psychological Review, 97,* 185–200.

Osherson, D.N., Smith, E.E., Myers, T.S., Shafir, E.B., & Stob, M. (in press). Extrapolating human probability judgment. *Theory and Decision.*

Osherson, D.N., Stern, J., Wilkie, O., Stob, M., & Smith, E.E. (1991). Default probability. *Cognitive Science, 15,* 251–269.

Rips, L.J. (1975). Inductive judgments about natural categories. *Journal of Verbal Learning and Verbal Behavior, 14,* 665–681.

Rothbart, M., & Lewis, P. (1988). Inferring category attributes from exemplar attributes. *Journal of Personality and Social Psychology, 55,* 861–872.

Shafir, E., Smith, E.E., & Osherson, D.N. (1990). Typicality and reasoning fallacies. *Memory & Cognition, 18,* 229–239.

Sloman, S.A. (1993). Feature based induction. *Cognitive Psychology, 25,* 231–280.

Sloman, S.A., & Wisniewski, E. (1992). Extending the domain of a feature-based model of property induction. *Proceeding of the 13th Annual Meeting of the Cognitive Science Society,* Bloomington, IN.

Smith, E.E., Lopez, A., & Osherson, D.N. (1992). Category membership, similarity, and naive induction. In A. Healy, S.M. Kosslyn, & R. Shiffrin (Eds.), *From learning processes to cognitive processes: Essays in honor of W.K. Estes* (Vol. 2, pp. 181–206). Hillsdale, NJ: Erlbaum.

Tversky, A. (1977). Features of similarity. *Psychological Review, 84*, 327–352.

Tversky, A., & Hutchinson, W. (1986). Nearest neighbor analysis of psychological spaces. *Psychological Review, 93*, 3–22.

Tversky, A., & Kahneman, D. (1983). Extensional versus intuitive reasoning: The conjunction fallacy in probability judgment. *Psychological Review, 90*, 293–315.

5 Debias the environment instead of the judge: an alternative approach to reducing error in diagnostic (and other) judgment

Joshua Klayman

Center for Decision Research, Graduate School of Business, University of Chicago

Kaye Brown

National Center for Health Program Evaluation, Victoria, Australia

Abstract

Questions about how to improve human judgment and reasoning are of theoretical and practical interest, notwithstanding the continuing controversy over whether people are "rational". Improving judgment may involve modifying people's processes to fit their environments better, or vice versa. We illustrate the latter approach in a study of diagnostic reasoning in which subjects learned to distinguish two fictitious diseases. Prior findings suggest that people may judge the likelihood of a diagnostic category on the presence or absence of features that are typical of, rather than diagnostic of, the category. We varied the structure of the information provided to subjects without attempting to modify their judgmental processes. In an "independent" format, subjects learned about each disease separately; in a "contrastive" format, information about the two diseases was juxtaposed to highlight distinctive features. Subjects in the two conditions formed different disease concepts. Diagnoses following contrastive training were much closer to the statistically prescribed judgments based on likelihood ratios. Interventions that modify the environment may provide an alternative approach where it is difficult to modify people's processes. Effective design of such interventions is one motivation

We thank Jackie Gnepp, Arthur Elstein, Michael Doherty, Craig McKenzie, F.R. Heath, Linda Ginzel, Selwyn Becker, Robin Hogarth, and an anonymous reviewer for their valuable comments on earlier drafts of this paper.

for directing research toward understanding how task characteristics affect the use of and the outcomes of judgment and reasoning processes.

Introduction

What is wrong with the way people think, and what can be done to improve it? A large proportion of the research on human judgment, reasoning, and decision making has been concerned with variations on these basic themes. Controversy continues not only over the answers, but also over the legitimacy of the questions themselves: is there anything systematically wrong with human thinking and if, in fact, it *ain't* broke, how can you fix it?

We will sidestep the debate over whether human thinking is fundamentally rational or irrational (see Abelson & Levi, 1985; Cohen, 1981; Edwards, 1990; Funder, 1987; Hammond, 1990; Hogarth, 1981; Jungerman, 1983; Kyburg, 1983), and the related question posed by Anderson (1990, 1991), "is human cognition adaptive?" We take an agnostic position: human judgment may be well *adapted*, but it is not always very *adaptable*. That is, cognitive processes may be well matched to the requirements of the average, modal, or typical task to which the process is applied, and yet not be ideally suited to the demands of the particular task at hand (e.g., see McKenzie, in press). Thus, error in judgment and reasoning can be viewed as indicative of mismatches between the cognitive processes people use and the tasks to which those processes are applied (see also Fischhoff, 1982). This view is not incompatible with the possibility that human cognitive processes are well suited to the general environment. Nevertheless, there may be identifiable subenvironments in which people could be doing better given their goals and their resources.

Modifying cognitive processes to fit the task

The view that problems come from discrepancies between tasks and processes suggests a taxonomy for interventions, based on how they attempt to bring processes and tasks into better alignment. A variety of approaches have been proposed to help change people's cognitive processes to fit their tasks better (see Fischhoff, 1982; Kahneman & Tversky, 1979; von Winterfeldt & Edwards, 1986):

Teach people more adaptable processes. One approach is to provide people with better cognitive tools. This may include training in general methods (e.g., statistical approaches to variance and sampling) that can replace intuitive heuristics (e.g., representativeness) in appropriate situations (Beyth-Marom,

Dekel, Gombo, & Shaked, 1985; Fong, Krantz, & Nisbett, 1986). Or, people may be taught to generalize useful "statistical heuristics" they have learned in specific domains (Nisbett, Krantz, Jepson, & Kunda, 1983).

Teach people to anticipate and correct their mistakes. Interventions can also focus on correcting, rather than avoiding, mistakes. For example, Koriat, Lichtenstein, and Fischhoff (1980) had subjects counter their tendency toward overconfidence in a chosen answer by explicitly listing reasons for and against their choice. Gaeth and Shanteau (1984) also found that correction was more feasible than avoidance in training people not to be influenced by irrelevant information in multiple-cue judgment tasks such as evaluating soil samples or job candidates. They found that people could not learn to ignore cues that were normatively irrelevant, but could learn to recognize the effects those cues had on their judgments, and to compensate for them.

Train people in task-specific processes. In some circumstances, it may be more feasible to teach not general problem-solving skills, but domain-specific heuristics. Such heuristics might be *less* well adapted in the overall environment, but would be better in a specific subenvironment. Smith and Kida (1991), for example, found that professional auditors had developed domain-specific strategies for testing and revising hypotheses (e.g., paying extra attention to any evidence of trouble, whether anticipated or not), and Dunbar (in press) observed that researchers in molecular biology learned, through observation, direct instruction, and painful experience, to distrust exciting positive findings. For both the auditors and the scientists, domain-specific training reduced the incidence of biases related to perseverance of beliefs. How well such training generalizes is unclear. How do Dunbar's scientists behave when developing ideas about child rearing, for example? Conventional wisdom in the expertise literature suggests transfer beyond the domain of training will be limited. Smith and Kida (1991) found, for example, that confirmatory biases in hypothesis testing and biases associated with the representativeness heuristic reappeared nearly full force if the experts were asked to make judgments they were not practiced at making, even when those judgments were relevant to their professional activities. On the other hand, Lee and Pennington (1992) report that expertise in debugging computer programs generalized well to unfamiliar problems in troubleshooting electronic circuits.

Provide people with analytical tools. Another widely used approach to improving judgment is to develop analytical techniques that people can use to supplement or supplant their intuitions. Examples include multi-attribute utility analysis, linear modeling, and Bayesian statistics. There is little doubt that people can be trained to use such techniques effectively to make better decisions under many circumstances. However, formal analysis is time consuming, effortful, and often difficult to do correctly (see von Winterfeldt & Edwards, 1986). For problems in which time, effort, and information are constrained, various hybrids of analytical and intuitive approaches may be more appropriate (see Hammond, Hamm, Grassia, & Pearson, 1987; Schoemaker & Russo, 1992).

All of these approaches hold promise for improving human judgment for all of the people some of the time. However, there is another, qualitatively different approach to improving judgments that has received relatively little attention. Rather than modifying cognitive processes to fit the environment better, one can modify the environment to fit the processes that people bring to it.

Modifying the environment to fit cognitive processes

In human factors and industrial design, one often thinks about modifying environments to fit people, as well as vice versa. If your operators have trouble reading their instruments, you might think about providing an easier-to-read instrument panel or making the operating manual easier to follow. Analogously, the knowledge that has accumulated concerning human judgment and reasoning processes could be used to design environments that avoid or compensate for anticipated errors.

One way to improve performance is to make the required processes easier to execute. In some cases, people may already be capable of more veridical processes, but are constrained by the costs of implementing them properly. Improving judgment in such cases may merely require designing an environment in which the cost of veridical strategies is lower (see Payne, Bettman, & Johnson, 1990).[1] Russo (1977), for example, presented supermarket shoppers with organized unit-price lists that were easier to use than item-by-item shelf tags. The change in format engendered a 2% decrease in shoppers' expenditures. In a laboratory task requiring choices among simple gambles, Johnson, Payne, and Bettman (1988) found that changing probability numbers from complicated fractions (e.g., 29/36) to simple decimals (e.g., 0.8) sharply reduced internally inconsistent choices ("preference reversals").

Performance is also affected by how judges encode, store, and retrieve the information they process. It may be possible to restructure the way information is provided so that it better suits the processes applied to it. For example, Klayman (1988) found that subjects were better able to learn from feedback in a multiple-cue task when they were allowed to choose their own combinations of cues to test than when they passively observed a representative set of instances. Another striking example involves hypothesis testing. People have a tendency toward

---

[1]Payne et al. (1990) use the term "adaptive" to refer to situations in which people profitably modify their strategies in response to local task conditions, such as the amount of time and information available. Thus, their use of the term is not equivalent to Anderson's (1990, 1991), and corresponds more closely to our "adaptable".

"positive testing" (Klayman & Ha, 1987). That is, they test instances they think will fit their hypothesis, paying less attention to instances they think will not fit. Thus, they discover false positives more readily than false negatives, and tend toward overly narrow hypotheses (Klayman & Ha, 1989). Tweney et al. (1980) found a very simple way around this problem. Their subjects were required to infer a rule that designated a subset of instances (certain sets of three numbers, as in Wason, 1960). Instead of classifying instances as those that fit the rule and those that did not, they described the same instances as belonging to one of two mutually exclusive and exhaustive categories, "Med" and "Dax". This resulted in much better performance, probably because, when conceptualized this way, subjects conducted some positive tests of a hypothesized "Med" rule and some of a hypothesized "Dax" rule, and because they then were able to encode each datum as being a positive example of something (either Med or Dax).

Interventions like these do not involve attempts to teach people different ways of reasoning or to give them more information. Instead, the environment is adjusted to fit existing processes. Some interventions (e.g., Russo's manipulation of unit-price displays) work by making it easier to execute a given process well, or facilitating the use of a better one already in the judge's repertoire. Others (e.g., Tweney et al.'s Med–Dax framing) provide an information structure that works better with the processes people use. We do not wish to imply that changing environments instead of processes is always the best approach, or even that it is always feasible. However, in some circumstances it may prove to be the most effective means of improving judgment.

A case study: learning to diagnose

We applied the approach of modifying the environment rather than the cognitive processes to a problem in diagnostic reasoning. Research in a number of different contexts points to a general inferential strategy that can be characterized as follows: given a set of data and one or more hypotheses, people judge the likelihood of a hypothesis by judging how well the observed data conform to the pattern expected under the hypothesis. This inferential strategy has been proposed both as a general heuristic for judgment under uncertainty (an aspect of "representativeness", see Kahneman, Slovic, & Tversky, 1982, Part II) and as a basic mechanism for categorization (see Komatsu, 1992; Osherson, Smith, Wilkie, López, & Shafir, 1990).

It may be that this inferential strategy is generally well adapted to the environment (in the spirit of Anderson, 1991). However, it can also give rise to some systematic errors in diagnostic reasoning (see Fischhoff & Beyth-Marom, 1983). Investigators have expressed concern over related phenomena in medicine (see Elstein, Shulman, & Sprafka, 1978; Schwartz & Griffin, 1986), auditing (see

Smith & Kida, 1991), and law (e.g., Saks & Kidd, 1980). Many of the observed problems stem from the fact that representative features are not necessarily diagnostic, and vice versa. From a Bayesian perspective, a feature is representative or typical if p(Feature|Category) is high, but a feature is diagnostic to the extent that p(Feature|Category) differs from p(Feature|Out-of-category).[2] People sometimes confuse the former with the latter, a problem known as "pseudo-diagnosticity" (Doherty, Mynatt, Tweney, & Schiavo, 1979). This problem reflects a broader tendency among hypothesis testers to focus on the relation of the data to the focal or preferred hypothesis, giving less attention to their relation to alternative hypotheses (Fischhoff & Beyth-Marom, 1983; Klayman & Ha, 1987, 1989; Slowiaczek, Klayman, Sherman, & Skov, 1992).

Suppose, for example, that you are an archeologist who uncovers a piece of pottery that must come from either Shell Island or Coral Island (Doherty et al., 1979; Doherty, Schiavo, Tweney, & Mynatt, 1981). You observe features such as a narrow mouth and curved handles. What information would you most want to help you determine the probability that the pot came from Shell Island? Subjects often choose to ask about the proportion of Shell Island pots with narrow necks and with curved handles, and are less interested in the proportion of those characteristics on Coral Island. In other words, people base their confidence more on the typicality of the feature, p(Feature|Category), than on the likelihood ratio that indicates diagnosticity, p(Feature|Category)$/p$(Feature|Out-of-category).[3]

Our study uses the context of medical diagnosis (see also Kern & Doherty, 1982; Gruppen, Wolf, & Billi, 1991; Wolf, Gruppen, & Billi, 1985). Consider a fictitious patient known to suffer from one of two fictitious diseases, proxititis and zymosis, described in Table 1. The last feature listed is the type of cough observed. The clinician's concept of proxititis[4] might include the fact that a dry cough was somewhat more common than a harsh cough. Thus, if a harsh cough were observed in a patient, that might be taken as modest evidence against a proxititis diagnosis. From a Bayesian standpoint, that would be a significant error of judgment. Harsh coughs are much more common in proxititis than in zymosis, so that symptom is strong evidence *in favor of* the former disease. Given the

---

[2]Specifically, Bayes' equation species that $\Omega' = [p(f|c)/p(f|-c)] \cdot \Omega$, where $p(f|c)$ is the probability of observing feature f given that the case belongs to category c, $p(f|-c)$ is the probability of observing f given that the case does not belong to category c, Ω is the odds the judge gives that the case belongs to c before observing f, and Ω' is the odds the judge should give after observing f.

[3]Our discussion ignores two interesting related phenomena. First, we assume that a feature could represent the presence of something or the absence of something. People may not treat these two representations identically (Christensen-Szalanski & Bushyhead, 1983; Sherman & Corty, 1984). Second, Bayesian inference also requires consideration of the base rates of the hypotheses, and people may not always incorporate base rate information properly (see Bar-Hillel, 1990).

[4]We use the term *concept* rather than the more specific *prototype*, because we do not wish to (or need to) take a position in the ongoing controversy over whether category concepts are organized around specific prototypes or generalized representations of exemplars (see Komatsu, 1992; Medin & Smith, 1984; Oden, 1987).

Table 1.   *Conditional probabilities of feature given each disease*

Cue	Feature	Proxititis	Zymosis
Age	<18 years	.9	.6
	>18 years	.1	.4
Sex	Male	.3	.7
	Female	.7	.3
Race	White	.6	.9
	Black/brown	.4	.1
Fever	High-grade	.4	.1
	Low-grade	.6	.9
Anorexia	Nausea	.7	.3
	Diarrhea	.3	.7
Prostration	Severe	.1	.4
	Mild	.9	.6
Difficulty walking	Pain	.3	.7
	Tingling	.7	.3
Tongue texture	Smooth	.1	.4
	Cracked	.9	.6
Rash	Moist	.7	.3
	Scaly	.3	.7
Cough	Dry	.6	.9
	Harsh	.4	.1

conditional probabilities shown in Table 1, the odds of proxititis are six times higher with a harsh cough than with a dry one, even though most proxititis patients have dry coughs.[5]

Researchers in medical decision making have found that trained clinicians do, in fact, confuse the typicality of a case feature (or, equivalently, the "sensitivity" of a test) with its diagnosticity. This is especially so of novices (Bordage & Lemieux, 1991; Feltovich, Johnson, Moller, & Swanson, 1984; Patel, Evans, & Kaufman, 1989; Lemieux & Bordage, 1992). This tendency toward pseudo-diagnostic reasoning may be fostered, or at least reinforced, by the way in which medical knowledge is presented. Medical textbooks are usually organized around particular diseases or categories of diseases, presenting the symptomatology of each and the pathophysiological principles that explain the symptoms (Bordage & Lemieux, 1990; Kriel & A'Beckett-Hewson, 1986). Similarly, in ward rounds and grand rounds, much of the instruction revolves around a "disease of the week", with discussion of symptomatology and presentations of illustrative cases.

The upshot is that medical students are generally trained to know the pattern of signs and symptoms associated with a particular disease. However, the diagnostic task is to find the disease associated with a particular set of signs and

[5]The odds of proxititis (abbreviated prox) given a harsh cough are equal to the prior odds of prox (Ω_{prox}) times the likelihood ratio, $p(\text{harsh}|\text{prox})/p(\text{harsh}|\text{zymosis})$. This equals $(.4/.1) \cdot \Omega_{prox} = 4 \cdot \Omega_{prox}$. The odds of prox given a dry cough are $\Omega_{prox} \cdot p(\text{dry}|\text{prox})/p(\text{dry}|\text{zymosis}) = (.6/.9) \cdot \Omega_{prox} = 2/3 \cdot \Omega_{prox}$.

symptoms (i.e., the presenting problems of the patient). As Barrows and Bennett (1972) put it, the student must "synthesize all this information and apply it in reverse when confronted with a . . . patient [who] never presents as a textbook case of anything" (p. 277). Or, as Kriel and A'Beckett-Hewson (1986) state, "medical textbooks and classroom teaching abound in the presentation of detailed lists of disorders, features and therapeutic actions which fail to provide a categorization scheme that is best suited for their retrieval in a clinical problem-solving situation" (p. 95). The complaint is not that students receive too little information, or the wrong information. Rather, the worry is that medical education does not help students to process information in a manner that suits the task of diagnosis.

There have been a number of proposals to change medical training to improve diagnostic performance. The goal is generally to improve clinicians' reasoning processes. One major reform effort centers on the use of "problem-based learning" (Albanese & Mitchell, 1993; Barrows, 1986; Barrows & Tamblyn, 1980; Berkson, in press; Schmidt, Dauphinee, & Patel, 1987). Problem-based curricula focus on real or realistic cases. The instructor works through the process of diagnosis with students, using the clinical problems as a vehicle for integrating basic science and clinical practice. A problem-based approach provides opportunities to train students to avoid pseudodiagnostic thinking. For example, teachers could prompt students to cross-reference different diseases by asking questions such as, "What would you say if the patient had symptoms X and Y instead of A and B?" or "How can you tell this is rheumatoid arthritis, rather than osteoarthritis?" Generally, though, such pedagogic techniques are not a systematic part of the curriculum, and it is not clear how widely they are applied. Furthermore, problem-based curricula tend to present a long series of cases of one particular condition, instead of a mixed series including cases of other kinds (Norman, 1988). Overall, there is little evidence that problem-based learning effectively improves diagnostic accuracy (Albanese & Mitchell, 1993; Berkson, in press; Norman & Schmidt, 1992; Patel, Groen, & Norman, 1991; Schmidt, Dauphinee, & Patel, 1987).

Other educators recommend training students in the use of systematic methods of hypothetico-deductive reasoning (see Elstein, Shulman, & Sprafka, 1990; Kassirer, 1983). There is little evidence for or against the effectiveness of such direct training in the medical domain. However, several studies suggest that use of proper hypothetico-deductive logic does not differ appreciably between expert and non-expert diagnosticians, nor between more- and less-successful diagnosticians (Groen & Patel, 1985; Neufeld, Norman, Barrows, & Feightner, 1981; Norman, Tugwell, Feightner, Muzzin, & Jacoby, 1985). This suggests that training in logical techniques may not be providing a critical missing skill. Others have advocated training clinicians in the use of formal, normative techniques such as Bayes' theorem and decision analysis (Schwartz, Gorry, Kassirer, & Essig,

1973; Sox, Blatt, Higgins, & Marton, 1988; Weinstein & Fineberg, 1980). Here, too, there is little evidence about the effects of such training on practice.

In medical education, as in other domains, recommendations for improving judgment skills focus on changing the reasoning processes to better fit the task. In our study, we took the opposite tack, taking for granted the reasoning process that engenders pseudodiagnosticity, and redesigning the information provided to reduce the errors produced by those processes. We assumed that clinicians judge the likelihood of a diagnosis by testing how well the observed case features match the features associated with their concept of that disease. Judgments based on such a heuristic process could be much more accurate if the clinicians' disease concepts included lists of *distinctive* features, rather than lists of *typical* features. For example, the concept of proxititis would indicate that harsh coughs were much more common in that disease than in zymosis, and dry coughs somewhat less common than in zymosis. Then, harsh coughs, rather than dry coughs, would be associated with proxititis, and a patient's harsh cough would be seen, properly, as a good match to proxititis. Deviations from proper Bayesian thinking might still remain (e.g., misestimations of the relative strengths of different items of evidence, or insufficient attention to disease base rates). However, diagnostic judgments should be much closer to the Bayesian ideal than if one is *taught* what is typical, and must *infer* what is distinctive.

One way to accomplish this transformation might be to change the structure of information with which student diagnosticians have to work. Instead of disease concepts based on the likelihoods of features given a disease, students could learn concepts based on features that distinguish one disease from another. Cognitive research on categorization suggests that these sorts of "contrastive" concepts are not difficult to learn. The category concepts people develop from everyday experience are based on a combination of typicality and discriminability (Rosch & Mervis, 1975), and experienced clinicians develop disease concepts that include discriminant features (see Johnson, 1982).

To encourage the formation of contrastive concepts, training should emphasize the ways in which the disease in question differs from other diseases that are frequently alternative explanations for similar patterns of findings. An objection might be raised that learning contrastive concepts would be impractical because, for any n diseases, it would be necessary to learn $n(n-1)$ sets of contrasts between diseases. Two factors mitigate this problem. First, diseases tend to fall into relatively small sets of logical competitors (two, three, or four), so in practice, n is not usually large. Second, contrasts need not be pairwise. Knowledge of diseases can be effectively organized into hierarchical groupings of related diseases (Beck & Bergman, 1986; Feltovich et al., 1984; Lemieux & Bordage, 1992; Politser, 1987; Wortman, 1972); then each particular disease need be contrasted only with the average of the group (e.g., "harsh cough is seen more often in proxititis than is usual for this class of diseases"). Contrastive concepts would be especially useful if they included direct information about the degree of diagnosticity of each feature (i.e., likelihood ratios such as "four times as likely in proxititis as in ..."); however, the formation of contrastive concepts does not require any information that is not required for independent concepts. The key difference is one of structure rather than content.

In the present study, we demonstrate the potential benefits of a change in information structure by teaching subjects to recognize cases of the two fictitious diseases referred to in Table 1: proxititis and zymosis. Half the subjects learned each disease separately, using written materials and examples similar to those used in traditional medical education. The other half of the subjects received exactly the same information, but the two diseases were presented in parallel, so that subjects could easily infer the differences between them.

We hypothesized that training the two diseases independently would encourage the formation of independent concepts based on those features that are most frequent in patients with the given diseases. Juxtaposing the two diseases during training should encourage attention to *relative* typicality, and should thus produce concepts that incorporate contrastive information. We did not expect contrastive training to change the basic method by which subjects evaluated hypotheses. In judging how typical a given case is of one disease, or in making a choice between alternative diagnoses, we expected that subjects in both conditions would base their judgments on how well the features of the case matched the features associated with the disease concept. However, we expected subjects in the two conditions to form different disease concepts. Thus, both typicality judgments and differential diagnoses should show differences between the two training methods because subjects are matching to different concepts. Moreover, because contrastive concepts are closer to the Bayesian sense of diagnosticity based on likelihood ratios, the diagnostic judgments of the contrastive training group should be significantly closer to the statistically correct diagnostic judgments.

Method

Subjects

Subjects were 48 students at the University of Chicago who responded to advertisements placed on campus noticeboards. Subjects received a fixed fee for participating in the experiment, which took about 45 min to complete. The procedure was administered in groups of two to five subjects, with each group assigned randomly to either the independent training condition or the contrastive training condition (24 subjects in each). Within each training condition, 12 subjects performed a typicality judgment task, and 12 performed a categorization task.

Materials

Subjects were provided with an introductory information sheet indicating that the subject's goal was to learn to recognize cases of two equally common, fictitious diseases: proxititis and zymosis. They were also given a summary sheet listing the ten cues about which information would be available, and the two possible values that each cue might take (resembling Table 1, without the probabilities). The training procedure included written information about the diseases (described later), and 30 slides of cases of each disease (an example is provided in Fig. 1). The set of profiles for each disease was designed to reflect closely the conditional probabilities of each feature given the disease.

An additional set of 20 profiles was printed on separate sheets of paper for use in the judgment tasks following training. These cases were designed to match independent and contrastive disease concepts in different ways. In modeling the degree of match between a case and a concept, we assumed that the independent concept for a given disease comprised those features that were present more often than not for that disease, and the contrastive concept comprised those features that were more common in that disease than in the other. We then counted the number of case features that matched the features in each concept, ignoring the possibility of differential weighting of different features. Consider the case described in Table 2. According to our simple feature-matching model, this case fits the independent concept of proxititis better than zymosis (designate this $Prox_{indep}$). From the point of view of contrastive concepts, however, the fit is equal to each disease (designated $Equal_{contr}$). Thus, the case described in Table 2 is classified as $Prox_{indep}/Equal_{contr}$.

Because contrastive concepts are based on features that are diagnostic of the

ZYMOSIS

Age:	11 YEARS
Sex:	MALE
Race:	WHITE
Fever:	LOW-GRADE
Reason for anorexia:	DIARRHEA
Degree of prostration:	MILD
Difficulty walking due to:	TINGLING SENSATION
Texture of tongue:	CRACKED AND FISSURED
Appearance of rash:	SCALY
Type of cough:	HARSH, BARKING

Figure 1. *One of the sample cases presented to subjects during training.*

Table 2.   *Example of a case for which judgments based on independent concepts and contrastive concepts differ*

		Matches to independent concepts		Matches to contrastive concepts	
		Prox.	Zym.	Prox.	Zym.
Age	>18 years	−	−	−	+
Sex	Female	+	−	+	−
Race	White	+	+	−	+
Fever	Low-grade	+	+	−	+
Anorexia	Nausea	+	−	+	−
Prostration	Mild	+	+	+	−
Walking	Tingling	+	−	+	−
Tongue	Smooth	−	−	−	+
Rash	Moist	+	−	+	−
Cough	Dry	+	+	−	+
Matches to concept		8	4	5	5

disease, rather than features that are common given the disease, matching to contrastive concepts produces a fair approximation to Bayesian diagnostic judgment. In all of the presented cases, the disease favored by matching to contrastive concepts was also the more likely diagnosis by Bayesian calculation, and when the fit to the two disease concepts was equal, the probabilities of the two diseases were indeed close. Seven types of profiles were constructed, as summarized in Table 3.

Table 3.   *Types of cases used in typicality judgment and differential diagnosis tasks*

Type of cases[a]	Number of cases	Match to independent concepts	Match to contrastive concepts
$Prox_{indep}/Equal_{contr}$	4	proxititis > zymosis	proxititis = zymosis
$Zym_{indep}/Equal_{contr}$	4	zymosis > proxititis	zymosis = proxititis
$Equal_{indep}/Prox_{contr}$	4	proxititis = zymosis	proxititis > zymosis
$Equal_{indep}/Zym_{contr}$	4	zymosis = proxititis	zymosis > proxititis
$Equal_{indep}/Equal_{contr}$	2	proxititis = zymosis	proxititis = zymosis
$Prox_{indep}/Prox_{contr}$	1	proxititis > zymosis	proxititis > zymosis
Zym_{indep}/Zym_{contr}	1	zymosis > proxititis	zymosis > proxititis

[a]In labeling the types of cases, Prox(ititis) and Zym(osis) indicate which disease concept better fits the features of the case, according to either indep(endent) or contr(astive) concepts. "Equal" indicates that the case features are about equally well matched to the proxititis and zymosis concepts of that type.
Note: In all cases, ">" indicates that the match to the left-hand disease was better by four features (e.g., two features in the profile matched the proxititis concept, six matched zymosis), and "=" indicates an equal number of feature matches to each concept.

Training procedures

Independent training condition

Subjects in the independent training condition began by reading a "summary chapter" that described one of two fictitious diseases, either "proxititis" or "zymosis". They were instructed to study this summary chapter carefully and to form a general impression of what a case of this disease looked like, based on the general description and some case histories which they would be shown.

Each summary chapter provided information about the signs and symptoms associated with the disease (see Appendix A). These chapters were similar to descriptions found in medical digests. In order to parallel the type of information provided in medical texts, probabilities and frequencies were expressed verbally rather than numerically. The translation from the numerical probabilities shown in Table 1 to verbal expressions was done in accord with studies of the meaning of probability-related words (Beyth-Marom, 1982; Kenney, 1981; Nakao & Axelrod, 1983; Wallsten & Budescu, 1983). Additionally, each of the diseases was described as being of "relatively frequent" occurrence, so no differences in base rates were indicated. Neither of the introductory chapters made any reference to the other disease.

Subjects were given 5 min to study the summary chapter. Then they were shown a series of 30 slides presenting case histories of the disease they had just read about, as in Fig. 1. Prior to viewing the first slide subjects were reminded that their objective was to be able to recognize a case of the disease when they saw one and that they should form a general impression of patients with the disease rather than try to remember individual patients. They viewed the slides in random order for 10 s each, without taking notes. Then subjects were given a summary chapter and 30 case histories for the second disease, following the same procedure. Half the subjects were trained on proxititis first, half on zymosis. After this second set of presentations, subjects were asked to list the features of a typical case of the first disease, and then, separately, the features of a typical case of the second disease.

After subjects had finished writing descriptions of a typical case of proxititis and a typical case of zymosis, half were given a typicality judgment task and half were given a classification task. Subjects completed these tasks at their own pace.

Contrastive training condition

The information provided in contrastive training was the same as in independent training. The two conditions differed in how the information was organized in the written summaries and in the case presentations. Subjects in the contrastive condition began by reading a summary chapter that described the signs and symptoms associated with both diseases. In essence, this chapter was an amalgam of the two chapters seen by subjects in the independent condition (see Appendix B). Contrastive subjects were given 10 min to study the chapter, with instructions to form a general impression of what a case of proxititis looked like and what a case of zymosis looked like, on the basis of this summary chapter and the set of case histories they would see. They saw the same 60 case histories that their counterparts in the independent condition saw, except that proxititis and zymosis patients were randomly intermixed during a single viewing session. Otherwise the procedure followed was the same as that for subjects in the other training condition.

Judgment task procedures

Twelve subjects in each training condition rated 10 patient profiles on a 7-point scale with endpoints labeled "not at all like a typical case of [disease]" and "very much like a typical case of [disease]". They were given printed case summaries, similar in format to the slides they had viewed (see Fig. 1). Each case appeared on a separate page, with the scale printed at the bottom. The subjects first rated the 10 cases with regard to one disease, and then the cases were presented again in a different random order to be rated with respect to the other disease. The 10 cases were a subset of the 20 listed in Table 3: two each of types $Prox_{indep}/Equal_{contr}$, $Zym_{indep}/Equal_{contr}$, $Equal_{indep}/Prox_{contr}$, $Equal_{indep}/Zym_{contr}$, and $Equal_{indep}/Equal_{contr}$. The other 12 subjects in each training condition made different differential diagnoses. They received case summaries with the two disease names printed at the bottom instead of the rating scale. (The order of the names was counterbalanced across subjects.) Subjects indicated which of the two diseases they believed to be the correct diagnosis for each of the 20 cases listed in Table 3.

Results

Disease descriptions

The first hypothesis to be tested is that the structure of information presentation in training affects the nature of the category concepts formed by learners. We examined the lists of features subjects provided when asked to describe a typical case of each disease. In the independent condition, we expected that subjects' descriptions would be based on absolute typicality. In other words, the description of proxititis would consist of those features found in the majority of proxititis patients. In the contrastive condition, however, we expected that subjects would be influenced by *relative* typicality, and the description of proxititis would be more likely to include features that were more frequent in proxititis than in the alternative, zymosis. The feature discussed earlier, type of cough, is an example: proxititis patients are more likely to have a dry cough than a harsh one, but having a harsh cough is more common with proxititis than with zymosis (see Table 1). Thus, independent subjects should describe the typical proxititis patient as having a dry cough, but contrastive subjects may instead identify proxititis with a harsh cough.

Table 4 shows which features subjects included in their descriptions of the typical case of proxititis and zymosis. For the first three cues (race, fever, and cough), absolute and relative typicality pointed to opposite features in proxititis; for the next three (age, prostration, and tongue condition), absolute and relative typicality differed in zymosis. These six cues provided data for three planned comparisons. In the independent condition, subjects were significantly more likely to report features consistent with absolute typicality than with relative typicality, $t(23) = 2.24$, $p < .05$. On average, they named the feature with higher absolute typicality 3.5 times out of 6, and the feature with higher relative typicality 2.2

Table 4. *Number of subjects who included each value in descriptions of the typical case of each disease, by training condition*

Cue	Feature	Proxititis		Zymosis	
		Indep.	Contrast.	Indep.	Contrast.
Race[a]	White	14	7	15	16
	Black/brown	8	17	7	5
Fever[a]	Low	13	7	16	16
	High	9	15	6	5
Cough[a]	Dry	14	7	18	18
	Harsh	10	13	5	6
Age[b]	<18	17	17	14	7
	>18	7	2	8	15
Prostration[b]	Mild	19	14	15	9
	Severe	4	9	9	13
Tongue[b]	Smooth	9	9	10	13
	Cracked	13	13	13	10
Sex[c]	Female	19	20	8	3
	Male	5	4	15	20
Anorexia[c]	Diarrhea	7	8	16	19
	Nausea	15	15	7	5
Walking[c]	Pain	4	3	19	18
	Tingling	20	19	4	6
Rash[c]	Scaly	6	6	17	12
	Moist	17	17	7	11

Note: Numbers exclude instances in which subjects mentioned both features or neither.
[a]Contrastive and independent conditions predicted to differ for proxititis.
[b]Contrastive and independent conditions predicted to differ for zymosis.
[c]Contrastive and independent conditions predicted to agree within each disease.

times. (The other 0.3 times the descriptions included both features or neither.) In the contrastive condition, subjects named the absolute-typicality feature an average of 1.9 times, and the relative-typicality features 3.6 times, $t(23) = 4.79$, $p < .001$. The interaction between condition and feature choice was significant, $t(46) = 4.40$, $p < .001$.

These results indicate that the independent and contrastive modes of presentation produced qualitatively different independent and contrastive disease concepts. In the independent condition, subjects most often identified a disease with those features that were present in a majority of cases. Contrastive-condition subjects were strongly influenced by the relative frequency of occurrence of a feature in one disease versus the other: they were more likely to identify a disease with the minority feature than the majority feature if the minority feature had a higher relative frequency.

Judgments of typicality

Ratings of the typicality of individual cases provide further tests of the hypothesis that independent and contrastive training produce qualitatively different disease concepts. We assume that typicality ratings are influenced primarily by the extent to which features in the patient profile match the features of the disease concept. Thus, differences in disease concepts should produce differences in the typicality ratings provided by subjects in the two training conditions.

Recall that subjects rated five kinds of cases ($Prox_{indep}/Equal_{contr}$, $Zym_{indep}/Equal_{contr}$, $Equal_{indep}/Prox_{contr}$, $Equal_{indep}/Zym_{contr}$, and $Equal_{indep}/Equal_{contr}$) with respect to each disease. If subjects in the independent condition are matching to independent concepts, they should judge $Prox_{indep}/Equal_{contr}$ cases to be more typical of proxititis than of zymosis, and vice versa for $Zym_{indep}/Equal_{contr}$ cases. For the other three kinds of cases, they should rate the two diseases about equally. As shown in Table 5, the results fit the predictions for all five types of cases. If subjects in the contrastive condition are matching to contrastive concepts, they should rate proxititis higher in $Equal_{indep}/Prox_{contr}$ cases and zymosis higher in $Equal_{indep}/Zym_{contr}$ cases, and there should be no difference in the other three types of cases. In the contrastive condition, the predicted pattern was observed in four of five types of cases, the exception being the significant difference in $Prox_{indep}/Equal_{contr}$ cases.

These findings suggest that subjects in each condition are matching to different concepts. It is also possible to test condition differences directly, by testing for Disease × Condition interactions. Such interactions should exist for all types of cases except $Equal_{indep}/Equal_{contr}$, with subjects in one condition rating the two diseases about equal, and subjects in the other condition rating one disease higher than the other. The predicted interaction was significant in $Zym_{indep}/Equal_{contr}$

Table 5. *Ratings of typicality of cases with respect to proxititis and zymosis, by training condition and type of case*

Training condition	Disease rated	Type of case				
		Prox_{indep} /Equal_{contr}	Zym_{indep} /Equal_{contr}	Equal_{indep} /Prox_{contr}	Equal_{indep} /Zym_{contr}	Equal_{indep} /Equal_{contr}
Independent	Proxititis	5.1	3.0	4.4	4.2	3.8
	Zymosis	2.7**	4.8**	3.6^a	3.9^a	3.7^a
Contrastive	Proxititis	4.6	4.2	5.1	3.7	4.0
	Zymosis	3.5*	4.3^a	3.6**	5.0**	4.1^a

*Proxititis and zymosis ratings differ, $p < .05$.
**Ratings differ, $p < .005$.
^{a}Ratings not significantly different, $p > .10$.

cases, $F(1, 22) = 8.72$, $p < .008$, and Equal_{indep}/Zym_{contr} cases, $F(1, 22) = 12.64$, $p < .002$, marginally significant in Prox_{indep}/Equal_{contr} cases, $F(1, 22) = 4.21$, $p < .06$, and nonsignificant in Equal_{indep}/Prox_{contr} cases, $F(1, 22) = 1.35$, $p < .26$.

In sum, despite some evidence of overlap between the concepts formed in independent and contrastive groups, the results provide strong support for the conclusion that independent and contrastive training produced different disease concepts.

Differential diagnosis

Subjects in the independent and contrastive training conditions developed different concepts of what is typical for each disease, but how does this affect diagnostic judgment? Studies of representativeness and pseudodiagnosticity suggest that subjects will choose the disease with the best match between typical features and the features observed in the case. If so, then the different concepts formed by subjects in the independent and contrastive conditions should produce different diagnostic judgments. Data to test this hypothesis come from the differential diagnoses of 20 cases made by 12 subjects in each condition. These analyses use the 16 cases for which condition differences are predicted: four each of types Zym_{indep}/Equal_{contr}, Prox_{indep}/Equal_{contr}, Equal_{indep}/Zym_{contr}, and Equal_{indep}/Prox_{contr}.

As with typicality ratings, our feature-matching hypothesis predicts that subjects will find that some cases fit one disease much better than the other, whereas other cases fit both diseases about equally. When one disease matches better than the other there should be good consensus as to which are proxititis cases and which are zymosis; when they match about equally there should be no clear distinction. As before, whether a case is clear or equivocal should depend on which kind of disease concepts are used.

We analyzed the average diagnoses proportion of cases in which proxititis was the diagnosis. (The proportion of zymosis diagnoses was one minus this; there were no missing judgments.) In accord with predictions, independent subjects diagnosed proxititis more often in $Prox_{indep}/Equal_{contr}$ cases ($M = .72$) than in $Zym_{indep}/Equal_{contr}$ cases ($M = .42$), $t(11) = 3.19$, $p < .009$, but contrastive subjects did not distinguish the two types ($M = .54$ and $.58$, respectively), $t < 1$. The interaction between condition and case type was significant in a 2×2 ANOVA, $F(1, 22) = 8.59$, $p < .008$. Similarly, contrastive subjects chose proxititis more often in $Equal_{indep}/Prox_{contr}$ cases ($M = .71$) than in $Equal_{indep}/Zym_{contr}$ cases ($M = .38$), $t(11) = 3.75$, $p < .004$, but independent subjects did not ($M = .48$ and $.52$, respectively), $t < 1$. The Case-type $\times$ Condition interaction was again significant, $F(1, 22) = 10.48$, $p < .004$.

We also compared responses to each of the four case types in each condition to chance ($.50$). These are more stringent tests of our predictions. Of the eight comparisons, there were four in which one diagnosis was expected to predominate. Subjects made the predicted diagnosis more often than chance ($p < .05$) in three of these four instances: $Prox_{indep}/Equal_{contr}$ in the independent condition, and $Equal_{indep}/Prox_{contr}$ and $Equal_{indep}/Zym_{contr}$ in the contrastive condition. The exception was that the independent group found $Zym_{indep}/Equal_{contr}$ cases to be somewhat equivocal. The proportion of proxititis and zymosis choices did not differ significantly in any of the four instances that were expected to be equivocal.

The data on differential diagnostic judgments support our three basic hypotheses: (a) subjects make differential diagnoses by judging relative goodness of fit between features of the case and features of each disease concept; (b) the structure of information during training affects the concepts applied in diagnosis; and (c) contrastive concepts produce diagnoses that are closer to the statistically appropriate judgments.

Discussion

Our study provides some good news and some bad news about diagnostic reasoning. First the bad news. Novice subjects are not good at translating knowledge about what is typical into knowledge about what is diagnostic. Our results accord with a basic process that has been documented in a variety of reasoning tasks: People judge the likelihood that an instance is a member of a category by how well the features of the instance match the features seen as average or typical for the category.

The good news is that the negative consequences of this feature-matching process may be alleviated by a fairly straightforward change in the way information is presented during instruction. Feature matching is not such a bad method of making diagnostic judgments if one matches to diagnostic features rather than typical features.

It is not easy to change the basic reasoning processes by which people make diagnostic judgments. The results of the present study suggest that it may not be so hard to change the form of the concepts upon which those processes operate. A change from independent to contrastive concepts was accomplished with a simple restructuring of information, presenting information about two diseases in parallel within one descriptive text and one representative sample of cases. No information was used beyond that provided in independent concepts, taught one disease at a time. Nevertheless, subjects who received the contrastive training were more likely to associate each disease with its discriminant features than with its typical features, and their diagnostic judgments were significantly closer to normative standards.

The task we used is of course a very simple one compared to the complexities of training in medicine or other domains of expert judgment. We cannot be certain that our technique will scale up easily from two diseases and ten features learned in a half hour to hundreds of diseases and features learned in 2 years of preclinical training, or to similarly complex knowledge in other domains. As mentioned earlier, a larger contrastive structure would require a hierarchical organization to avoid the need for innumerable pairwise contrasts. However, our results suggest a direction worth trying. In medical education, for example, teaching basic disease information in a contrastive format could provide novices with a knowledge structure that is closer to that of experts and better adapted to the task of differential diagnosis. A contrastive knowledge structure might also put students in a better position to profit from problem-based training and instruction in Bayesian principles, because there would be less discrepancy between the concepts being taught and the structure of information in memory.

Conclusions

Non-optimalities in judgment can be thought of as mismatches between people's environments and the processes they use to attain their goals in those environments. A better match between processes and environments can be achieved through changes in either or both. Most efforts to improve judgment focus on changing cognitive processes or enhancing them through the use of analytical tools. There are a number of potential advantages to that approach. Under favorable circumstances, training to avoid errors in one context may generalize to other contexts. For example, a person who learned to think about diagnosticity rather than typicality in diagnosing diseases might carry the lesson to problems in automobile repair or human relations. Furthermore, training in more effective processes could yield more wide-ranging benefits. For example, a skilled

Bayesian reasoner would presumably avoid the ill effects of pseudodiagnosticity, base rate neglect, and conjunction fallacies simultaneously.

On the other hand, it may sometimes be more effective to take the processes as given, and think about how the environment can be adapted to suit them. We advocate devoting more attention to this approach as an alternative means of intervention. Given the non-intuitive nature of many statistical principles and decision analysis techniques, it may often be easier to modify the environment than the person. Moreover, whereas better thinking must be taught to each individual, the benefits of a modified environment are likely to generalize across the range of individuals who encounter it.

To be effective, though, improvements in the environment must be targeted to specific goals. In our study, for example, teaching contrastive concepts without changing the basic judgment process might reduce pseudodiagnosticity, but create "pseudotypicality". That is, contrastive-trained subjects may identify a low-frequency feature as typical of a disease if its frequency given the other diseases is lower. Where accurate diagnostic judgment is a more central goal than accurate judgments of typicality, the trade-off between pseudodiagnosticity and pseudo-typicality would be favorable.

Thinking about the design of favorable environments highlights the importance of research into environment–person interactions. When and how do people adapt their cognitive processes in response to environmental characteristics? The answers to this question can guide the design of environments that facilitate the use of better strategies. How do environmental characteristics affect the performance of different processes? Answers here can guide the design of the environmental inputs to human cognition to obtain the best performance from given strategies.

Some critics of "heuristics and biases research" complain that researchers are too interested in demonstrating irrationality, and are not impressed enough with what well-fashioned cognitive machines people are. Indeed, many of the biases, fallacies, and imperfections of human judgment and reasoning seem to come and go, depending on the wording of the problem, the goals of the subject, the subject's expertise in the problem domain, etc. One possible interpretation is that the purported biases are not robust, or are artifacts of the laboratory. An alternative view is this: most of the environments people face in life are artificial; a great many are ambiguously defined, present conflicting goals, and are unfamiliar. Sometimes people manage quite well, by standards that are important to them, sometimes they do not.

It is reasonable to expect human cognition to be well adapted to the general environment, but not completely adaptable to each subenvironment encountered. One can recognize human judgmental errors as real and perhaps remediable, while also acknowledging that evolution, social transmission, and learning are powerful forces for shaping appropriate behavior. In other words, it is possible to be very impressed with both the successes and the failures of human judgment, and to wonder why there is not more of the former and less of the latter. Knowing more about what makes the difference is important for being able to design effective interventions that can improve performance. And seeing what does and does not aid performance can reveal a good deal about underlying processes, too.

References

Abelson, R.P., & Levi, A (1985). Decision making and decision theory. In G. Lindzey & E. Aronson (Eds.), *The Handbook of Social Psychology* (3rd ed., Vol. 1, pp. 231–309). New York: Random House.

Albanese, M.A., & Mitchell, S. (1993). Problem-based learning: a review of literature on its outcomes and implementation issues. *Academic Medicine, 68*, 52–81.

Anderson, J.R. (1990). *The Adaptive Character of Thought.* Hillsdale, NJ: Erlbaum.

Anderson, J.R. (1991). Is human cognition adaptive? *Behavioral and Brain Sciences, 14*, 471–517.

Bar-Hillel, M. (1990). Back to base rates. In R. Hogarth (Ed.), *Insights in decision making: a tribute to Hillel J. Einhorn* (pp. 200–216). Chicago: University of Chicago Press.

Barrows, H.S. (1986). A taxonomy of problem-based learning methods. *Medical Education, 20*, 481–486.

Barrows, H.S., & Bennett, K. (1972). The diagnostic (problem solving) skill of the neurologist. *Archives of Neurology, 26*, 273–277.

Barrows, H.S., & Tamblyn, R.N. (1980). *Problem-based learning: an approach to medical education.* New York: Springer.

Beck, A.L., & Bergman, D.A. (1986). Using structured medical information to improve students' problem-solving performance. *Journal of Medical Education, 61*, 749–756.

Berkson, L. (in press). Problem-based learning: have the expectations been met? *Academic Medicine.*

Beyth-Marom, R. (1982). How probable is probable? A numerical translation of verbal probability expressions. *Journal of Forecasting, 1*, 257–269.

Beyth-Marom, R., Dekel, S., Gombo, R., & Shaked, M. (1985). *An elementary approach to thinking under uncertainty.* Hillsdale, NJ: Erlbaum.

Bordage, G., & Lemieux, M. (1990). Which medical textbook to read? Emphasizing semantic structures. *Academic Medicine, 65*, S23–S24.

Bordage, G., & Lemieux, M. (1991). Semantic structures and diagnostic thinking of experts and novices. *Academic Medicine, 66*, S70–S72.

Christensen-Szalanski, J.J.J., & Bushyhead, J.B. (1983). Physicians' misunderstanding of normal findings. *Medical Decision Making, 3*, 169–175.

Cohen, L.J. (1981). Can human irrationality be experimentally demonstrated? *Behavioral and Brain Sciences, 4*, 317–331.

Doherty, M.E., Mynatt, C.R., Tweney, R.D., & Schiavo, M.D. (1979). Pseudodiagnosticity. *Acta Psychologica, 49*, 111–121.

Doherty, M.E., Schiavo, M.D., Tweney, R.D., & Mynatt, C.R. (1981). The influence of feedback and diagnostic data on pseudodiagnosticity. *Bulletin of the Psychonomic Society, 18*, 191–194.

Dunbar, K. (in press). How scientists really reason: scientific reasoning in real-world laboratories. In R.J. Sternberg & J. Davidson (Eds.), *Insight.* Cambridge, MA: MIT Press.

Edwards, W. (1990). Unfinished tasks: a research agenda for behavioral decision theory. In R. Hogarth (Ed.), *Insights in decision making: a tribute to Hillel J. Einhorn* (pp. 44–65). Chicago: University of Chicago Press.

Elstein, A.S., Shulman, L.S., & Sprafka, S.A. (1978). *Medical problem solving: an analysis of clinical reasoning.* Cambridge, MA: Harvard University Press.

Elstein, A.S., Shulman, L.S., & Sprafka, S.A. (1990). Medical problem solving: a ten year retrospective. *Evaluation and the Health Professions, 13*, 5–36.

Feltovitch, P.J., Johnson, P.E., Moller, J.H. & Swanson, D.B. (1984). The role and development of medical knowledge in diagnostic expertise. In W. Clancey & E.H. Shortliffe (Eds.), *Readings in medical artificial intelligence* (pp. 275–319). New York: Addison-Wesley.

Fischhoff, B. (1982). Debiasing. In D. Kahneman, P. Slovic, & A. Tversky (Eds.), *Judgment under uncertainty: heuristics and biases* (pp. 422–444). New York: Cambridge University Press.

Fischhoff, B., & Beyth-Marom, R. (1983). Hypothesis evaluation from a Bayesian perspective. *Psychological Review, 90,* 239–260.

Fong, G.T., Krantz, D.H., & Nisbett, R.E. (1986). The effects of statistical training on thinking about everyday problems. *Cognitive Psychology, 18,* 253–292.

Funder, D.C. (1987). Errors and mistakes: evaluating the accuracy of social judgment. *Psychological Bulletin, 101,* 75–90.

Gaeth, G.J., & Shanteau, J. (1984). Reducing the influence of irrelevant information on experienced decision makers. *Organizational Behavior and Human Performance, 33,* 263–282.

Groen, G.J., & Patel, V.L. (1985). Medical problem-solving: some questionable assumptions. *Medical Education, 19,* 95–100.

Gruppen, L.D., Wolf, F.M., & Billi, J.E. (1991). Information gathering and integration as sources of error in diagnostic decision making. *Medical Decision Making, 11,* 233–239.

Hammond, K.R. (1990). Functionalism and illusionism: can integration be usefully achieved? In R. Hogarth (Ed.), *Insights in decision making: a tribute to Hillel J. Einhorn* (pp. 227–261). Chicago: University of Chicago Press.

Hammond, K.R., Hamm, R.M., Grassia, J., & Pearson, T. (1987). Direct comparison of the efficacy of intuitive and analytical cognition in expert judgment. *IEEE Transactions on Systems, Man, and Cybernetics, SMC-17,* 753–770.

Hogarth, R.M. (1981). Beyond discrete biases: functional and dysfunctional aspects of judgmental heuristics. *Psychological Bulletin, 90,* 197–217.

Johnson, E.J., Payne, J.W., & Bettman, J.R. (1988). Information displays and preference reversals. *Organizational Behavior and Human Decision Processes, 42,* 1–21.

Johnson, P.E. (1982). Cognitive models of medical problem solvers. In D.C. Connelly, E. Benson, & D. Burke (Eds.), *Clinical decision making and laboratory use* (pp. 39–52). Minneapolis: University of Minnesota Press.

Jungerman, H. (1983). The two camps on rationality. In R.W. Scholz (Ed.), *Decision making under uncertainty* (pp. 63–86). Amsterdam: Elsevier.

Kahneman, D., Slovic, P., & Tversky, A. (Eds.) (1982). *Judgment under uncertainty: heuristics and biases.* New York: Cambridge University Press.

Kahneman, D., & Tversky, A. (1979). Intuitive predictions: biases and corrective procedures. *TIMS Studies in Management Science, 12,* 313–327.

Kassirer, J.P. (1983). Teaching clinical medicine by iterative hypothesis testing: let's practice what we preach. *New England Journal of Medicine, 309,* 921–923.

Kenney, R.M. (1981). Between never and always. *New England Journal of Medicine, 305,* 1097–1098.

Kern, L., & Doherty, M.E. (1982). Pseudodiagnosticity in an idealized medical problem-solving environment. *Journal of Medical Education, 57,* 110–114.

Klayman, J. (1988). Cue discovery in probabilistic environments: uncertainty and experimentation. *Journal of Experimental Psychology: Learning, Memory, and Cognition, 14,* 317–330.

Klayman, J., & Ha, Y.-W. (1987). Confirmation, disconfirmation, and information in hypothesis testing. *Psychological Review, 94,* 211–228.

Klayman, J., & Ha, Y.-W. (1989). Hypothesis testing in rule discovery: strategy, structure and content. *Journal of Experimental Psychology: Learning, Memory, and Cognition, 15,* 596–604.

Komatsu, L.K. (1992). Recent views of conceptual structure. *Psychological Bulletin, 112,* 500–526.

Koriat, A., Lichtenstein, S., & Fischhoff, B. (1980). Reasons for confidence. *Journal of Experimental Psychology: Human Learning and Memory, 6,* 107–118.

Kriel, J., & A'Beckett-Hewson, M. (1986). Conceptual frameworks in preclinical and clinical textbooks. *Medical Education, 20,* 94–101.

Kyburg, H.E., Jr (1983). Rational belief. *Behavioral and Brain Sciences, 6,* 231–273.

Lee, A.Y., & Pennington, N. (1992, November). *Across-domain transfer from program debugging to electronic troubleshooting*. Paper presented at the meeting of the Psychonomic Society, St. Louis.

Lemieux, M., & Bordage, G. (1992). Propositional versus structural semantic analyses of medical diagnostic thinking. *Cognitive Science, 16*, 185–204.

McKenzie, C.R.M. (in press). The accuracy of intuitive judgment strategies: covariation assessment and Bayesian inference. *Cognitive Psychology*.

Medin, D.L., & Smith, E.E. (1984). Concepts and concept formation. *Annual Review of Psychology, 35*, 113–138.

Nakao, M.A., & Axelrod, S. (1983). Numbers are better than words: verbal specifications of frequency have no place in medicine. *American Journal of Medicine, 74*, 1061–1065.

Neufeld, V.R., Norman, G.R., Barrows, H.S., & Feightner, J.W. (1981). Clinical problem-solving of medical students: a longitudinal and cross-sectional analysis. *Medical Education, 15*, 26–32.

Nisbett, R.E., Krantz, D.H., Jepson, C., & Kunda, Z. (1983). The use of statistics in everyday inductive reasoning. *Psychological Review, 90*, 339–363.

Norman, G.R. (1988). Problem-solving skills, solving problems and problem-based learning. *Medical Education, 22*, 279–286.

Norman, G.R., & Schmidt, H.G. (1992). The psychological basis of problem-based learning: a review of the evidence. *Academic Medicine, 67*, 557–565.

Norman, G.R., Tugwell, P., Feightner, J.W., Muzzin, L., & Jacoby, L. (1985). Knowledge and clinical problem solving. *Medical Education, 19*, 344–356.

Oden, G.C. (1987). Concept, knowledge, and thought. *Annual Review of Psychology, 38*, 203–228.

Osherson, D.N., Smith, E.E., Wilkie, O., López, A., & Shafir, E. (1990). Category-based induction. *Psychological Review, 97*, 185–200.

Patel, V.L., Evans, D.A., & Kaufman, D.R. (1989). A cognitive framework for doctor–patient interaction. In D.A. Evans & V.L. Patel (Eds.), *Cognitive science in medicine: biomedical modeling* (pp. 257–312). Cambridge, MA: MIT Press.

Patel, V.L., Groen, G.J., & Norman, G.R. (1991). Effects of conventional and problem-based medical curricula on problem solving. *Academic Medicine, 66*, 380–389.

Payne, J.W., Bettman, J.R., & Johnson, E.J. (1990). The adaptive decision maker: effort and accuracy in choice. In R. Hogarth (Ed.), *Insights in decision making: a tribute to Hillel J. Einhorn* (pp. 129–153). Chicago: University of Chicago Press.

Politser, P.E. (1987). Medical education for a changing future: new concepts for revising texts. *Medical Education, 21*, 320–333.

Rosch, E., & Mervis, C.B. (1975). Family resemblances: studies in the internal structure of categories. *Cognitive Science, 7*, 573–605.

Russo, J.E. (1977). The value of unit price information. *Journal of Marketing Research, 14*, 193–201.

Saks, M.J., & Kidd, R.F. (1980). Human information processing and adjudication: trial by heuristics. *Law and Society Review, 15*, 123–160.

Schmidt, H.G., Dauphinee, W.D., & Patel, V.L. (1987). Comparing the effects of problem-based and conventional curricula in an international sample. *Journal of Medical Education, 62*, 305–315.

Schoemaker, P.J.H., & Russo, J.E. (1992). *A pyramid of decision approaches* (working paper no. 246). Chicago: University of Chicago Graduate School of Business, Center for Decision Research.

Schwartz, S., & Griffin, T. (1986). *Medical thinking: the psychology of medical judgment and decision making*. New York: Springer.

Schwartz, W.B., Gorry, G.A., Kassirer, J.P., & Essig, A. (1973). Decision analysis and clinical judgment. *American Journal of Medicine, 55*, 459–472.

Sherman, S.J., & Corty, E. (1984). Cognitive heuristics. In R.S. Wyer & T.K. Srull (Eds.), *Handbook of social cognition* (Vol. 1, pp. 189–286). Hillsdale, NJ: Erlbaum.

Slowiaczek, L.M., Klayman, J., Sherman, S.J., & Skov, R.B. (1992). Information selection and use in hypothesis testing: what is a good question, and what is a good answer? *Memory & Cognition, 20*, 392–405.

Smith, J.F., & Kida, T. (1991). Heuristics and biases: expertise and task realism in auditing. *Psychological Bulletin, 109*, 472–489.

Sox, H.C., Blatt, M.A., Higgins, M.C., & Marton, K.I. (1988). *Medical decision making*. Boston: Butterworths.

Tweney, R.D., Doherty, M.E., Worner, W.J., Pliske, D.B., Mynatt, C.R., Gross, K.A., & Arkkelin, D.L. (1980). Strategies of rule discovery in an inference task. *Quarterly Journal of Experimental Psychology, 32*, 109–123.

von Winterfeldt, D., & Edwards, W. (1986). *Decision analysis and behavioral research*. Cambridge, UK: Cambridge University Press.

Wallsten, T.S., & Budescu, D.V. (1983). Encoding subjective probabilities: a psychological and psychometric review. *Management Science, 29*, 151–173.

Wason, P.C. (1960). On the failure to eliminate hypotheses in a conceptual task. *Quarterly Journal of Experimental Psychology, 12*, 129–140.

Weinstein, M.C., & Fineberg, H.V. (1980). *Clinical decision analysis*. Philadelphia: W.B. Saunders.

Wolf, F.M., Gruppen, L.D., & Billi, J.E. (1985). Differential diagnosis and the competing-hypothesis heuristic: a practical approach to judgment under uncertainty and Bayesian probability. *Journal of the American Medical Association, 253*, 2858–2862.

Wortman, P.M. (1972). Medical diagnosis: an information processing approach. *Computational Biomedical Research, 5*, 315–328.

Appendix A: summary chapter from the independent training condition (zymosis)

Identification: Zymosis is an acute disease of short duration and varying severity. Onset is sudden and characterized by fever, cough, prostration (physical weakness) and anorexia (loss of appetite). Anorexia is commonly associated with diarrhea, although the underlying cause is sometimes nausea. The degree of prostration is more likely to be mild than severe. Zymosis patients experience difficulty in walking; the cause is usually pain in the lower extremities, especially the feet. Sometimes, though, the patient's difficulty in walking is attributed to a "pins-and-needles" or tingling sensation in the legs and feet. Fever is constantly elevated for 5 to 7 days, and is very likely to be low-grade (i.e., temperatures in the range of 99–101°F). Patients normally develop a dry cough, although they occasionally experience a harsh, barking cough instead. More often than not, the tongue is cracked and fissured. As the disease progresses, a rash appears on the chest and abdomen and then spreads to the body generally. This rash commonly has a scaly consistency, although it sometimes can be moist and "weepy".

Occurrence: Worldwide and relatively frequent. More common in males than females, and somewhat more common in children than adults. There are pronounced racial differences, with White people being much more susceptible than Black or Brown people, for reasons that are not clear.

Mode of transmission: From person to person by direct contact. Highly contagious.

Incubation period: Highly variable and difficult to ascertain; usually 7 to 21 days.

Susceptibility and resistance: Susceptibility is universal among those not previously infected. One infection confers long-term immunity. Immunity is sometimes conferred by subclinical infection (i.e., without the disease being obvious).

Appendix B: summary chapter from the contrastive training condition

Identification: Proxititis and zymosis are both acute diseases characterized by sudden onset of fever, cough, prostration (physical weakness) and anorexia (loss of appetite), and later development of a rash. Illness is of short duration, with constantly elevated temperature for about 5 to 7 days. The two diseases have similar symptomatology.

With zymosis, anorexia is commonly associated with diarrhea, although the underlying cause is sometimes nausea. The degree of prostration is more likely to be mild than severe. Patients experience difficulty in walking; the cause is usually pain in the lower extremities, especially the feet. Sometimes, though, the patient's difficulty in walking is attributed to a "pins-and-needles" or tingling sensation in the legs and feet. Fever is very likely to be low-grade (i.e., temperatures in the range of 99–101°F). Zymosis patients normally develop a dry cough, although they occasionally experience a harsh, barking cough instead. More often than not, the tongue is cracked and fissured. As the disease progresses, a rash appears on the chest and abdomen and then spreads to the body generally. This rash commonly has a scaly consistency, although it sometimes can be moist and "weepy".

With proxititis, fever is more often low-grade than high. Patients are somewhat more likely to have a dry cough than a harsh, barking one. The tongue is usually cracked and fissured but occasionally will have a smooth appearance. Anorexia is commonly due to nausea. Prostration is normally mild, although proxititis patients occasionally will experience more severe physical weakness. In addition, most patients experience difficulty in walking due to a tingling sensation in the lower extremities, particularly the feet. Later, a rash appears. The rash is usually moist and "weepy", although proxititis patients sometimes have a scaly rash.

Occurrence: Both diseases occur worldwide and are relatively frequent. Zymosis is more common in males than females, and somewhat more common in children than adults. There are pronounced racial differences, with White people being much more susceptible to zymosis than Black or Brown people, for reasons that are not clear. Proxititis is more common in females than in males. Racial differences are not pronounced, but Whites are somewhat more susceptible than Black and Brown people. Proxititis is normally a disease of children and adolescents, but is sometimes seen in adults.

Mode of transmission: From person to person by direct contact. Both diseases are highly contagious.

Incubation period: Highly variable and difficult to ascertain; usually 7 to 21 days for both diseases.

Susceptibility and resistance: Susceptibility is universal among those not previously infected. One infection confers long-term immunity. Immunity is sometimes conferred by subclinical infection (i.e., without the disease being obvious).

6 Reasoning in explanation-based decision making

Nancy Pennington, and Reid Hastie
Psychology Department, University of Colorado, Boulder

Abstract

A general theory of explanation-based decision making is outlined and the multiple roles of inference processes in the theory are indicated. A typology of formal and informal inference forms, originally proposed by Collins (1978a, 1978b), is introduced as an appropriate framework to represent inferences that occur in the overarching explanation-based process. Results from the analysis of verbal reports of decision processes are presented to demonstrate the centrality and systematic character of reasoning in a representative legal decision-making task.

Introduction

Many important decisions are made under conditions where a large base of implication-rich, conditionally dependent pieces of evidence must be evaluated as a preliminary to choosing a course of action. We propose that a model of *explanation-based* decision making describes behavior under these conditions (Pennington, 1981; Pennington & Hastie, 1981, 1986, 1988, 1991, 1992, 1993). According to the explanation-based model, decision makers begin their decision process by constructing a causal model to explain the available facts. The decision maker is also engaged in a separate activity to learn, create, or discover a set of alternatives from which an action will be chosen. A decision is made when the causal model of the evidence is successfully matched to an alternative in the choice set. The three processing stages in the general explanation-based decision model are shown in Fig. 1.

Distinctive assumptions in our explanation-based approach to decision making are the hypotheses that decision makers *reason about* the evidence in order to

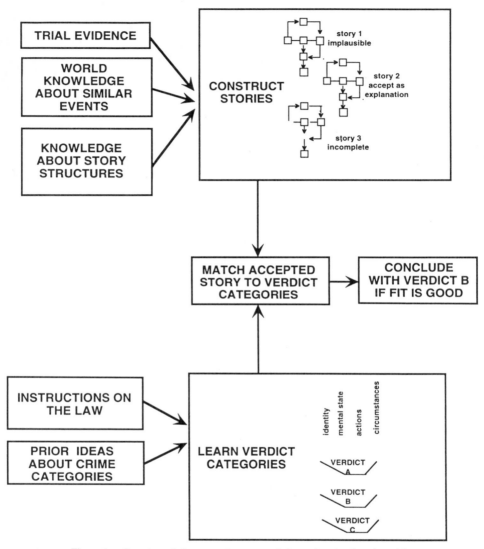

Figure 1. *Overview of the processing stages of the explanation-based model.*

construct an intermediate summary representation of the evidence, that this intermediate representation is an *interpretation* of the original evidence, and that this representation, rather than the original "raw" evidence, is the basis of the final decision. Interposition of this organized representation facilitates evidence comprehension, directs inferencing, enables the decision maker to reach a decision, and contributes substantially to the confidence assigned to the accuracy or success of the decision. Our approach to decision processes parallels work demonstrating the role of explanation in categorization behavior (Murphy & Medin, 1985; Rips, 1989a), category learning (e.g., Schank, Collins, & Hunter, 1986), planning (Wilensky, 1983), and learning by generalization from examples (e.g., Lewis, 1988).

According to our theory of explanation-based decision making, the structure of the causal model constructed to explain the evidence will depend on the decision domain. Domain-specific causal rules and knowledge structures will underlie an internist's causal model of a patient's medical condition and its precedents (Pople, 1982), an engineer's mental model of an electrical circuit (de Kleer & Brown, 1983), an epidemiologist's model of the effect of radon contamination on health (Bostrom, Fischhoff, & Morgan, 1992), a merchant's image of the economic factors in a resort town (Hogarth, Michaud, & Mery, 1980), or a diplomat's causal map of the political forces in the Middle East (Axelrod, 1976; and see Klein, Orasanu, Calderwood & Zsambok, 1993, for additional examples). In the case of juror decision making we have established that a juror uses narrative story structures to organize and interpret evidence in criminal trials (Pennington & Hastie, 1986, 1988). In the present paper we will go beyond discussions of the *structure* of the model generated from the evidence to examine some of the *reasoning processes* that are involved in the creation and utilization of that mental representation.

The juror's decision task

The juror's decision task is a prototype of the tasks to which the explanation-based model should apply: First, a massive "database" of evidence is encountered at trial, frequently requiring several days to present. Second, the evidence comes in a scrambled order in which several witnesses and exhibits convey pieces of a historical puzzle in a jumbled temporal sequence. Third, the evidence is piecemeal and there are many gaps in its depiction of the historical events that are the focus of reconstruction: event descriptions are incomplete, usually some critical events were not observed by the available witnesses, and information about personal reactions and motivations is not presented (often because of the rules of evidence). Finally, subparts of the evidence (e.g., individual sentences or statements) are interdependent in their probative implications for the verdict. The meaning of one statement cannot be assessed in isolation because it depends on the meanings of related statements.

The general explanation-based model accounts for decision making by jurors through the following three component processes corresponding to those shown in Fig. 1: (a) constructing an explanation that accounts for the evidence in the form of a "story"; (b) representation of the decision alternatives by learning verdict category attributes; and (c) reaching a decision through the classification of the story into the best-fitting verdict category. In addition to descriptions of processing stages, one central claim of the model is that the story the juror constructs *determines* the juror's decision. As part of the theory, we also propose four certainty principles – coverage, coherence, uniqueness, and goodness-of-fit – that govern which story will be accepted, which decision will be selected, and the confidence or level of certainty with which a particular decision will be made.

In order to illustrate our ideas with examples, we will draw on one of the simulated trials that we have used in our research, *Commonwealth of Massachusetts v. Johnson*. In this trial, the defendant Frank Johnson is charged with first-degree murder. The undisputed background events include the following: the defendant Johnson, and the victim, Alan Caldwell, had a quarrel early on the day of Caldwell's death. At that time, Caldwell threatened Johnson with a razor. Later in the evening, they were again at the same bar. They went outside together, got into a fight, and Johnson knifed Caldwell, resulting in Caldwell's death. The events under dispute include whether or not Caldwell pulled a razor in the evening fight, whether Johnson actively stabbed Caldwell or merely held his knife out to protect himself, how they got outside together, whether or not Johnson intentionally went home and got his knife, whether Johnson went back to the bar to find Caldwell or went to the bar because it was his habit, etc.

Constructing an explanation

Our empirical research has focused on the claim that the juror's explanation of legal evidence takes the form of a "story" in which causal and intentional relations among events are prominent (see also Bennett & Feldman, 1981; Hutchins, 1980; Pennington, 1981; Pennington & Hastie, 1986, 1988, 1992). Furthermore, we have shown that, under the conditions that hold in a typical criminal jury trial, jurors spontaneously construct story structures (and not other plausible structures); jurors who choose different verdicts construct different stories; and the story summary is a *cause* of the juror's decision.

According to the theory, the story will be constructed from three types of knowledge: (a) case-specific information acquired during the trial (e.g., statements made by witnesses about past events relevant to the decision); (b) knowledge about events similar in content to those that are the topic of dispute (e.g., knowledge about a similar crime in the juror's community); and (c) generic expectations about what makes a complete story (e.g., knowledge that human actions are usually motivated by goals). This constructive mental activity results in one or more *interpretations* of the evidence that have a narrative story form. One of these interpretations (stories) will be accepted by the juror as the best explanation of the evidence. The story that is accepted is the one that provides the greatest coverage of the evidence and is the most coherent, as determined by the particular juror.

Stories involve human action sequences connected by relationships of physical causality and intentional causality between events. In its loosest form, a story could be described as a "causal chain" of events in which events are connected by causal relationships of necessity and sufficiency (Trabasso & van den Broek, 1985). However, psychological research on discourse comprehension suggests that story causal chains have additional higher-order structure both when considering the discourse itself and when considering the listener's or reader's "mental representations" of the discourse. Stories appear to be organized into units that are often called *episodes* (Mandler, 1984; Pennington & Hastie, 1986; Rumelhart, 1977; Schank, 1975; Stein & Glenn, 1979; Trabasso & van den Broek, 1985). An episode should contain events which fulfill particular roles and are connected by certain types of causal relationships. In stories and in episodes, events considered to be *initiating events* cause characters to have psychological *responses* and to form *goals* that motivate subsequent *actions* which cause certain *consequences* and accompanying *states*. An example of an episode in the Johnson case is the following sequence: Johnson and Caldwell are in Gleason's bar. Caldwell's girlfriend, Sandra Lee, goes up to Johnson and asks him for a ride to the race track the next day (initiating events). Caldwell becomes angry (internal response), pulls his razor, and threatens Johnson (actions, note that a goal is missing). Johnson backs off (consequence).

Stories may have further structure by virtue of the fact that each component of an episode may be an episode itself. For example, the entire episode above (characterized as Caldwell threatens Johnson) is the initiating event in one version of the Johnson story. In this version, the afternoon "threat" episode causes Johnson to be angry, and want to pay Caldwell back. Thus, a story may be thought of as a hierarchy of embedded episodes (Rumelhart, 1977; Trabasso & van den Broek, 1985). The highest-level episode characterizes the most important features of "what happened". Components of the highest-level episode are elaborated in terms of more detailed event sequences in which causal and intentional relations among subordinate story events are represented.

The structure of stories, according to our theory, plays an important role in the juror's comprehension and decision-making processes. The story constructed by the juror will consist of some subset of the events and causal relationships referred to in the presentation of evidence, *and* additional events and causal relationships inferred by the juror. Some of these inferences may be suggested by the attorney and some may be constructed solely by the juror. Whatever their source, the inferences will serve to fill out the episode structure of the story. Thus, expectations about the kinds of information necessary to make a story tell the juror when important pieces of the explanation structure are missing and when inferences must be made. Knowledge about the structure of stories allows the juror to form an opinion concerning the completeness of the evidence – the extent to which a story has all its parts. Second, the structure of episodes in a story corresponds to the structure of our knowledge about human action sequences in the world. That is, story construction is a general comprehension strategy for understanding human action. Thus the juror can easily compare the structure that is being imposed on the evidence to already encoded prior knowledge. Finally, the hierarchical episode and causal structure of the story provides an "automatic" index of the importance of different pieces of evidence (Trabasso & Sperry, 1985). In the example above, the details of the embedded "threat" episode are subordinate in importance to the details of the top-level episode that reveal what Johnson did in order to pay Caldwell back. However, this indexing of importance is something that emerges from the *structure* of the story.

Learning the choice set

The decision maker's second major task is to learn or to create a set of potential solutions or action alternatives that constitute the choice set. In criminal trials the legal information for this processing stage is given to jurors at the end of the trial in the judge's instructions on the law and the verdict alternatives available to the juror. These instructions provide only a sketchy outline of the decision categories and jurors may also have prior ideas concerning the meaning of the verdict alternatives. The verdict definition information in the judge's instructions is usually abstract and often couched in unfamiliar language: a crime is named and then abstract features are presented that define the crime. Features typically describe requirements of *identity*, *mental state*, *circumstances*, and *actions* that constitute the crime (Kaplan, 1978).

Again, constructive inference processes are rampant and it is common for prior conceptions of the verdicts (e.g., from news media and fictional accounts of trials) to intrude into the verdict representations (see Smith, 1991, for additional empirical results on verdict representation). But, many gaps and errors remain in the jurors' operative conceptualizations of the law (cf. Elwork, Sales, & Alfini, 1977; Hastie, Penrod, & Pennington, 1983).

Matching the story to the verdicts

The final stage in the global decision process involves matching decision alternatives to the summary evidence representation to find the most successful pairing. Because verdict categories are unfamiliar concepts, the classification of a story into an appropriate verdict category is likely to be a deliberate inferential process. For example, a juror may have to decide whether a circumstance in the story such as "pinned against a wall" constitutes a good match to a required circumstance, "unable to escape", for a verdict of not guilty by reason of self-defense. In this example, these inferences would depend on knowledge from the trial evidence, from the judge's instructions, and from the juror's background knowledge of human motivations (was the person "trying" to escape?), mental processes (was the person incapacitated?), and the physical world (was it physically possible for the person to escape?).

The story classification stage also involves the application of the judge's procedural instructions on the presumption of innocence and the standard of proof. That is, if not all of the verdict attributes for a given verdict category are satisfied "beyond a reasonable doubt", by events in the accepted story, then the juror should presume innocence and return a default verdict of not guilty.

Confidence in decisions

More than one story may be constructed by the juror. However, one story will usually be accepted as the "best" story. And the juror will have a level of confidence in that "best" story that may be quite high or quite low. The principles that determine acceptability of a story, and the resulting level of confidence in the story, we call *certainty principles*. According to our theory, two certainty principles govern acceptance: *coverage* and *coherence*. An additional certainty principle – *uniqueness* – will contribute to confidence (see Pennington, Messamer, & Nicolich, 1991, for elaboration and formalization of these principles; see Collins, Brown, & Larkin, 1980, for a similar set of principles proposed to determine global confidence in one alternative interpretation of an ambiguous text).

A story's *coverage* of the evidence refers to the extent to which the story accounts for evidence presented at trial. Our principle states that the greater the story's coverage, the more acceptable the story as an explanation of the evidence, and the greater confidence the juror will have in the story as an explanation, if accepted. An explanation that leaves a lot of evidence unaccounted for is likely to have a lower level of acceptability as the correct explanation. Poor coverage should lower the overall confidence in a story and consequently lower confidence in the decision.

A story's *coherence* also enters into its acceptability, and level of confidence given that the story is accepted. However, coherence is a concept in our theory that has three components: *consistency*, *plausibility*, and *completeness*. A story is consistent to the extent that it does not contain internal contradictions either with evidence believed to be true or with other parts of the explanation. A story is plausible to the extent that it corresponds to the decision maker's knowledge about what typically happens in the world and does not contradict that knowledge. A story is complete when the expected structure of the story "has all of its parts" (according to the rules of the episodic structure and discussion above). Missing information or lack of plausible inferences about one or more major components of the story structure will decrease confidence in the explanation. Thus, the coherence of the explanation reflects the consistency of the explanation with itself and with world knowledge, and the extent to which parts of the explanation can be inferred or assembled. These three ingredients of coherence (consistency, plausibility, and completeness) may be fulfilled to a greater or lesser degree and the values of the three components will combine to yield the overall level of coherence of a story. Combination of these ingredients, however, is not strictly additive (Pennington, Messamer, & Nicolich, 1991). For example, completeness interacts with plausibility. If a story is plausible, then the completeness increases confidence. However, if a story is implausible, completeness does not increase confidence (it might be thought that completeness of an implausible story would actually decrease confidence but this is not the case; see Pennington, Messamer, & Nicolich, 1991).

Finally, if more than one story is judged to be coherent, then the stories will lack *uniqueness*, which contributes to confidence in a story and in a decision. If there are multiple coherent explanations for the available evidence, belief in any one of them over the others will be lessened (Baltzer & Pennington, 1993; Einhorn & Hogarth, 1986; Van Wallendael, 1989). If there is one coherent story, this story will be accepted as the explanation of the evidence and will be instrumental in reaching a decisions.

Reasoning to construct representations

It is a trite but profound insight that "perception is only half of perception". The inevitable gaps in our sensory connections with the outside world are filled with information that is inferred. When we attempt to perceive the world second- or third-hand, as a juror or judge must, the gaps are larger and the role of inference is even more dominant. If we listen to jurors thinking aloud on their way to a decision, retrospectively reflecting on their verdicts, or discussing their decisions in a social context such as the jury room, we observe a flood of inferences; most of them directed at constructing a summary of "what happened", but many also drawn in support of a deliberate classification of the story into a verdict category. In this paper, we will focus on the reasoning to construct a story representation that accounts for as much of the trial evidence as possible.

We have hypothesized that jurors *impose* a narrative organization on evidence. By this, we mean that jurors engage in an active, constructive comprehension process in which evidence is organized, elaborated, and interpreted by them during the course of the trial. In part, this activity occurs because comprehension is inherently a constructive process for even the simplest discourse (Crothers, 1979; Collins, Brown & Larkin, 1980; Kintsch, 1974, 1988).[1] This is especially true in the context of legal trials in which characteristics of the trial evidence make comprehension unwieldy. First there is a lot of evidence, often presented over a duration of several days. Second, evidence presentation typically appears in a disconnected question and answer format; different witnesses testify to different pieces of the chain of events, usually not in temporal or causal order; and witnesses are typically not allowed to speculate on necessary connecting events such as why certain actions were carried out, or what emotional reaction a person had to a certain event.

Our concept of reasoning to construct story representations is shown in Fig. 2. According to the theory, stories are constructed by reasoning from world knowledge and from evidence. Some potential story elements are accepted as true directly on the basis of their appearance as evidence from one or more credible sources; they are reasonably well established as fact. For example, an evidence item, "Caldwell was in Gleason's Bar", is direct testimony, is not a matter of dispute, and it appears in all jurors' individual stories. In Fig. 2, this is shown as a piece of evidence (e1) appearing directly in the story. Which of these events will appear as relevant depends on the interpretation assigned to the fact from its causal relatedness to other events. The inclusion in the story of other evidence, inferred events, and causal relations between them is the result of a wide variety of deductive and inductive reasoning procedures applied to the evidence and world knowledge (Collins, 1978a, 1978b; Collins & Michalski, 1989). For example, a typical deduction from world knowledge in the "Johnson case" consists of the following premise (P1–P3) and conclusion (C) structure:

P1. A person who is big and known to be a troublemaker causes people to be afraid. (from world knowledge)
P2. Caldwell was big. (from evidence)
P3. Caldwell was known to be a troublemaker. (previous inference)

C. Johnson was afraid. (inferential conclusion)

[1]This is a dominant view in cognitive psychology today. To illustrate, a listener is told a simple narrative: "Billy went to Johnny's birthday party. When all the children were there, Johnny opened his presents. Later, they sang Happy Birthday and Johnny blew out the candles." Many listeners will infer spontaneously, and most will agree when asked, that there was a cake at the birthday party. Yet, no cake is mentioned in the sentences above; indeed it is not certain that there was a cake. The cake is inferred because we share knowledge about birthday party traditions and about the physical world (the candles had to be on something). Another illustration comes with the comprehension of the sentence, "The policeman held up his hand and stopped the car". Most of us understand this sentence in the cultural context of the policeman's authority, shared signals, a driver watching the policeman but controlling the car, etc. Indeed, this is a sentence that would be puzzling to a person from a different culture.

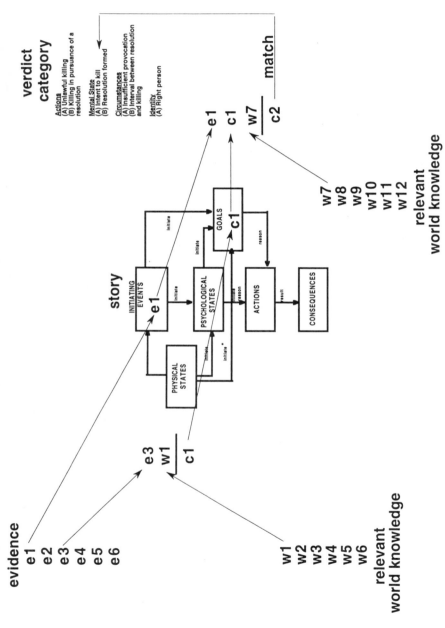

Figure 2. *Inferences connect evidence with world knowledge and with the evolving story, and they connect the story with world knowledge and with verdict category features.*

In this example, the juror matches features of Caldwell from undisputed evidence (P2) and a previous inferential conclusion (P3) to world knowledge about the consequences of being confronted with such a person (P1) to infer that Johnson was afraid (C). In Fig. 2, we have represented abstractly that a piece of evidence (e3) combined with world knowledge (w1) can produce a conclusion (c1) that becomes an element of the story. This story conclusion might then be involved in a later stage of inferential reasoning required to match the story to a decision alternative. In Fig. 2, the story element (c1) coming from an earlier inference and the story element (e1) coming directly from evidence might be combined with world knowledge (w7) to produce an inferential conclusion allowing those story attributes to be mapped more directly onto the verdict category definition.

In the present research, we have used a taxonomic system to describe inference procedures based on a system for informal reasoning proposed by Allan Collins and his colleagues (Collins, 1978a, 1978b; Collins, Brown, & Larkin, 1980; Collins, Warnock, Aiello, & Miller, 1975). Collins' goal was to develop a system of forms of plausible inference that can be implemented as a well-defined computer program to answer questions based on reasoning from world knowledge in the reasoner's long-term memory. His most recent papers have expressed the system in a formalism consistent with Michalski's variable-valued logical calculus (Collins & Michalski, 1989) and some versions of the system have been implemented as operational programs (Baker, Burnstein, & Collins, 1987; Dontas & Zemankova, 1987; Kelly, 1988).

We have simplified the Collins system and use his general (and traditional) categories of the major inference forms to label the variety of inference types that occur in our analyses of inference in juror decision protocols. In general terms the inference forms include and extend traditional logic inference forms in several ways. The basic inferential forms of deduction, analogy, induction, generalization, and abduction are included in the theory in premise–conclusion form. But the rules of logic are generalized from two values of certainty (true or false) to a continuum of certainty, creating plausible inference forms that would constitute fallacies in logic (e.g., affirming the consequent).

In later sections, in which we discuss our analyses of inference chains in example jurors' reasoning, we outline the inference types and show sample applications in some detail. The theory of reasoning in decision making that we promote has some higher-level claims that we explicate here. First, we lean towards an inclusive definition of the concept of inference, and would include most mental activities that result in adding a new piece of information to the reasoner's current model of a situation. But we would also like to exclude the unconscious, "raw", associative mental activation processes that may underlie many memory retrieval achievements. Although we cannot draw definitive conceptual or operational distinctions between inference processes and other types of mental processes, we can point to the familiar premise–conclusion propositional form as the prototype of inference processes. Second, although our explanation-based decision-making theory is based on the idea that decision makers construct a model of the situation specific to the decision, our treatment of reasoning processes is based on the idea that we use inference procedures that are fairly general across content domains and contexts in order to construct the model of the situation (cf. Collins, 1978a, 1978b; Collins & Michalski, 1989; Rips, 1986). Thus, the basic inference procedures will be generalizations of syllogistic forms. We also propose, following Collins (1978a, 1978b), that people use several different inference patterns and converging chains of reasoning to establish their conclusions.

Relationship of explanation-based decision making and the story model to other approaches

Our approach has much in common with the "mental models" approaches to deductive reasoning (Johnson-Laird, 1983; Johnson-Laird & Byrne, 1991) and discourse comprehension (Bower & Morrow, 1990; Bransford, Barclay, & Franks, 1972; Perrig & Kintsch, 1985; van Dijk & Kintsch, 1983). Like these researchers we propose that people construct mental representations of situations, in the course of normal comprehension and reasoning, that are concrete in the sense that they are constituted of "individuals" with external referents (not abstract "variables") and in that the structure of the representation corresponds to the structure of the relevant situation. Our account of reasoning in decision making is also similar to the process models of deduction and comprehension proposed by these researchers. We claim that a model is constructed, "in the head", of the situation referred to in a problem or text. Additional conclusions are inferred, usually in the form of new relations among elements cited in the original text or problem, and checked for consistency with the source text and world knowledge. We also propose that, sometimes, alternate counter-example models are constructed and evaluated for veracity.

Like the Johnson-Laird and Kintsch representations, the explanation models we have proposed are relatively static, although they usually have a temporal dimension (ordering the events in an alleged crime, a medical case history, or the historical development of a military or economic scenario). But we have not suggested that they can be "run" or "simulated" to project future outcomes. ("Dynamic" mental models have been proposed, but plausible mental procedures have not been spelled out to explain how the models "run". But it seems that sensible "forward inference" procedures could be added to the basic claims about representation to produce the desired "dynamic" models; see Gentner & Stevens, 1983; Kahneman & Tversky, 1982; Rouse & Morris, 1986, for examples.)

The fundamental difference between our explanation-based approach and traditional algebraic approaches, such as cognitive algebra (Anderson, 1981), the lens model (Hammond, Stewart, Brehmer, & Steinman, 1975), and utility theory (von Neumann & Morgenstern, 1947), is that we view *reasoning about the evidence* and *construction of an intermediate, semantic representation of the evidence* to be the central process in decision making, in contrast to an emphasis on the computation that occurs once evidence has been selected, augmented, and evaluated. We also depart from the common assumption that, when causal reasoning is involved in judgment, it can be described by algebraic computations that lead directly to a decision (e.g., Anderson, 1974; Einhorn & Hogarth, 1986; Kelley, 1973). In our model causal reasoning plays a subordinate but critical role by guiding inferences in evidence evaluation and construction of the intermediate explanation.

We can also relate our approach to the cognitive heuristics analysis of judgment under uncertainty (Kahneman, Slovic, & Tversky, 1982; Tversky & Kahneman, 1974). We claim that evaluations of uncertainty, estimates of probability, etc., are secondary judgments that occur in the context of primary inference processes. For example, when set membership relationships are involved in inductive, deductive, abductive or analogical inference processes, "representativeness" or the typicality of instances or subsets provides one type of cue about the certainty with which conclusions have been established (see Cherniak, 1984; Osherson, Smith, Wilkie, Lopez, & Shafir, 1990; and Rips, 1975, for similar views). Following Collins (1978a, 1978b), we label these secondary considerations "certainty conditions" and postulate additional conditions, beyond the similarity, typicality, ease of recall or generation factors from the Tversky and Kahneman heuristics.

In sum, the basic claim of explanation-based decision making is that constructing an explanation that accounts for evidence (a story in the case of juror decisions) enables critical interpretive processing and organization of the evidence so that evidence can be meaningfully evaluated against multiple judgment dimensions. The story model provides a psychological account for the assignment of relevance to presented and inferred information for juror decisions. Precise claims are made concerning the representational form of the evidence and a mediating role is claimed for stories in subsequent decisions and confidence in those decisions. Uncertainty in the decision is centered in assessments of the coverage, coherence, and uniqueness of the story and on the goodness-of-fit of the story with reference to the verdict categories. Detailed summaries of empirical studies supporting the claims of the story model are provided in other reports (Baltzer & Pennington, 1993; Pennington, 1981; Pennington & Hastie, 1981, 1986, 1988, 1992; Pennington, Messamer, & Nicolich, 1991; Wolfe & Pennington, 1993).

In the present paper we focus on explicating some of the *forms of reasoning* that occur during the story construction phases of the decision process. In the juror's decision, there is no question that this component dominates the time spent by jurors deciding criminal cases. Our initial approach is descriptive and taxonomic because we believe that it is necessary to have a sample of everyday inferences in hand before it is appropriate to attempt to develop a detailed processing model (see Collins et al., 1975; and Voss, Perkins, & Segal, 1991, for similar approaches).

Research

In previous research, we have established that jurors construct narrative representations of evidence spontaneously in the course of reaching a decision, and that these representations determine their decisions. In the present analyses, our claim is that numerous inferences are made in order to construct and justify these narrative evidence summaries during and after the decision process, that jurors use converging lines of reasoning to establish their major story conclusions, and that the forms of reasoning are well captured by a general theory of plausible reasoning developed by Collins and his colleagues (Collins, 1978a, 1978b; Collins et al., 1975, 1980).

We use Collins' system of categories of major inference forms to label the variety of inference types that occur in juror decision protocols. The basic inference forms we are concerned with involve the mapping of patterns of knowledge onto a conclusion. Four major mapping relations occur frequently in the protocols, as shown in Table 1: deduction, analogy, induction and abduction. A fifth mapping relation, generalization, occurs seldom in this context. These forms vary in terms of whether the mapping is from instance or subset to superordinate category (generalization, abduction), from one set or instance to another (analogy, induction), or from a superordinate set to a subset (deduction).

For each inference mapping shown in Table 1A, there are two forms. The first is a categorical or "set" form in which a property of one set is mapped onto another set. The second is a functional (causal/correlational) form in which the property to be mapped depends on other properties. This dependency is a directional relationship between variables that includes notions of implication, correlation, and causal relationships (see Collins, 1978a).

Collins (1978b) also identifies two causal reasoning principles. One is functional *attribution* (see Table 1B) – a form of induction concerning causes. In its full form, a general causal rule is affirmed (e.g., if the causes $c_1 \ldots c_i$ occur then effect e will follow). When the antecedent events occur and the effect occurs, then conclude that the effect occurred *because of* the causes. A second, functional *alternative* is a type of "discounting" reasoning whereby knowledge that one causal antecedent was present, and that an effect occurred, leads to the conclusion that another causal antecedent was probably not present (this form would assume as a premise an appropriate general causal rule). A final principle applies more to sets and properties, *contradiction*, in which knowledge of the presence of one property leads to the inference that contradictory or incompatible values could not also be present.

For each inference form in Collins' theory of plausible reasoning, *certainty conditions* are specified. For example, consider the deduction in Table 1A: P1 = People who frequent bars are loud and impulsive. P2 = Caldwell frequented bars. C = Maybe Caldwell was loud and impulsive. One condition affecting certainty would be how typical (or representative) Caldwell was of people who frequent bars. Thus, this looks like a "representativeness heuristic" judgment under certainty (Tversky & Kahneman, 1983) in that features of a concrete situation (premises 2) is matched against features of a prototypic situation (premise 1), and the certainty of the conclusion is related to the goodness of the match. However, following Collins (1978a, 1978b; Collins et al., 1975) we propose that each inference procedure is associated with appropriate "certainty conditions" (some, but not all, of which have been identified in the literature on judgment under uncertainty; Kahneman, Slovic, & Tversky, 1982). For example, certainty conditions for deductive inferences include: (a) typicality of the instances within the relevant categories (e.g., how typical is Caldwell of those who frequent bars?); (b) base rates of the properties under consideration (e.g., how frequently are people loud and impulsive in general?); (c) variability in properties attributed to general categories (e.g., for the category of people who frequent bars, how variable is the "loud and impulsive" quality?); and (d) dissimilarity between cited instances and the most similar group that behaves in a contradictory manner (e.g., how similar is Caldwell to the kind of person who frequents bars but is *not* loud and impulsive?).

In Collins' (1978a, 1978b) taxonomy of inferences, there are approximately 40 inference forms. In addition to the categorical and functional forms of many of the inferences, many of the mappings also have a *temporal* and *spatial* form in which deductive or abductive mappings are applied to temporal and spatial knowledge. Our goal in this research was to go beyond our previous analyses of the representations of evidence during juror decision making and to characterize the inference structure and lines of argumentation used to coordinate trial information, world knowledge, verdict category information and major story conclusions, in order to produce the representational forms that we have previously analyzed. The 11 inference forms shown in Table 1A and 1B, with a few temporal and spatial variations that are not shown, were adequate to capture most of the juror reasoning we analyzed.

Table 1. *Example inference forms. After Collins (1978a, 1978b)*

Table 1A	Deduction: maps properties of a set onto subsets[a]	Analogy: maps properties from one set onto a similar set	Induction:[b] maps properties of subsets onto other subsets of the same set	Abduction: maps a subset with the same property as a set into the set
Categorical form	Set X has property A1. X1 is subset of X.	Set X has property A1. Set Y is like set X.	X1, X2 have A1. X1, X2, X3 subsets of X.	Set X has property A1. X1 has property A1.
	Maybe X1 has A1.	Maybe Y has A1.	Maybe X3 has A1.	Maybe X1 is subset of X
Example	People who frequent bars are loud and impulsive. Caldwell frequented bars,	I am quick tempered. Johnson is probably like me.	Two different friends of mine got in fights in a bar and didn't intend any harm. Johnson got in a fight in a bar.	Gentle people speak softly. Johnson spoke softly.
	Maybe Caldwell was loud and impulsive.	Johnson is probably quick tempered.	Possibly Johnson didn't intend any harm.	Maybe Johnson was a gentle person.
Functional dependency (causal/correlational) form	A1 depends on B, C. X1 has B, C.	(A1 depends on B, C.) Y is like X on B, C. X has A1.	(A1 depends on B, C.) X1, X2 have B. C. X1, X2 have A1. X3 has B. C. X1, X2, X3 subsets of X.	A1 depends on B, C. X1 has A1.
	Maybe X1 has A1.	Maybe Y has A1.	Maybe X3 has A1.	Maybe X1 has B, C.
Example (positive)	If someone embarrassed Johnson, he would probably go back with malice and do a job on him. Caldwell embarrassed Johnson.	My father carried a knife for protection because he had to come and go in a rough neighborhood. It sounds like Johnson also frequented a rough neighborhood.	None observed	Going to the park with your family, being home, eating supper, depend on a calm frame of mind. Johnson went to the park with his family, came home, had supper.
	Probably, Johnson went back with malice to do a job on Caldwell. (modus ponens)	Maybe Johnson carried a knife for protection.		Probably Johnson was in a calm frame of mind.
Example (negative)	If Johnson went back out of pride, he would not need a knife. Johnson took a knife.	None observed	None observed	None observed
	Johnson probably did not go back out of pride. (modus tollens)			

Table 1. *continued*

Table 1B	Attribution: for a given subset, when all properties are present, a causal relationship is inferred for the case	Alternative: when two causes are possible and one is known to be true, the other is considered unlikely	Contradiction: when two causes or properties are possible, but contradictory, and one is known to be true, then the other is inferred to not be true
Categorical or functional dependency form	A1 depends on B, C. X1 has B, C. X1 has A1. ___ X1 has A1 *because* B, C.	A1 depends on B or C. X1 has A1 and B. ___ X1 may not have C.	X has A1. A1 implies not B1. X1 is a subset of X. ___ X1 does not have B1.
Example	One reason for carrying a weapon is being afraid. Johnson carried a knife. Johnson was afraid of Caldwell. ___ Johnson carried his knife *because* he was afraid of Caldwell.	Johnson went back either out of pride or to fix Caldwell. Johnson went back to fix him. ___ Johnson did not go back out of pride.	Johnson was trying to stay away from Caldwell. Staying away from someone is incompatible with trying to find the person. ___ Johnson was not trying to find Caldwell.

[a] Subset may mean either several instances or one individual instance.

[b] A fifth standard form, generalization, maps properties of subsets of a set onto the set. This would have the categorical form: X1, X2 have A1; X1, X2 are subsets of X; (conclusion) maybe all X have A1. The functional (causal correlational) form would be: X1, X2 have B, C; X1, X2 have A1; X1, X2 subsets of X; (conclusion) maybe A1 depends on B, C for all X. Generalizations did not occur in the protocols.

Research method

Procedure

Adult subjects were randomly sampled from a pool of more than 200 volunteers who had been called for jury duty in the major trial court in Boston, Massachusetts, and shown a 3-hour videotaped re-enactment of a criminal case (see Pennington & Hastie, 1986, for more details on the method). Following the videotaped trial, the jurors were individually interviewed and asked to talk about their decisions. For present purposes we have selected two jurors' post-decision interviews and will provide detailed analyses of the forms of reasoning and argumentation that occur in their verbal reports.

Subjects

The two example jurors were selected on the basis of their decisions: one chose the most lenient (not guilty) verdict and the other chose the harshest (first-degree murder) verdict. In terms of the lengths and contents of their protocols, they are representative of the other jurors who were interviewed about their decisions. But we must note that the present report relies on two protocols that are being presented to *illustrate* the forms of inference and the roles of inference in the juror decision task. These post-decision interviews contain a mixture of inferences made in the service of the decision and inferences made to communicate or justify the decision. The present method does not allow us to discriminate between these two sources of inferences. Finally, the verbal report interview may omit, even systematically omit, certain classes of difficult-to-report or embarrassing-to-report inferences. We can assert that our current research, including the analysis of verbal reports collected during the presentation of the stimulus trial, replicates the essential richness and variety of inference forms that were obtained in the post-trial presentation method.

Stimulus trial

The specific characteristics of the task will exert a dominant influence on the types and forms of inferences that occur in the decision process. The legal case used in our research, labeled *Commonwealth* v. *Johnson*, represents a typical serious felony trial (it is based on the transcript of a Massachusetts trial) in which the defendant Frank Johnson was charged with killing Alan Caldwell with deliberate premeditation and malice aforethought. We have already briefly summarized to the stimulus trial, but include a fuller description here in order to highlight the major issues about which subjects would be led to reason.

The first witness for the prosecution, a police officer, testified that one evening from a distance of about 75 feet he saw Caldwell (the victim) hit the defendant Johnson in the face and then Johnson plunged a large knife downward into Caldwell's chest. Because of the distance and the angle of view he was unable to see Caldwell's right hand (to observe whether or not the victim was armed). When arrested, Johnson said, "Caldwell pulled a razor on me so I stuck him".

The second witness, a state pathologist, testified about the cause of death (a stab wound to the heart); that the victim's blood alcohol level rendered him legally drunk; and that the victim's body was marked in several places with scars that may or may not have been surgical in origin. The pathologist also noted that the victim carried a straight razor in his left rear pants pocket.

The owner of the bar outside of which the killing occurred testified that he observed, through a partially obstructed window, and also saw Johnson stab Caldwell. He said that Johnson and a friend (Dennis Clemens) arrived in the bar before Caldwell and that sometime later Caldwell and Johnson left the bar together. The bar owner also reported that earlier on the afternoon of the same day the two men had quarreled and that Caldwell had threatened Johnson with a straight razor and chased him out of the bar. Finally, he noted that Johnson had never caused trouble in the bar before.

The defense opened with testimony from Dennis Clemens, a friend of Johnson's who indicated that he initiated the evening visit to the bar by asking Johnson to join him for a drink. Johnson was reluctant to go into the bar, but when the two men saw no trace of Caldwell, they entered. After they had been in the bar for about half an hour, Caldwell came in and then asked Johnson to step outside with him. Clemens saw the fight start and described Caldwell knocking Johnson to the ground and then drawing a straight razor. Johnson tried to hold Caldwell off (Clemens never saw a weapon in Johnson's hand) and then Caldwell staggered back and fell to the ground.

The second defense witness, a waitress from the bar, corroborated the timing of the fight events and also reported that a car was parked illegally in front of the bar in a location that would have interfered with the police officer's view of the altercation from across the street.

The defendant, Frank Johnson, testified last and said that he had a quarrel with Caldwell in the bar in the afternoon, when a woman asked him (Johnson) for a ride to the dog track. He was frightened and left the bar after Caldwell threatened him with a straight razor. Johnson did not remember having a knife with him at that time; but after going fishing later that day, his wife asked him not to leave his fishing knife around the house where children might find it and he must have put the knife in his pocket. Johnson also reported that he had spent the afternoon with his children at the park.

Later that evening Dennis Clemens invited him to go to the bar again, but he hesitated because he was afraid of Caldwell. After he was convinced that Caldwell was not in the bar, Johnson entered, but later Caldwell came in and sat at the bar. He invited Johnson to step outside, in a friendly way, but then became angry and struck him. The blow knocked Johnson off balance and he was cornered against the wall of the bar; then Caldwell drew his straight razor. Unthinkingly, Johnson drew his fishing knife to protect himself, but Caldwell rushed in and lunged onto the blade, killing himself.

The trial judge's instructions on the law, especially definitions of the four verdicts (choice set alternatives: murder in the first degree, murder in the second degree, manslaughter, and not guilty by reason of self-defense), also exert considerable influence on the jurors' reasoning. For example, to conclude with a verdict of murder in the first degree the juror must be convinced (beyond a reasonable doubt) that a killing was committed with deliberately premeditated malice aforethought. Malice includes feelings of hatred or ill will, but it also includes any intentional infliction of an injury where there is a likelihood of causing death. Malice may be inferred from the intentional use of a deadly weapon without just provocation or legal excuse. In addition, deliberate premeditation is a sequence of thought processes: the plan to murder is formed, then the resolution to kill, then the killing in pursuance of the resolution. On the other end of the spectrum, the juror might find that the killing was in self-defense and the defendant is not guilty of a crime. The right to self-defense arises from a threat to the defendant's life or fear of great bodily harm. The right comes into existence only after the defendant has exhausted all reasonable means to escape from the confrontation and the method of defense can rely on only reasonable force.

In the context of this stimulus trial and the form of the decision prescribed by the judge's instructions, we can anticipate the contents of many of the inferences that will be elicited. The largest subset of the inferences expressed in the protocols were directed at completing a collection of coherent episodes linked by the motivations of the defendant (i.e., to construct a narrative summary of the evidence): What was the defendant's state of mind when he left the bar after the first encounter with the victim in the afternoon? Why did the defendant return to the bar on the evening of the killing? Why did the defendant carry a knife when he returned? How did the fight outside the bar start? Did the defendant attempt to avoid the fatal fight with the decedent? The second most frequent type of inference was directed at questions raised by the legal terms in the judge's instructions: Did the defendant's (inferred) state of mind fit the legal concept of "malice"? Had the defendant "formed a resolution to injure or kill" the victim? Did the defendant "exhaust all means to avoid combat" in the confrontation outside the bar? The third most frequent collection of inferences was concerned with evaluations of the witnesses' credibility: Was the police officer telling the truth? Could the defendant's friend have seen what he claimed to have observed?

Protocol collection and story analysis procedures

Following their exposure to the videotaped trial each juror was instructed: "I would like for you to be a juror in this case and to decide on a verdict. You do not need to decide right away. I would like for you to talk out loud as you think about what to decide." This general solicitation was followed by more specific questions asking jurors if they had considered alternate verdicts, what aspects of the evidence they felt were most important, and what they could recall from the judge's instructions on the law.

The interviews were transcribed (approximately 9,000 words for each juror's responses) and systematic analyses were conducted to extract the summary of the historical events referred to in testimony (the juror's "story") that each juror had constructed from the trial evidence. Detailed reports of these analyses are available elsewhere (Pennington, 1981; Pennington & Hastie, 1986) and we provide diagrammatic summaries of the two example jurors' stories in Figs. 3 and 4.

In Figs. 3 and 4, the stories constructed by these two jurors are shown as the coordination of two streams. The first stream is the event chain showing events that occurred (such as Caldwell threatens Johnson at the bar; Johnson goes home; Johnson goes back to the bar; Johnson takes knife; Caldwell hits Johnson; etc.). This stream looks similar for the two different stories. The second stream represents the interpretation of the event chain or *why* the events occurred as they did; it is the set of goals that explain the events. For example, the first-degree murder juror (Fig. 4) has a goal to stab Caldwell that is the reason for Johnson taking the knife. In contrast, the self-defense juror (Fig. 3) has Johnson taking the knife because he was afraid. It is these goals, internal states, and causal connections between goals and events that are the major story conclusions we propose are derived through the inference procedures that are the topic of our analyses in this report.

Inference analysis procedures

Recall that our claim is that numerous inferences are made to construct and justify these narrative evidence summaries during and after the decision process; that these inferences can be identified according to the general inference forms proposed by Collins (1978a, 1978b); and that inference structures can be identified as lines of reasoning that converge on certain major inferential conclusions. Our first analysis concentrated on identifying the inference *forms* that were used to reach or justify certain story conclusions. These conclusions are concerned with *why the defendant returned to the bar* and *why the defendant was carrying a knife*. Our second analysis concentrated on identifying the *chains* of

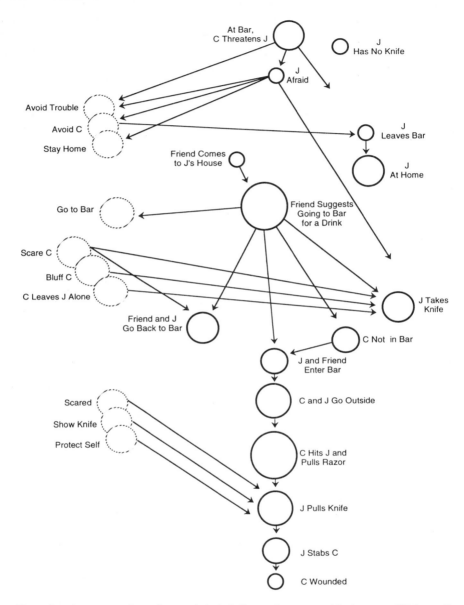

.Figure 3.   *A summary of causal event chain including goals constructed by juror no. 109 (not-guilty verdict) while making a decision in the Commonwealth* v. *Johnson case. Events and episodes are represented by solid circles and the diameters of the circles indicate the degree of elaboration provided of events by the juror; broken border circles represent the defendant's goals, inferred by the juror. The arrows connect events that were explicitly linked by causal relations in the juror's verbal report. The letters J and C refer to the defendant Johnson and the victim Caldwell respectively.*

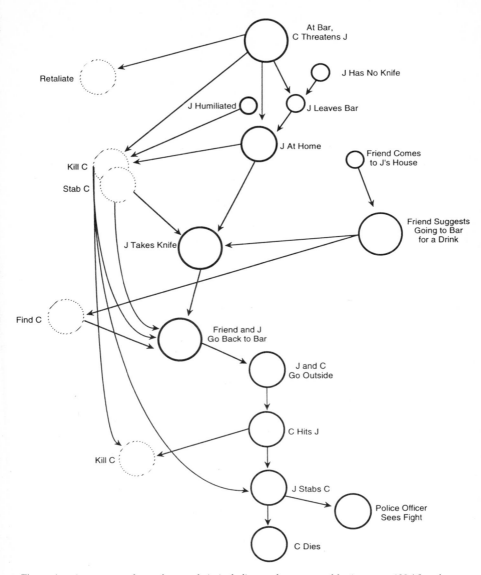

Figure 4. *A summary of causal event chain including goals constructed by juror no. 128 (first-degree murder verdict) while making a decision in the Commonwealth v. Johnson case. Events and episodes are represented by solid circles and the diameters of the circles indicate the degree of elaboration provided of events by the juror; broken border circles represent the defendant's goals, inferred by the juror. The arrows connect events that were explicitly linked by causal relations in the juror's verbal report. The letters J and C refer to the defendant Johnson and the victim Caldwell, respectively.*

inferences that were generated by jurors reasoning about the two central conclusions of the stories represented in Figs. 3 and 4. Our final analysis concentrated on identifying the reasoning *strategies* represented by these inference structures.

Tables 2 and 3 list the content and form of the inferences that we identified in each of the two protocols leading to story conclusions concerning why the defendant returned to the bar and why the defendant was carrying a knife. We did this by first identifying each assertion concerning the return to the bar and then identifying all arguments leading to the assertion. We then rewrote the juror's words in the form of an inference consisting of at least two premises and a conclusion.

Jurors don't speak in terms of premises and conclusions. The sentences in the tables are abstracted from the exact words used by jurors during the interview, but we also filled in "missing premises" to make complete inference forms. For example, the not-guilty juror's words concerning the reason Johnson took the knife to the bar were:

"...I think he took the knife with him because he was scared..."
"...I think he did it because he was afraid, the gentleman was a big gentleman, did he say 200 pounds, he was well known as a troublemaker..."

These words were translated into two inferences listed as inferences A and B in Table 2. For inference A, the premises "Caldwell was big" and "Caldwell was known to be a troublemaker" were taken from the juror's assertions. However, the premise that "A person who is big and known to be a troublemaker causes people to be afraid" was inferred as the world knowledge premise that allowed the juror to infer that Johnson was afraid of Caldwell. Sometimes jurors would explicitly state such beliefs, but often such beliefs would be implicit in the argument, as in the excerpt above.

A second coding example is drawn from the protocol of the first-degree-murder juror, who said:

"...That Mr. Johnson, when he came back, he was looking for Mr. Caldwell. Because if somebody had threatened me four or five hours earlier with a straight edge razor, I would not go back to Mr. Gleason's place again, unless I was going to be out for revenge..."
"...If Mr. Johnson wasn't looking for revenge for this, he would never go back to the same place, even with his friend Mr. Clemens, knowing that Mr. Caldwell had the razor, and he knew he had it from four or five hours ago, if he wasn't going back for revenge and to kill the man..."

These inferences, as coded in our analysis, are shown in Table 3 as inferences

Table 2. *Inferences for not-guilty juror (inference types from Table 1 are shown in parentheses)*

A.	(Functional deduction)	

A person who is big and known to be a troublemaker causes people to be afraid.
Caldwell was big.
Caldwell was known to be a troublemaker.

Johnson was afraid of Caldwell.

B. (Functional attribution)
One reason for carrying a weapon is being afraid.
Johnson carried a knife.
Johnson was afraid of Caldwell.

Johnson took his knife *because* he was afraid of Caldwell.

C. (Functional abduction)
Going to the park with your family, being home, eating supper . . . depend on a calm frame of mind.
Johnson went to the park with his family, came home, had supper . . . .

Johnson was in a calm frame of mind.

D. (Contradiction)
Johnson was in a calm frame of mind.
Being in a calm frame of mind is incompatible with being out for revenge.

Johnson was not out for revenge.

E. (Negative functional deduction – modus tollens)
If Johnson were going home to get his knife for revenge, he would have gone back to the bar immediately.
Johnson didn't go back to the bar immediately.

Johnson did not get his knife for revenge.

F. (Contradiction)
Johnson was trying to avoid Caldwell.
Avoiding Caldwell is incompatible with seeking revenge.

Johnson was not seeking revenge.

G. (Categorical deduction)
Asthma is associated with nervous problems.
Johnson has asthma.

Johnson has nervous problems.

H. (Contradiction)
Johnson had nervous problems.
Johnson was afraid of Caldwell.
Being nervous and afraid is incompatible with looking for Caldwell.

Johnson was not looking for Caldwell.

continued

Table 2. *continued*

I.	(Self-analogy)	

I.   (Self-analogy)
If someone were going to fight with me, I wouldn't want to go anywhere near them.
Johnson is like me.

If someone were going to fight with Johnson, he wouldn't want to go anywhere near them.

J.   (Functional deduction – modus ponens)
If someone were going to fight with Johnson, he wouldn't want to go anywhere near them.
Caldwell wanted to fight with Johnson.

Johnson did not want to go anywhere near Caldwell.

K.   (Contradiction)
Johnson was trying to stay away from Caldwell.
Staying away from someone is incompatible with planning to find them.

Johnson didn't plan and think about finding Caldwell.

L.   (Abduction)
A favorite place is where you go all the time.
They drink at Gleason's all the time.

Gleason's is their favorite place.

M.   (Functional deduction – modus ponens)
People like to go to their favorite place for relaxation.
Gleason's is Johnson's favorite place.

Johnson likes to go to Gleason's.

N.   (Functional attribution)
Going somewhere depends on liking the place and being invited.
Clemens asked Johnson to go to Gleason's.
Johnson likes to go to Gleason's.
Johnson went to Gleason's.

Johnson went to Gleason's *because* Clemens asked and Johnson likes to go to Gleason's.

A, B, C, and D. Again, many world knowledge premises must be inferred by the coders to complete the inference forms. Although our analyses were highly inferential, two coders independently applied similar coding methods to identify the inferences in Tables 2 and 3. For these inferences and others in the two protocols, there was substantial agreement (over 80%) on the contents and forms of the inferences abstracted by the two coders.

One question we posed in these analyses was the extent to which we could

Table 3.   *Inferences generated by first-degree murder juror (inference types from Table 1 are shown in parentheses)*

A.	(Self-analogy)

If somebody threatened me with a razor, I would not go back to the same place unless I were looking for revenge.
Johnson is like me.

If somebody threatened Johnson with a razor, he would never go back to the same place unless he were looking for revenge.

B.	(Functional deduction – modus ponens)

If somebody threatened Johnson with a razor, he would never go back to the same place unless he were looking for revenge.
Caldwell threatened Johnson with a razor.
Johnson returned to the same place.

Johnson was looking for revenge.

C.	(Negative functional deduction – modus tollens)

If Johnson wasn't looking for revenge, he would never go back to the same place.
Johnson went back to the same place.

Johnson was looking for revenge.

D.	(Temporal analogy)

Johnson knew Caldwell had a razor on him in the afternoon.
The evening is near in time to the afternoon.

Johnson knew that Caldwell would have a razor in the evening.

E.	(Deduction)

A friend is not much help when confronted by a razor.
Johnson knew Caldwell would have a razor.

Johnson's friend would not be much help.

F.	(Deduction)

Places where people have razors are dangerous.
Johnson knew that Caldwell would have a razor in the evening.

Gleason's would be dangerous in the evening.

G.	(Functional attribution)

One reason for returning to a place known to be dangerous without much help is to get revenge.
Gleason's would be dangerous in the evening.
Clemens would not be much help.
Johnson returned to Gleason's.
Johnson was looking for revenge.

Johnson returned to Gleason's *because* he wanted revenge.

H.	(Abduction)

A renitent person says things like . . .
Johnson (in testimony) said things like . . .

Johnson is a renitent person (doesn't like to back down).

continued

Table 3. *continued*

I.	(Negative functional deduction – modus tollens) Having to back down makes you an underdog. Johnson didn't want to be an underdog.
	Johnson wasn't going to back down.
J.	(Functional abduction) Not backing down depends on going back and showing Caldwell who is boss by killing him. Johnson is not going to back down.
	Johnson went back to show Caldwell who is boss by killing him.
K.	(Self-analogy) If anybody pulled a razor on me in a bar, I would never go back unless I was going to retaliate with another weapon. Johnson is like me.
	If anybody pulled a razor on Johnson in a bar, he would never go back unless he was going to retaliate with another weapon.
L.	(Functional attribution) If anybody pulled a razor on Johnson in a bar, he would never go back unless he was going to retaliate with another weapon. Caldwell pulled a razor on Johnson. Johnson went back with a knife.
	Johnson went back with a knife *because* he was going to retaliate with a weapon.
M.	(Negative functional deduction – modus tollens) If Johnson went back out of pride, he would not need a knife. Johnson took a knife.
	Johnson did not go back out of pride.
N.	(Functional alternative) Johnson went back either out of pride or to fix Caldwell. Johnson went back to fix him.
	Johnson did not go back out of pride.
O.	(Self-analogy) If someone embarrassed me, I would go back with malice and do a job on him. Johnson is like me.
	If someone embarrassed Johnson, he would probably go back with malice and do a job on him.
P.	(Functional deduction – modus ponens) If someone embarrassed Johnson, he would probably go back with malice and do a job on him. Caldwell embarrassed Johnson.
	Probably, Johnson went back with malice to do a job on Caldwell.

successfully capture the inferential reasoning of the jurors by the inference forms proposed by Collins. We have shown the forms we used most frequently in Table 1, along with examples. A typical *deduction* from world knowledge (Table 2, inference A) consists of the following three premises and conclusion from the not-guilty juror's protocol:

Premise 1: Reasons to be afraid of someone include if that person is a trouble-maker and is big. (source: world knowledge)
Premise 2: Johnson new Caldwell was a troublemaker. (source: trial testimony)
Premise 3: Caldwell was big. (source: trial testimony)

Conclusion: Johnson was afraid of Caldwell.

Typically, for central decision-relevant conclusions several lines of inference were attempted and their success or failure contributed to the juror's confidence in the common conclusion. Thus, the juror who initially concluded "Johnson was afraid" develops another line of support, in the form of an *analogy* to himself, followed by a deduction, for the conclusion about Johnson's motivational state (Table 2, inferences I and J):

Premise 1: If someone were going to fight with me, I would not go anywhere near them. (source: personal knowledge)
Premise 2: Johnson is like me. (source: matching to personal knowledge)

Conclusion: If someone were going to fight with Johnson, *he* wouldn't go anywhere near them.

Premise 1: If someone were going to fight with Johnson, he wouldn't go anywhere near them. (source: prior inference)
Premise 2: Caldwell wanted to fight with Johnson. (source: trial testimony)

Conclusion: Johnson did not want to go anywhere near Caldwell.

There is also a substantial amount of reasoning by *contradiction*, especially by the juror who concluded with the not guilty verdict (Table 2, inference D):

Premise 1: Johnson was in a calm state of mind. (source: prior inference)
Premise 2: Being in a calm state of mind is incompatible with being out for revenge. (source: general world knowledge)

Conclusion: Johnson was *not* out for revenge.

There was also a substantial amount of reasoning by *negative deduction* (or modus tollens, Table 2, inference E):

Premise 1: If Johnson were going home to get his knife for revenge, he would
   have gone back to the bar immediately (source: general world knowledge)
Premise 2: Johnson did not go back immediately. (source: trial testimony)

Conclusion: Johnson was *not* out for revenge.

Comparable examples of the same inference forms can be found in the
protocol of the juror who concluded with the contrasting decision, first-degree
murder. For example, a self-analogy form followed by a deduction supports the
conclusion that Johnson was motivated by malice when he returned to the bar
(Table 3, inferences O and P):

Premise 1: If someone embarrassed me, I would go back with malice and do a job
   on him. (source: personal knowledge)
Premise 2: Johnson is like me. (source: matching to personal knowledge)

Conclusion: If someone embarrassed Johnson, he would probably go back with
   malice and do a job on him.

Premise 1: If someone embarrassed Johnson, I would go back with malice and do
   a job on him. (source: prior inference)
Premise 2: Caldwell embarrassed Johnson. (source: prior inferences)

Conclusion: Probably, Johnson went back with malice to do a job on Caldwell.

For our second analysis, we again focused on the conclusions, for the not-guilty
juror: *the defendant returned to the bar on the evening of the killing because his
friend invited him and he likes to drink in that locale* (Table 2, inference N) and *he
carried a knife because he was afraid* (Table 2, inference B). And for the juror
who found the defendant guilty of first-degree murder, we focused on the parallel
inferences relevant to his conclusion that *the defendant returned to the bar on the
evening of the killing because he wanted revenge* (Table 3, inferences G and P)
and the conclusion that *he carried a knife because he intended to assault and kill
the victim* (Table 3, inferences L and P). In this analysis, we linked inferences
together in chains any time a prior inferential conclusion appeared as one of the
premises in a subsequent inference. Inference chains are shown in Fig. 5 for the
not-guilty juror and in Fig. 6 for the first-degree murder juror.

Some general properties of everyday inferences are suggested by diagrams of
the inference chains leading to central conclusions (Figs. 5 and 6). First, at least
under conditions where a reasoner is motivated to think hard about conclusions,
we see the tendency to create multiple independent inference chains relevant to
central conclusions. Thus, in the present example, two to four chains are
generated for each of the major decision-relevant conclusions concerning the

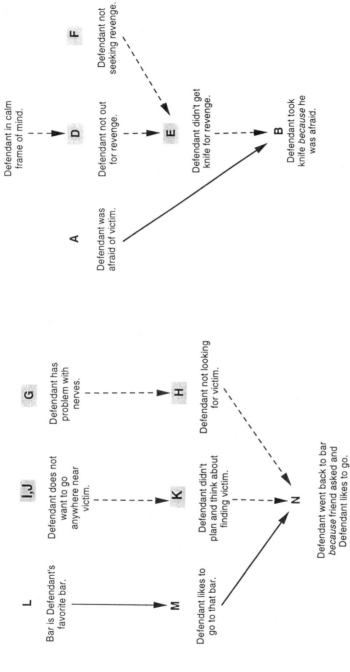

Figure 5. *Example inference structures for juror no. 109 (not-guilty verdict), underlying conclusions concerning the defendant's motivations to return to the bar and to carry a knife in the evening of the killing. Only inference conclusions are listed. Key: Letters A–N refer to inferential conclusions from Table 2. The two conclusions (B and N) correspond to episodes on the causal chain maps (Fig. 4). A solid line connecting inferences indicates a directly confirming argument. The dotted line and the shaded letters indicate an argument for a position by disconfirming opposing arguments. Collins' inference types are not fully illustrated here since the premises for each inference are not shown (see Table 2).*

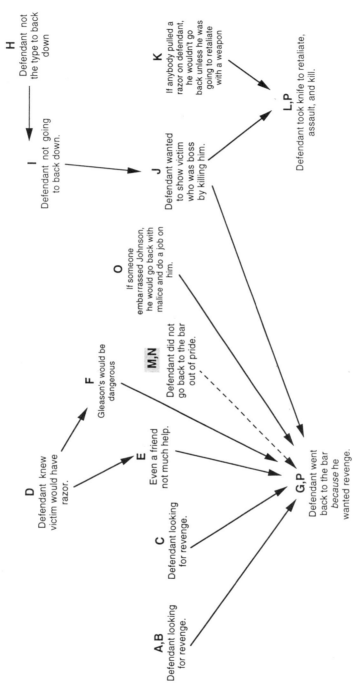

Figure 6.   *Example inference structures for juror no. 128 (first-degree murder verdict), underlying conclusions concerning the defendant's motivations to return to the bar and to carry a knife on the evening of the killing. Only inference conclusions are listed. Key: Letters A–P refer to inferential conclusions from Table 3. The two conclusions (G, P and L, P) correspond to episodes on the causal chain maps (Fig. 3). A solid line connecting inferences indicates a directly confirming argument. The dotted line and the shaded letters indicate an argument for a position by disconfirming opposing arguments. Collins' inference types are not fully illustrated here since the premises for each inference are not shown (see Table 3).*

defendant's motives for returning to the bar and for carrying a weapon. The chains are also relatively short; the longest example contains three inferential steps.

Differences in strategies can also be detected from the inference structures created by the linked inferences. In Fig. 5, the not-guilty juror displays a single confirmatory argument (arguing *for* her conclusion) and two disconfirming arguments (arguing *against* competing conclusions, indicated in the figure by dotted lines). In contrast, the first-degree murder juror, shown in Fig. 6, uses converging confirmatory arguments almost exclusively. In addition, this juror relies much more heavily on the self-analogy strategy in which inferences are based on imagining himself in the place of the defendant.

Our analyses show that explanation-based decision makers' thought processes are full of connected chains of propositions that can be reliably classified into the categories of inference forms provided by Collins' system of plausible inference. Our current research shows that the wealth of inferences revealed in the post-trial interviews reported here is also present in on-line verbal reports, elicited after each witness during the trial. Evidence for the utility of a system like Collins' is provided by the finding that only a few general inference forms suffice to classify a large portion of the inferences in the protocols; the same forms keep reappearing within and between protocols, regardless of the ultimate verdict decision reached by the juror. The links between elements in the chains are more than simple semantic associations; rather they repeatedly fit the premise–conclusion categories prescribed by Collins' system.

In the context of the juror's decision task and the particular case materials, certain interesting inference forms frequently appear: (a) reasoning in terms of "negation" (by contradiction, and by negative deduction (modus tollens)) is surprisingly common; (b) reasoning by analogy to (hypothetical) self behavior is frequent and appears to be a very common basis for inferences of social motives (cf. Dawes, 1990; Ross, Greene, & House, 1977); and (c) there is extensive "discounting" of alternate causes ("functional alternative" in Collins' terms; Kelley, 1973).

Local confidence

It is the certainty of the conclusion C as a function of the levels of certainty of P1, P2, and P3, and the strengths of the relationships between the premises and conclusion that probabilistic (and heuristic) theories of inference were designed to model. It is at this point, that Bayesian or fuzzy set or heuristic calculations could be incorporated into our theory to yield the level of certainty with which a juror believes in any particular proposition (and consequently in the ultimate decision proposition). As we have already noted, deductive inferences such as inference A from

Table 2 looks like a "representativeness heuristic" judgment under uncertainty (Tversky & Kahneman, 1983) in that features of a concrete situation (premises 2 and 3) are matched against features of a prototypic situation (premise 1), and the certainty of the conclusion is related to the goodness of the match. We have proposed, following Collins (1978a, 1978b; Collins et al., 1975) that each inference procedure is associated with additional certainty conditions that will determine local confidence in inferential conclusions. For example, certainty conditions for deductive inferences include: (a) typicality of the instances within the relevant categories (e.g., How typical a troublemaker is Caldwell? How big is Caldwell? How typical a person is Johnson?); (b) base rates of the properties under consideration (e.g., How frequently are people afraid of other people?); (c) variability in properties attributed to general categories (e.g., What is the range of emotional reactions to big troublemakers?); and (d) dissimilarity between cited instances and the most similar group that behaves in a contradictory manner (e.g., How similar is Johnson to the kind of person who would *not* be afraid of a big troublemaker?).

Because of lack of empirical support for Bayesian calculations as a *description* of human judgment under uncertainty, and because of the incompleteness of the heuristic approach, we have adopted a set of simple assumptions that will allow us to perform calculations over a network of relationships and that we believe are closer to actual juror judgment processes. Our main assumption is that at the time that an inferential conclusion is being considered as a potential story event, certainty evaluations render it certainly true (and therefore as data, e.g., Premise 2), or as uncertain (and therefore as a hypothesis, e.g., premise 3, conclusion), or as rejected and therefore certainly untrue. The final level of acceptability of any given proposition is hypothesized to be a function of its inferential support (with reference to certainty conditions and the evaluation of contradictory conclusions), its plausibility with reference to known "facts" about the world, and its role in the larger story structure.

We do not deny the significance of confidence or probability evaluation processes; but we believe that their role is secondary and embedded in logic-like inference procedures. One sign of the secondary role of these factors is their shadowy appearance in think-aloud reports of judgment under uncertainty. For example, in the empirical analyses we report, discussion of degrees of certainty, confidence, or probability accounts for a small percentage (less than 5%) of the verbal report protocols.

Global confidence

We have already outlined features of the semantic representation of decision-relevant evidence that we believe contribute to global confidence in the decision.

According to our theory, two certainty principles govern acceptance of a story: *coverage* and *coherence*. An additional certainty principle, *uniqueness*, will contribute to confidence.

A very important direction for development of the story model and for explanation-based decision making involves elaborating and formalizing the principles that we suggest determine confidence in decisions: coverage, coherence (completeness, consistency, and plausibility), uniqueness, and goodness-of-fit. One part of the puzzle involves examining these principles separately and in interaction. For example, in actual case materials, the coverage of the story and its completeness would often be correlated, although in principle they need not be. Experiments can examine the effects of these variables independently. Our empirical work so far has suggested that there will be interactions we have not anticipated. For example, we suggested that uniqueness (the extent to which there is only one coherent story) will enhance confidence. Yet, we found that in one set of case materials, mock-jurors were most confident when they were able to easily construct both stories (Pennington & Hastie, 1988). We suspect this was because one of the stories was less plausible (and thus less coherent) than the other. On the other hand, it could be that knowing both stories will always increase confidence, regardless of plausibility. These are clearly empirical questions that are currently being addressed through experimentation (Pennington et al., 1991).

A second goal in pursuing determinants of confidence is to formalize these principles in order to understand how confidence in a decision can result from a computation across semantic features of a mental representation of evidence. Toward this end, we have adopted a formalization of the goodness-of-fit, coverage, coherence, and uniqueness ideas, based on an adaptation of Thagard's model of explanatory coherence, ECHO (Thagard, 1989). We call our modification of Thagard's (1989) explanatory coherence model STORY-ECHO, for the obvious reason that we hypothesize that explanations of the evidence in legal trials take the form of stories (see Pennington et al., 1991, for preliminary reports of this work). The model is an interactive activation model that represents hypotheses and supporting evidence in a network of interconnected propositions (Rumelhart & McClelland, 1986). Similar models have been implemented to describe comprehension processes and representations in non-decision-making tasks (e.g., Kintsch, 1988) and proposed for analogical and deductive reasoning tasks that are similar to our legal judgment task (Holyoak & Thagard, 1989). Although our modeling work is preliminary, we expect to be able to provide more explicit comparisons between our ideas about confidence and uncertainty and those proposed by probability calculi as applied to the legal decision task (see Thagard, 1991, for such a comparison in the area of belief in scientific theories).

Concluding comments

Our primary goal in this paper was to delineate the roles of inference procedures in explanation-based decision processes with illustrations of the pervasiveness and variety of inferences in this type of decision. Considerable psychological research has focused on the question of the generality of inference rules or procedures (Smith, Langston, & Nisbett, 1992). Are very general inference rules, like those represented in the system we applied in our analysis, sufficient to account for most everyday reasoning (Johnson-Laird, 1983; Rips, 1983, 1990)? Or must we postulate intermediate-level domain-specific schemas (Cheng & Holyoak, 1985; Cosmides, 1989; Gigerenzer & Hug, 1992) or even situation-specific rules or case-based procedures (Evans, 1989; Kolodner, 1992; Pollard, 1982) to account for everyday reasoning?

Although we cannot claim to have shown that less general pragmatic schemas or concrete situation-based rules are not relevant, we have been able to account for a substantial portion of the contents of our protocols with the general procedures in Collins' system. The contents of premises and conclusions do matter (e.g., we predict they will have large effects on the confidence with which conclusions are asserted), but the basic forms of reasoning seem always to fit into Collins' forms. The one possible elaboration of Collins' system that we might propose would be to attribute a special status to the "analogy to self" form that appears to be ubiquitous in social inference processes.

We also want to emphasize that in the context of explanation-based decision making, for the types of general rules and knowledge structures we have proposed, some of the disputes between proponents of general inference rules and proponents of mental models (Johnson-Laird, 1983, and Johnson-Laird & Byrne, 1990; vs. Rips, 1986, 1989b) are resolved by embracing both points of view in one framework. Our claim is that general inference rules are the primary tools for the construction, interpretation, and application of an explanatory mental model to perform an overarching decision task. Thus, we suggest that there are complementary roles for inference rules (*construction* of a model of the judgment-relevant situation) and situation models (*representation* of the situation implied by the judgment-relevant evidence).

If general inference rules and situation-specific explanatory models are involved in a cooperative process, we need to further specify the roles of these components. One advantage of the combination of rules and models in the explanation-based framework is that it suggests a solution to the frequently raised issue of the unconstrained generativity of simple forms of the inference rule and mental model approaches. Our claim is that the decision maker's goal is to construct a complete representation of the judgment-relevant situation that "covers" the available valid evidence. In a sense, this is a specification of some "extra-logical constraints", to indicate which of the many possible models will be constructed and, indirectly, which inferences are likeliest to be drawn (cf. Johnson-Laird & Byrne, 1991).

We also need to say something about the types of rules or operators that can be applied to an explanation model once it is constructed. In the juror decision, we have concluded that the primary operations are feature comparisons to determine if the constructed story fits any of the verdict categories. However, we would also like to allow inference rules to take "parts" of the model as premises for forward inferences. For example, many jurors in the Johnson case reason that if Johnson has five children and Johnson is convicted and incarcerated it will mean a substantial hardship for his family. At present, without more empirical research to illuminate these processes, we can only indicate where in the larger framework the relevant specifications would occur.

A secondary goal of the paper is to present additional detailed examples of explanation-based decision making. However, we do not claim that explanation-based decision making is the only decision-making strategy available to decision makers, nor do we claim it will be applied everywhere. Elsewhere we have shown that even in the context of a juror decision task other general models (i.e., anchor and adjust inductive processes) can be induced by appropriate instructions and response requirements (Pennington & Hastie, 1992). Furthermore, in many popular laboratory research tasks where a decision is based on a relatively small set of independent evidence items, where the required judgment dimension is unidimensional and known prior to hearing evidence, or where the to-be-judged outcome is "caused" by a random process (e.g., where subjects are asked to assess the attractiveness of lottery gambles or to make repeated evaluations of personality descriptions), it is difficult to see why a subject would be motivated to construct a complex causal model of the relevant situation. Under such conditions, we believe that algebraic models such as those based on linear additive, anchor-and-adjust updating processes provide an adequate picture of the judgment strategy (Anderson, 1981; Einhorn & Hogarth, 1986; Hammond et al., 1975; Lopes, 1982).

However, for decisions in which a complex base of interdependent evidence items is considered and in which the features of the ultimate decision are not all known prior to evaluation of the evidence, we would expect the explanation-based model to describe behavior and expect to observe the rich display of plausible reasoning processes we have found in legal decisions.

Acknowledgements

Support for this research was provided by NSF Grant SES-9113479 to the first author and by NSF Grant BNS-8717259 to the second author.

References

Anderson, N.H. (1974). Cognitive algebra: Integration theory applied to social attribution. In L. Berkowitz (Ed.), *Advances in experimental social psychology* (Vol. 7, pp. 1–101). New York: Academic Press.

Anderson, N.H. (1981). *Foundations of information integration theory.* New York: Academic Press.

Axelrod, R. (Ed.) (1976). *Structure of decision: The cognitive maps of political elites.* Princeton: Princeton University Press.

Baker, M., Burnstein, M.H., & Collins, A. (1987). Implementing a model of human plausible reasoning. In *Proceedings of the Tenth International Joint Conference of Artificial Intelligence* (Vol. 1, pp. 185–188). Los Altos, CA: Morgan Kaufman.

Baltzer, A.J., & Pennington, N. (1983). *Reasoning about conjunctions and disjunctions of events: An explanation-based account.* Unpublished manuscript, Psychology Department, University of Colorado, Boulder.

Bennett, W.L., & Feldman, M. (1981). *Reconstructing reality in the courtroom.* New Brunswick, NJ: Rutgers University Press.

Bostrom, A., Fischhoff, B., & Morgan, M.G. (1992). Characterizing mental models of hazardous processes. A methodology and an application to radon. *Journal of Social Issues, 48,* 85–100.

Bower, G.H., & Morrow, D.G. (1990). Mental models in narrative comprehension. *Science, 247,* 44–48.

Bransford, J.D., Barclay, J.R., & Franks, J.J. (1992). Sentence memory: A constructive versus interpretive approach. *Cognitive Psychology, 3,* 193–209.

Cheng, P.W., & Holyoak, K.J. (1985). Pragmatic reasoning schemas. *Cognitive Psychology, 17,* 391–416.

Cherniak, C. (1984). Prototypicality and deductive reasoning. *Journal of Verbal Learning and Verbal Behavior, 23,* 625–642.

Collins, A. (1978a). Fragments of a theory of human plausible reasoning. In D. Waltz (Ed.), *Theoretical issues in natural language processing II* (pp. 194–201). Urbana, IL: University of Illinois Press.

Collins, A. (1978b). *Human plausible reasoning* (Report No. 3810). Cambridge, MA: Bolt, Beranek & Newman Inc.

Collins, A., Brown, J.S., & Larkin, K.M. (1980). Inference in text understanding. In R.J. Spiro, B.C. Bruce, & W.F. Brewer (Eds.), *Theoretical issues in reading comprehension* (pp. 385–407). Hillsdale, NJ: Erlbaum.

Collins, A., & Michalski, R. (1989). The logic of plausible reasoning: A core theory. *Cognitive Science, 13,* 1–49.

Collins, A., Warnock, E.H., Aiello, N., & Miller, M.L. (1975). Reasoning from incomplete knowledge. In D. Bobrow & A. Collins (Eds.), *Representation and understanding: Studies in cognitive science* (pp. 383–415). New York: Academic Press.

Cosmides, L. (1989). The logic of social exchange: Has natural selection shaped how humans reason? *Cognition, 31,* 187–276.

Crothers, E.J. (1979). *Paragraph structure inference.* Norwood, NJ: Ablex.

Dawes, R.M. (1990). The potential nonfalsity of the false consensus effect. In R.M. Hogarth (Ed.), *Insights in decision making* (pp. 179–199). Chicago: University of Chicago Press.

de Kleer, J., & Brown, J.S. (1983). Assumptions and ambiguities in mechanistic mental models. In D. Gentner & A.L. Stevens (Eds.), *Mental models* (pp. 155–190). Hillsdale, NJ: Erlbaum.

Dontas, K., & Zemankova, M. (1987). APPLAUS: An implementation of the Collins–Michalski theory of plausible reasoning. In *Proceedings of the Third International Symposium on Methodologies for Intelligent Systems,* Torino, Italy, 1987.

Einhorn, H.J., & Hogarth, R.M. (1986). Judging probable cause. *Psychological Bulletin, 99,* 3–19.

Elwork, E., Sales, B.D., & Alfini, J.J. (1977). Juridic decisions: In ignorance of the law or in light of it? *Law and Human Behavior, 1,* 163–189.

Evans, J.St.B.T. (1989). *Bias in human reasoning: Causes and consequences.* Hove, UK: Erlbaum.

Gentner, D., & Stevens, A.L. (Eds.) (1983). *Mental models.* Hillsdale, NJ: Erlbaum.

Gigerenzer, G., & Hug, K. (1992). Domain-specific reasoning: Social contracts, cheating, and perspective change. *Cognition*, *43*, 127–171.

Hammond, K.R., Stewart, T.W., Brehmer, B., & Steinman, D. (1975). Social judgment theory. In M. Kaplan & S. Schwartz (Eds.), *Human judgment and decision processes*. New York: Academic Press.

Hastie, R., Penrod, S.D., & Pennington, N. (1983). *Inside the jury*. Cambridge, MA: Harvard University Press.

Hogarth, R.M., Michaud, C., & Mery, J.L. (1980). Decision behavior in urban development: A methodological approach and substantive considerations. *Acta Psychologica*, *45*, 95–117.

Holyoak, K.J., & Thagard, P. (1989). Analogical mapping by constraint satisfaction. *Cognitive Science*, *13*, 295–356.

Hutchins, E. (1980). *Culture and inference*. Cambridge, MA: Harvard University Press.

Johnson-Laird, P.N. (1983). *Mental models: Towards a cognitive science of language, inference, and consciousness*. Cambridge, MA: Harvard University Press.

Johnson-Laird, P.N., & Byrne, R.M.J. (1990). Meta-logical puzzles: Knights, knaves, and Rips. *Cognition*, *36*, 69–84.

Johnson-Laird, P.N., & Byrne, R.M.J. (1991). *Deduction*. Hove, UK: Erlbaum.

Kahneman, D., Slovic, P., & Tversky, A. (Eds.) (1982). *Judgment under uncertainty: Heuristics and biases*. New York: Cambridge University Press.

Kahneman, D., & Tversky, A. (1982). The simulation heuristic. In D. Kahneman, P. Slovic, & A. Tversky (Eds.), *Judgment under uncertainty: Heuristics and biases* (pp. 201–210). New York: Cambridge University Press.

Kaplan, J. (1978). *Criminal justice: Introductory cases and materials* (2nd Edn.). Mineola, NY: Foundation Press.

Kelley, H.H. (1973). The processes of causal attribution. *American Psychologist*, *28*, 107–128.

Kelly, J. (1988). *PRS: A system for plausible reasoning*. Master's thesis, Computer Science Department, University of Illinois, Champaign.

Kintsch, W. (1974). *The representation of meaning in memory*. Hillsdale, NJ: Erlbaum.

Kintsch, W. (1988). The role of knowledge in discourse comprehension: A construction-integration model. *Psychological Review*, *95*, 163–182.

Klein, G.A., Orasanu, J., Calderwood, R., & Zsambok, C.E. (Eds.) (1993). *Decision making in action: Models and methods*. Norwood, N.J.: Ablex.

Kolodner, J. (1992). An introduction to case-based reasoning. *Artificial Intelligence Review*, *6*, 3–34.

Lewis, C.H. (1988). Why and how to learn why: Analysis-based generalization of procedures. *Cognitive Science*, *12*, 211–256.

Lopes, L.L. (1982). *Toward a procedural theory of judgment*. Technical Report No. 17, Wisconsin Human Information Processing Program, Madison.

Mandler, J.M. (1984). *Stories, scripts, and scenes: Aspects of schema theory*. Hillsdale, NJ: Erlbaum.

Murphy, G.L., & Medin, D.L. (1985). The role of theories in conceptual coherence. *Psychological Review*, *92*, 289–316.

Osherson, D.N., Smith, E.E., Wilkie, O., Lopez, A., & Shafir, E. (1990). Category-based induction. *Psychological Review*, *97*, 185–200.

Pennington, N. (1981). *Causal reasoning and decision making: The case of juror decisions*. Unpublished doctoral dissertation, Harvard University.

Pennington, N., & Hastie, R. (1981). Juror decision making models: The generalization gap. *Psychological Bulletin*, *89*, 246–287.

Pennington, N., & Hastie, R. (1986). Evidence evaluation in complex decision making. *Journal of Personality and Social Psychology*, *51*, 242–258.

Pennington, N., & Hastie, R. (1988). Explanation-based decision making: The effects of memory structure on judgment. *Journal of Experimental Psychology: Learning, Memory, and Cognition*, *14*, 521–533.

Pennington, N., & Hastie, R. (1991). A cognitive theory of juror decision making: The story model. *Cardozo Law Review*, *13*, 519–557.

Pennington, N., & Hastie, R. (1992). Explaining the evidence: Tests of the story model for juror decision making. *Journal of Personality and Social Psychology*, *62*, 189–206.

Pennington, N., & Hastie, R. (1993). A theory of explanation-based decision making. In G.A. Klein, J. Orasanu, R. Calderwood, & C.E. Zsambok (Eds.), *Decision making in action: Models and methods* (pp. 188–204). Norwood, NJ: Ablex.

Pennington, N., Messamer, P.J., & Nicolich, R. (1991). *Explanatory coherence in legal decision making.* Unpublished manuscript, Psychology Department, University of Colorado, Boulder.

Perrig, W., & Kintsch, W. (1985). Propositional and situational models of text. *Journal of Memory and Language, 24,* 503–518.

Pollard, P. (1982). Human reasoning: Some possible effects of availability. *Cognition, 12,* 65–96.

Pople, H.E., Jr. (1982). Heuristic methods for imposing structure on ill-structured problems: The structuring of medical diagnostics. In P. Szolovits (Ed.), *Artificial intelligence in medicine* (pp. 119–190). Boulder, CO: Westview Press.

Rips, L.J. (1975). Inductive judgments about natural categories. *Journal of Verbal Learning and Verbal Behavior, 14,* 665–681.

Rips, L.J. (1983). Cognitive processes in propositional reasoning. *Psychological Review, 90,* 38–71.

Rips, L.J. (1986). Mental muddles. In M. Brand & R.M. Harnish (Eds.), *The representation of knowledge and belief* (pp. 258–286). Tucson: University of Arizona Press.

Rips, L.J. (1989a). Similarity, typicality, and categorization. In S. Vosniadu & A. Ortony (Eds.), *Similarity and analogy* (pp. 21–59). Cambridge, UK: Cambridge University Press.

Rips, L.J. (1989b). The psychology of knights and knaves. *Cognition, 31,* 85–116.

Rips, L.J. (1990). Reasoning, *Annual Review of Psychology, 41,* 321–353.

Ross, L., Greene, D., & House, P. (1977). The "false consensus effect": An egocentric bias in social perception and attribution process. *Journal of Experimental Social Psychology, 13,* 279–301.

Rouse, W.B., & Morris, N.M. (1986). On looking into the black box: Prospects and limits on the search for mental models. *Psychological Bulletin, 100,* 349–363.

Rumelhart, D.E. (1977). Understanding and summarizing brief stories. In D. LaBerge & S.J. Samuels (Eds.) *Basic processes in reading: Perception and comprehension* (pp. 265–303). Hillsdale, NJ: Erlbaum.

Rumelhart, D.E., & McClelland, J.L. (Eds.) (1986). *Parallel distributed processing: Explorations in the microstructure of cognition.* Cambridge, MA: MIT Press.

Schank, R.C. (1975). The structure of episodes in memory. In D.G. Bobrow & A.M. Collins (Eds.), *Representation and understanding studies in cognitive science* (pp. 237–272). New York: Academic Press.

Schank, R.C., Collins, G.C., & Hunter, L.E. (1986). Transcending inductive category formation in learning. *Behavioral and Brain Sciences, 9,* 639–686.

Smith, E.E., Langston, C., & Nisbett, R.E. (1992). The case for rules in reasoning. *Cognitive Science, 16,* 1–40.

Smith, V.L. (1991). Prototypes in the courtroom: Lay representations of legal concepts. *Journal of Personality and Social Psychology, 61,* 857–872.

Stein, N.L., & Glenn, C.G. (1979). An analysis of story comprehension in elementary school children. In R.O. Freedle (Ed.), *New directions in discourse processing* (Vol. 2, pp. 53–120). Norwood, NJ: Ablex.

Thagard, P. (1989). Explanatory coherence. *Behavioral and Brain Sciences, 12,* 435–502.

Thagard, P. (1991). *Probabilistic networks and explanatory coherence.* Unpublished manuscript, Cognitive Science Laboratory, Princeton University.

Trabasso, T., & Sperry, L.L. (1985). Causal relatedness and importance of story events. *Journal of Memory and Language, 24,* 612–630.

Trabasso, T., & van den Broek, P. (1985). Causal thinking and the representation of narrative events. *Journal of Memory and Language, 24,* 612–630.

Tversky, A., & Kahneman, D. (1974). Judgement under uncertainty: Heuristics and biases. *Science, 185,* 1124–1131.

Tversky, A., & Kahneman, D. (1983). Extensional versus intuitive reasoning: The conjunction fallacy in probability judgment. *Psychological Review, 90,* 293–315.

van Dijk, T.A., & Kintsch, W. (1983). *Strategies of discourse comprehension.* New York: Academic Press.

Van Wallendael, L.B. (1989). The quest for limits on noncomplementarity in opinion revision. *Organizational Behavior and Human Decision Processes, 43,* 385–405.

von Neumann, J., & Morgenstern, O. (1947). *Theory of games and economic behavior* (2nd ed.). Princeton, N.J.: Princeton University Press.

Voss, J.F., Perkins, D.N., & Segal, J.W. (Eds.) (1991). *Informal reasoning and education.* Hillsdale, NJ: Erlbaum.

Wilensky, R. (1983). *Planning and understanding: A computational approach to human reasoning.* Reading, MA: Addison-Wesley.

Wolfe, M., & Pennington, N. (1983). *Memory and judgment: Availability versus explanation-based accounts.* Unpublished manuscript, Psychology Department, University of Colorado, Boulder.

7 Reasoning, decision making and rationality

J.St. B.T. Evans

Department of Psychology, University of Plymouth, UK

D.E. Over

School of Social and International Studies, University of Sunderland, UK

K.I. Manktelow

School of Health Sciences, University of Wolverhampton, UK

Abstract

It is argued that reasoning in the real world supports decision making and is aimed at the achievement of goals. A distinction is developed between two notions of rationality: rationality₁ which is reasoning in such a way as to achieve one's goals – within cognitive constraints – and rationality₂ which is reasoning by a process of logic. This dichotomy is related to the philosophical distinction between practical and theoretical reasoning. It is argued that logicality (rationality₂) does not provide a good basis for rationality₁ and some psychological research on deductive reasoning is re-examined in this light. First, we review belief bias effects in syllogistic reasoning, and argue that the phenomena do not support the interpretations of irrationality that are often placed upon them. Second, we review and discuss recent studies of deontic reasoning in the Wason selection task, which demonstrate the decision making, and rational₁ nature of reasoning in realistic contexts. The final section of the paper examines contemporary decision theory and shows how it fails, in comparable manner to formal logic, to provide an adequate model for assessing the rationality of human reasoning and decision making.

Introduction

The psychological fields of reasoning and of decision making are reported in different literatures, mostly by different authors and with little cross-reference. Is this just a matter of research traditions, or are the cognitive processes involved fundamentally different? On the face of it, a reasoning task is significantly different from a decision task. In the study of deductive reasoning, for example, subjects may be presented with the premises of some argument and asked whether or not a conclusion follows. For example, a subject may be asked to evaluate a syllogism such as

No A are B
Some B are not C
Therefore, some C are not A

and to indicate whether or not the conclusion follows. This is presumed to involve a process of reasoning from the premises which may or may not support the conclusion. If the subject has *deductive competence* – discussed below – it should be possible for him or her to solve the problem set without further information. In this sense, deductive reasoning tasks can be viewed as a special case of well-defined problem-solving tasks, whose main purpose is to investigate people's ability to understand and apply logical principles.

Decision-making tasks, on the other hand, involve choices between actions and normally involve commitment to particular acts at one point in time, whose consequences will only later be apparent. A simple example might be deciding whether or not to place a bet on a horse. One might think that a "good" decision is one that works out, that is, placing the bet on a horse who wins, or withholding on one who loses, but it is not that simple. Because real-world events are uncertain, good and bad decisions must be judged on their theoretical merits, not on their outcomes (see von Winterfeldt & Edwards, 1986). The standard normative principle is that of *subjective expected utility* (SEU). Subjects are assumed to make the choice that maximizes the expression $\Sigma s_i U_i$, where s represents the subjective probability of an outcome associated with a choice and U represents its utility, that is, subjective value or pay-off to the decision maker. Hence an objectively good decision is one which would pay off best on average if the decision could be made under the same circumstances a large number of times.

Both reasoning and decision-making literatures involve assessing people's actions against normative theories of "correct" behaviour but in so doing they imply different notions of rationality. In one case it is apparently rational to reason logically, and in the other case it is rational to achieve maximization of expected utility. This distinction is discussed in the following section and we believe it is critical to understanding the relation between the two fields. Leaving this aside for the moment, it is clear that both reasoning and decision tasks involve high-level thought processes. On further reflection it is apparent that reasoning tasks usually involve making decisions, and that choosing between actions often requires one to make inferences. In real-world situations the distinction between reasoning and decision making is blurred.

Decision making, or at least rational decision making, usually involves *forecasting*. That is to say, one action is preferred to another because the chooser believes that he or she would rather live in the slightly different world that will exist when this action is taken. But what does forecasting consist of, if not reasoning? Consider the situation of a school leaver deciding which university to apply to for degree study. A number of factors will influence such a decision, including the academic merits of the courses offered and the advantages and disadvantages of different geographical locations. In reading prospectuses of different universities the chooser is trying to infer which course he or she will most benefit from. The sophisticated chooser will make allowances for the promotional techniques and biases in the literature read – this too is reasoning.

If we look at deductive reasoning in the laboratory, we find that the great majority of tasks given to subjects involve decision making (see the reviews of Evans, 1982; Evans, Newstead, & Byrne, 1993). Subjects are asked whether a given conclusion follows or not, or which of a list of conclusions is the best candidate, or on the famous Wason selection task (of which more later) which of several cards should be turned over. (Researchers who ask subjects simply to generate inferences are in the minority, but see Johnson-Laird & Byrne, 1991, for good examples.) These decisions have a goal structure, albeit one that is often implicit. If the subjects are trying to find the logically correct answer it is because the instructions have motivated them to do precisely that, or because they do not wish to look foolish, or because they want to enhance their self-esteem.

It is difficult to think of cases in the real world when we make inferences *except* to make a decision or achieve a goal of some kind. The apparent exception is that of inferences drawn in order to enhance our knowledge or revise our beliefs in some way. However, maintenance of coherent and accurate belief systems is fundamental to our survival and achievement of goals in the real world and is clearly motivated in its own right. Hence some of our goals are *epistemic* or knowledge serving.

In the following section we lay out our thoughts about rationality in reasoning and decision making and relate this to the distinction between theoretical and practical inference. We argue that the separation of the psychology of reasoning from that of decision making is primarily due to emphasis on the study of logical competence and theoretical reasoning, and that more attention to practical reasoning will not only develop the link with the study of decision making but also enhance the ecological validity of reasoning research. To illustrate our arguments we present discussions of two major areas within the psychology of deductive reasoning – belief bias in syllogistic inference and deontic reasoning on the Wason selection task – whose findings are interpreted within the framework proposed. Finally, we present a critical examination of the value of decision theory as a criterion for rational choice and reasoning.

Rationality and practical inference

Evans (1993) has argued that the debate about rationality in human reasoning and decision making is confused by two different, but implicit definitions of rationality. These can be defined as follows:

rationality$_1$ (rationality of purpose): reasoning in a way which helps one to achieve one's goals;
rationality$_2$ (rationality of process): reasoning in a way which conforms to a supposedly appropriate normative system such as formal logic.

In the classical decision-making literature (e.g., Savage, 1954) the primary definition of rationality has been an idealized version of rationality$_1$: a rational person is believed to be one who chooses in such a way as to maximize their subjective expected utility (SEU). (We shall, however, later question the adequacy of decision theory defining rational choice.) In the literature on deductive reasoning, however, the rationality argument has focused on the concept of *logicality*, that is, validity or deductive correctness in reasoning, with the consequent adoption of the rationality$_2$ concept. There is, of course, a further implicit assumption, namely that rationality$_2$ serves rationality$_1$: in particular that logical reasoning will lead to the achievement of goals. This idea resembles Dennett's (e.g., 1978) "argument from natural selection" which is criticized by Stich (1985; see also Manktelow & Over, 1987).

Leading researchers continue to equate rationality with deductive competence, as the following quotations from three very recent sources illustrate:

> At the heart of rationality is the capacity to make valid deductions. (Johnson-Laird, 1993, p. 2)
> The concept of rationality assumes that people can engage in abstract deductive arguments and derive valid conclusions from a set of premises. (Stevenson, 1993)
> The classical Greek view of human nature included a rationality that allows for logical reasoning. My colleagues and I have argued elsewhere ... that we have no adequate reason to abandon this view, and that this rationality includes a mental logic that accounts for our basic logical intuitions. (O'Brien, 1993)

However, it is true that in addition to the current authors (Evans, 1993; Over & Manktelow, 1993) others have started to adopt a rationality$_1$ perspective in the study of reasoning. For example:

> ... what counts as human rationality: reasoning processes that embody content-independent formal rules, such as propositional logic, or reasoning processes that are well designed for solving important adaptive problems, such as social contents or social regulations? (Gigerenzer & Hug, 1992, p. 129).

Many authors have argued that we should regard rationality as axiomatic (e.g., Cohen, 1981; Dennett, 1978). Humans are the most intelligent species on earth and have evolved into creatures extraordinarily capable of flexible response to their environment. Our ability to solve problems and to achieve goals is self-evident. The present authors accept this premise with two important reservations: (a) rationality is only axiomatic in the sense of rationality$_1$, not rationality$_2$; and (b) the rationality we hold is highly *bounded* by cognitive constraints. Our position is thus similar to the argument for bounded rationality proposed by Newell and Simon (e.g., 1972): we assume that people try to achieve goals, and when they fail it is indicative of limitations in their processing capacity or ability. Due to cognitive limitations we also propose that goals are more likely to be achieved by *satisficing*, that is, finding an adequate solution, rather than by optimizing or maximizing utility across all possible choices and outcomes as proposed in classical decision theory. (For a philosophical treatment of satisficing, see Slote, 1989.)

Recently, there has been increasing interest in a type of thinking in which the relation between reasoning and decision making, and between rationality$_1$ and rationality$_2$, has been brought into sharp focus. This is the type actually known in philosophy as practical reasoning, and distinguished from so-called theoretical reasoning, the centre of so much earlier psychological research. (See Audi, 1989, on the history of the philosophical study of practical reasoning, which goes back to Aristotle.) People use practical reasoning to try to achieve their goals in the actions they perform, and when they do this in the right way, they display rationality$_1$. They use so-called theoretical reasoning to try to acquire true beliefs about matters of fact, and they have rationality$_2$ when they do this in the right way.

Theoretical reasoning, despite its name, does not have to be about scientifically theoretical entities, like subatomic particles, but may concern ordinary material objects, like cats and mats. You are engaged in theoretical reasoning if you are just trying to discover whether the cat is on the mat; you are engaged in practical reasoning if you are trying to decide whether you should kick the cat off your new mat. You have to have some basic ability to do theoretical reasoning, otherwise you would not know, for one thing, what is presupposed by your practical reasoning: that the cat is on your new mat. But only a quite bounded or limited logical ability is necessary to acquire such knowledge, and not even a much more sophisticated ability at deductive logic would be sufficient for it. Inductive inferences are also necessary, in general, to acquire empirical knowledge.

It is our purpose in this paper to concentrate on rationality$_1$ and practical reasoning. Before doing so, however, a little more must be said about the nature of rationality$_2$ and theoretical reasoning. We concede that the literature on deductive reasoning does contain evidence of deductive competence and that is one aspect of the evidence that theories of reasoning must explain (see Evans, 1991). However, we also believe that an undue emphasis on rationality$_2$ and the belief in the logicality = rationality equation has not only dominated theoretical effort in the psychology of reasoning but has also led to widespread misinterpretation of much of the data which demonstrate "biases" and content effects. Detailed arguments against the "rationality = logicality" thesis are presented by Evans (1993) and will not be repeated here. Reinterpretation of literature in terms of practical reasoning will, however, be offered in the review sections of this paper.

The belief bias effect in syllogistic reasoning

Real-life reasoning is not, in general, well modelled by laboratory reasoning tasks. In everyday life we do not reason in order to be logical, but are logical (when we are) in order to achieve our goals. We often do not restrict ourselves to information given in premises, and frequently go beyond any information we have in inductive reasoning. Rational$_1$ reasoning in the real world means that it is applied to the achievement of a practical goal, or the selection of a decision, and that as much relevant knowledge as possible is retrieved and applied to the problem at hand. It is in this context that laboratory studies must be interpreted. If logical errors occur then we must ask first whether these result from processes which would be adaptive (i.e., goal-fulfilling) in application to real-world problems. Only if the answer to this is negative is it sensible to consider what the "errors" tell us about the cognitive constraints on human inference.

We illustrate the problem of illogicality in experimental studies of reasoning by reference to the belief bias effect in deductive reasoning – a phenomenon which appears on first inspection to render people inherently irrational. First, we will present a brief review of the recent research findings in this area and then we will offer an interpretation of the effect in the context of the current argument. In a typical deductive reasoning task, subjects are presented with the premises of an argument and asked whether a particular conclusion follows logically from them. Alternative procedures involve asking subjects to choose from a list of putative conclusions or asking them to generate a conclusion of their own. With the first method, belief bias consists in tending to endorse conclusions which are *a priori* believable as valid and those which are unbelievable as invalid, regardless of the logic of the problem.

Belief bias: the phenomena

The belief bias effect was first reported by Wilkins (1928) and replicated a number of times during the following 30 years or so. Unfortunately, a number of these studies were marred by methodological errors (see Evans, 1982, pp.

107–111; Revlin, Leirer, Yopp, & Yopp, 1980). Paradoxically, recent interest in the phenomenon was revived by Revlin et al. (1980), whose motivation was apparently to discredit the belief bias effect. In particular they argued that subjects might be converting premises, for example, reading "All A are B" as "All B are A". In their own experiments, with new controls, they did produce significant, if small, effects of belief bias which they play down in discussion. Revlin et al. asked subjects to choose from a list of conclusions which leads to problems of interpretation as to what is the correct answer and may have led them to underestimate the size of the bias.

Evans, Barston and Pollard (1983) used carefully constructed syllogisms whose premises were logically unaffected by conversion, and presented a single conclusion for evaluation. Instructions to subjects included the following sentences, intended explicitly to preclude the use of prior beliefs about the problem material:

You should answer the question on the assumption that the two statements are, in fact, true. If you judge that the conclusion necessarily follows from the statements, you should answer "yes" otherwise "no".

An example of an invalid syllogism with a believable conclusion used by Evans et al. is the following:

No addictive things are inexpensive
Some cigarettes are inexpensive
Therefore, some addictive things are not cigarettes

By reordering the words, the same logical form can produce a syllogism with an unbelievable conclusion as follows:

No cigarettes are inexpensive
Some addictive things are inexpensive
Therefore, some cigarettes are not addictive

If the terms in the conclusion are reordered without altering the premises then the argument is valid. Thus it is possible to construct four classes of syllogism: valid–believable, valid–unbelievable, invalid–believable and invalid–unbelievable. In spite of the use of explicit deductive reasoning instructions and an intelligent undergraduate student population, massive effects of belief bias were observed. The basic acceptance rate of conclusions in these four categories observed by Evans et al. is shown in Table 1. There are three substantial and highly significant effects: (a) subjects endorse more conclusions which are logically valid than invalid; (b) subjects endorse more conclusions which are believable than unbelievable; and (c) logic and belief interact in their effect on subjects'

Table 1.   *Percentage conclusions accepted by subjects in the study of Evans, Barston & Pollard (1983) averaged over three experiments*

	Believable	Unbelievable
Valid	89	56
Invalid	71	10

choices. The latter finding reflects the fact that the belief bias effect is much larger for invalid syllogisms.

Subsequent research has been mostly theory driven. Evans et al. (1983) favoured an account of the findings which was later named as the selective scrutiny model (see Barston, 1986; Evans, 1989). The other major account is based upon the mental models theory of reasoning (Johnson-Laird, 1983; Johnson-Laird & Byrne, 1991) and was first developed by Oakhill and Johnson-Laird (1985). The selective scrutiny model assumes that subjects first evaluate the believability of the conclusion. If it is believable, they usually accept it without an attempt to assess the logic of the syllogisms. If it is unbelievable, then they are more likely to check the logic. This predicts the interaction shown in Table 1 due to the "selective scrutiny" of arguments with unbelievable conclusions.

Evidence in favour of the selective scrutiny model is provided first by verbal protocol analyses reported by Evans et al. (1983). They found that subjects who referred only to the conclusion showed most belief bias, whilst those who referred to the premises and then the conclusion showed the least belief bias. Intermediate levels were associated with subjects who referred to the premises *after* reference to the conclusion. Hence, belief bias was associated with conclusion rather than premise-based reasoning. A second source of evidence was that of Evans and Pollard (1990), who predicted and found that increasing the logical complexity of the problems – and hence the overall error rate – did *not* increase the size of the belief bias effect. This surprising finding is predicted on the grounds that in the selective scrutiny model belief bias occurs prior to an attempt at reasoning. Hence, any subsequent failures in reasoning due to logical complexity will add only random error.

The mental model theory of deductive reasoning (see Johnson-Laird & Byrne, 1991) assumes that subjects attempt to build models compatible with the premises from which putative conclusions are formed. Invalid conclusions are generally avoided by searching for counter-examples, that is, by attempting to generate models compatible with premises but incompatible with the putative conclusions. Oakhill and Johnson-Laird (1985) argued that where putative conclusions are believable subjects may neglect the third stage of seeking counter-examples. This would lead to precisely the high acceptance of invalid–believable conclusions which is typical of findings in the area (see Table 1). Whilst a kind of selective scrutiny argument itself, the mental model account differs from the proposals of Evans et al. (1983) in assuming that some reasoning always occurs prior to the influence of belief.

A variety of types of evidence have been claimed in favour of the mental models account. Oakhill and Johnson-Laird (1985) and Oakhill, Johnson-Laird, and Garnham (1989) have shown that subjects may be biased in favour of *producing* believable conclusions when given only the premises of the argument, hence showing that the effect is not simply due to the evaluation of presented conclusions. However, Oakhill et al. (1989) also found that subjects may withhold unbelievable conclusions on one-model valid problems, where no counter-examples exist, and are only able to offer an ad hoc account in terms of "conclusion filtering". In fact, there are several sources of evidence demonstrating a negative belief bias, that is, preference for neutral over unbelievable conclusions (Evans & Perry, 1990; Evans & Pollard, 1990; Newstead, Pollard, Evans, & Allen, 1992) which present theoretical problems for both accounts considered here.

A recent paper by Newstead et al. (1992) reports five new experiments which fail to support the original selective scrutiny model and which provide evidence for a modified mental model account. One new finding reported (Experiments 1 and 2) was that little belief bias occurs, and the belief by logic interaction disappears, when the invalid syllogisms used have conclusions which are determinately *false* rather than indeterminate as in the Evans et al. (1983) study. This cannot be explained on the assumption that belief bias precedes an attempt at reasoning. However, the mental model account proposes that initial modelling and formation of a putative conclusion precede the influence of belief. In these cases a believable–invalid conclusion could not survive the initial stage since *no* model of the premises will permit it. Another finding reported (Experiment 5) was that the belief by logic interaction was removed by elaborated instructions emphasizing logical necessity, which would presumably discourage premature conclusions and stimulate a search for counter-examples. (For discussion of this paper, and a reply, see Oakhill & Garnham, 1993; Newstead & Evans, 1993).

Is belief bias rational$_1$?

Now what should we make of these findings in terms of our argument for rationality$_1$ in human reasoning? These findings do appear to provide evidence of highly irrational reasoning. In the Evans et al. study, for example, subjects were told to base their reasoning only on the information presented and to endorse only conclusions which necessarily followed from the premises. Despite the fact that subjects *can* figure out the logic – as the large effect of validity shows – they were nonetheless quite unable to ignore the believability of the conclusions. Can the belief bias effect be explained within the notion of bounded rationality$_1$ presented earlier? We believe it can. First, we have to recognize that mechanisms of reasoning have evolved to facilitate the achievement of goals in the real world rather than to solve problems in the psychological laboratory. Second, we have to be sensitive to relevant cognitive constraints.

The first question, then, is whether belief bias effects could result from a normally adaptive process. Both major theoretical accounts considered above involve the notion of selective scrutiny. Only conclusions which are *unbelievable* to the reasoner appear likely to get a full process of logical evaluation. Other invalid conclusions are often accepted unless they are incompatible with the premises or unless elaborated instructions are provided. In general, both believable and even neutral conclusions tend to be accepted without adequate search for counter-examples.

Why would it be adaptive to reason only selectively and more so when the argument goes against rather than for one's beliefs? The maintenance of a large and stable set of beliefs is essential for intelligent behaviour, since this forms the basis for any actions which one may take to achieve one's goals. When arguments are encountered which support existing beliefs, the evidence suggests that we do not examine them closely. This is surely rational$_1$ since (a) it is advantageous to maintain beliefs unless there is good reason to revise them, and (b) the processing effort required constantly to question the evidence of current beliefs would be enormous. The situation when confronted with argument or evidence for a statement which contradicts one's beliefs is quite different. To accept such an argument uncritically would be damaging to the individual since this would introduce a contradiction and disrupt the internal consistency of their belief system. Hence, it is quite rational that such arguments should be subjected to the closest possible scrutiny and refuted if at all possible.

A distinct but related phenomenon to belief bias is that of confirmation bias, although some controversy surrounds the evidence claimed for the phenomenon (see Evans, 1989; Klayman & Ha, 1987). Confirmation bias consists of a tendency to seek out evidence which confirms rather than contradicts current beliefs and thus runs counter to the rational$_2$ falsification model of science espoused by the philosopher Karl Popper (1959, 1962). The two phenomena together constitute belief-maintaining biases which are often portrayed as evidence of high irrationality in human reasoning. However, Baron (1985) in discussing possible causes of belief-preserving biases offers an argument related to our above comment on belief bias:

"... when beliefs are integrated with each other, so that each provides support (evidence) for the others, a change in one belief might weaken others as well. If we are also motivated to have consistent beliefs, such a change might require reevaluation of other beliefs than the one under attack at the moment. Such reevaluation will require thinking, which has a cost. Thus, revision of a single belief might lead either to inconsistency or to further thinking, both undesirable consequences, although perhaps not equally undesirable for all people. (pp. 165–166)

The problem with viewing confirmation bias as evidence of irrationality is first that this is based upon rationality$_2$, and second that it regards any act of confirmation as illogical. Beliefs that hold on most occasions and which maintain consistency with other beliefs may benefit the individual, even though occasional exceptions show them to be strictly false.

Consider the example of falsifying evidence in scientific research. Reading the arguments of some psychologists discussing belief and confirmation biases, you would think that abandonment of a theory was required by a single failed prediction. These psychologists are apparently presupposing quite a naive Popperian scientific methodology, which has been heavily criticized by philosophers of science in recent years, in large part for rejecting any notion of confirmation or inductive reasoning (Earman, 1992; Howson & Urbach, 1989). A prediction is usually inferred, not from a theory on its own, but from the theory along with an indefinite number of background beliefs, for example, about the conditions under which the experiment is conducted, and the reliability of the experimental equipment. It is also rare for the prediction to be certain given all these beliefs or hypotheses. For these reasons, it can be far from certain that there is a serious problem at the heart of a previously well-confirmed theory when there has been a failed prediction.

In this section we have offered an interpretation of one of the most reliable biases in the experimental literature on reasoning which is compatible with our notion of rationality$_1$ in reasoning. We now turn to another area of the experimental literature on deductive reasoning in order to discuss recent work on reasoning with deontic conditionals. This work, we believe, directly demonstrates the decision-making nature of subjects' inferences using laboratory tasks.

Deontic reasoning

The primary purpose of most of our ordinary reasoning is to help us make good decisions, so that we can have reasonable success in achieving our goals. This point was brought out clearly by Grice (1975), who noted that efficient communication has to be a goal-directed process, in which the participants must infer each other's purposes and then make appropriate decisions about their own speech acts and other actions. Similarly, the purpose of reasoning is best served by drawing inferences from *all* our beliefs, not just from an artificially restricted set of premises, as in most psychological experiments on reasoning.

On this basis, we should also expect people to display rationality$_1$ in experiments calling for something like ordinary practical reasoning, which is aimed at realistic goals and not at abstract theoretical ones. Striking results of changing the nature of experimental reasoning tasks in this way can be observed in the recent history of work on the Wason selection task. The developments in question have focused selection task research on a type of *deontic* reasoning which is directly and immediately practical. The object of deontic reasoning is to infer what actions ought to be taken, or may be taken, and it calls for cognitions of probability, utility and social perspective – aspects of thought which hitherto were the prime concern of research on decision making. Thus in deontic-reasoning research we have a premier case of cross-pollination between the two fields of reasoning and decision making.

The indicative and deontic selection tasks

As many readers will be aware, a typical selection task experiment involves presenting a conditional sentence of the form *if p then q* with four cards, each of which has a *p* or *not-p* value one one side and a *q* or *not-q* value on the other (see Evans et al. 1993, Chapter 4, for a comprehensive review of work on this problem). In the standard – what we describe as *indicative* – form of the selection task, the conditional is couched in abstract materials (e.g., "If there is an A on one side of a card then there is a 3 on the other") and the subject is asked to decide which cards would need to be turned over in order to decide *whether the conditional is true or false*. The correct answer is *p* and *not-q* since only the combination of these two values on the same cards could disprove the conditional. However, typically fewer than 10% of intelligent adult subjects give the correct response when the task is presented in this way: most often they say *p* and *q* or just *p*. In recent times most researchers' attention has been concentrated on facilitating the production of the logically warranted response by changing the content and context in which the problem is presented. Many of these involve a *deontic* version of the task in which subjects decide which cards will tell if *a rule has been followed or violated*, as opposed to deciding whether it is true or false.

For the purposes of the present discussion, the crucial development was the use of a generalized deontic context by Cheng and Holyoak (1985). To explain why the use of such a context has the effect of facilitating the "correct" response, Cheng and Holyoak introduced the theory of *pragmatic reasoning schemas*. It is held that in situations clearly perceived by the reasoner as deontic (in their research, they referred specifically to situations of *permission* and *obligation*, though there are some problems with their definition of these terms; see Manktelow & Over, 1991), a set of generalized production rules was activated in which the relation between preconditions and actions was specified. Mapping these on to the specific task content would deliver the appropriate selections.

For example, a version which reliably facilitates performance is that of the drinking age rule (Griggs & Cox, 1982). Subjects are asked to imagine that they are police officers checking whether the rule "If a person is drinking beer then that person must be over 19 years of age" has been violated, by inspecting cards which have a beverage on one side and the age of the drinker on the other. Most subjects correctly turn over "beer" (p) and an age under 19 years ($not-q$). This is attributed by Cheng and Holyoak to use of a permission schema in which the rule is mapped to "If you perform an action (*in this case drinking beer*) then you must fulfil a precondition (*in this case being over 19 years of age*)."

This theory has led to an upsurge in research on deontic reasoning, and dominated the explanations of its findings, but it has not gone unchallenged. Its two principal competitors are the theory of mental models (derived from Johnson-Laird & Byrne, 1991) and the social contract theory of Cosmides (1989). We shall defer discussion of the former for the moment, and pause briefly on the latter before looking in detail at some of the most recent work. Cosmides' theory has sustained serious criticism, making it no longer tenable in its original form (see, for example, Cheng & Holyoak, 1989; Manktelow & Over, 1987, 1991). However, it is of singular importance in one respect: its emphasis on benefits and costs in the explanatory framework. Cosmides' theory holds that the essence of the kinds of deontic thinking explored by reasoning researchers, for example permissions, lies in social exchange; this in turn boils down to an implicit or explicit contract held by its parties, that *if you take a benefit then you pay a cost*. Human life would be impossible without an innate understanding of this contract, says Cosmides, which entails an immediate ability to detect its violation: instances of people taking a benefit without paying a cost, or *cheaters* as she calls them.

Recent studies of deontic reasoning

Recent experimental work has enlarged our understanding of the nature of deontic reasoning, and enabled us to look not only at the particular issue of explaining what goes on in selection tasks of this type, but also at the implications of these findings for theory and for the relation between reasoning and decision making. Let us take these issues in turn.

Gigerenzer and Hug (1992), for example, distinguish between two core components of Cosmides' theory: social contracts and cheating. They found that casting a task in social contract form was not sufficient to produce facilitation of the p, $not-q$ response. This only occurred when a cheating context was specified. When the cheating conditions are clearly set out, this form of deontic reasoning becomes very straightforward, as Light, Girotto, and Legrenzi (1990) found: children of 12 or younger are adept at such reasoning tasks. Detection of the violation of a clearly specified deontic rule such as a permission (Gigerenzer & Hug, 1992; Manktelow & Over, 1991), promise (Light et al., 1990), obligation (Gigerenzer & Hug, 1992), or warning (Politzer and Nguyen-Xuan, 1992) has been demonstrated to be a natural cognitive process by these studies.

Such research has also elucidated the role of social cognition in this form of practical thought. All the studies just cited have pointed out the role of two fundamental parties in deontic reasoning: the one who lays down the rule, and the one whose behaviour is its target, termed the *agent* and the *actor*, respectively, by Manktelow and Over (1991). These authors have shown that violations of a rule such as permission can be performed by either party and in more than one way. Take the use of a standard conditional permission rule, *if you do p then you may do q*, which in many contexts pragmatically implies that the only way you get permission to do *q* is by doing *p*. Subjects readily understand that, in realistic contexts of this general type, the actor goes wrong by doing *q* without fulfilling *p* and not doing *q*; while the agent goes wrong by not allowing the actor to do *q* although *p* has been fulfilled, or by allowing *q* without *p* being fulfilled. Note that these are not all cases of someone being *cheated*, but they are all cases in which someone suffers a cost because of the failure to conform to the rule, or what is pragmatically conveyed by its use, in a realistic context. Permission has, as Gigerenzer and Hug term it, *bilateral* options for violation; some deontic relations are *unilateral* in that they can generally only be violated by the agent (e.g., in the case of promises) or the actor (in the case of obligations).

These observations have forced a reconsideration of the traditional facilitation effect in selection task research, and consequently to an appreciation of the relation between what has always been seen as a reasoning task and its role in explaining decision making, hence to the relation between rationality$_1$ and rationality$_2$, as set out above.

As we saw, the idea of the facilitation effect arises from the original use of the selection task in research on theoretical reasoning, using indicative conditionals, for which a correct response has generally been taken to be to select the *p* and *not-q* cards. The recent studies outlined above have shown that it is routinely possible to elicit high rates of *not-p*, *q* selections in certain well-defined contexts. For instance, Manktelow and Over (1991) used a permission rule, "If you spend more than £100 then you may take a free gift"; subjects were readily cued to select the *not-p*, *q* combination (spent less than £100, took the gift) when the scenario referred to a store giving out more than it should, or customers taking more than they were entitled to (see also Politzer & Nguyen-Xuan, 1992, who independently used similar materials and reported similar effects). It is clear then that what is being facilitated here is not something corresponding to the truth conditions of the material conditional.

A rational$_1$ interpretation of deontic reasoning

The notion of testing the truth conditions of a conditional does not apply to deontic reasoning at all. In the experiments discussed above, people are not being asked to test the truth of rules, but are being asked to detect violations (a form of action) of rules whose truth status is not in question. This leads to further questions: what counts as a correct response in this case? And what counts as a true deontic rule?

The first question leads us to focus again on the relation between reasoning and decision making, and between rationality$_1$ and rationality$_2$. As Light et al. (1990) put it, responses in deontic selection tasks should be judged as correct if they lead to the detection of the possible violators, independent of the values that the corresponding cases would have under a formal heading. Detecting violation is an important practical matter. If we could not do this, we would fail to achieve many of our prudential, social, and moral goals.

As for the truth of deontic rules, this gives us reason to part from the schema theories (derived from Cheng & Holyoak, which most current theorists adhere to) on the grounds that the theory of pragmatic reasoning schemas is a non-semantic production rule theory: it contains no component which could specify why a deontic utterance should be made or accepted in the first place, or when it would be felicitous to do so. We have put forward elsewhere an alternative based on the theory of mental models (see Manktelow & Over, 1991; and Over & Manktelow, 1993, for details) which addresses this and other points. It is based on the semantic notion of modelling the state of affairs specified by the particular deontic context and content, and the notion of preference between these states.

Suppose that a mother is trying to decide whether to let her son to go out to play. She might think that he is likely to get into trouble if he goes out, and in that case, she will prefer him to stay in. She will then announce her decision by saying, "You must stay in", which places her son under an obligation. Another possibility is that she is indifferent to whether he goes out or not, and she might even prefer him to go out (where he will not be under her feet). Expressing a permission, she will consequently say, "You may go out". A slightly more complex case would be one in which she is indifferent to whether her son goes out provided that he satisfies some condition which she has as a goal, say, that of getting his room tidy. She will now utter a conditional permission, that is, a deontic conditional like "If you tidy your room, you may go out."

The mother will consider the above conditional permission true just in case she is indifferent to whether her son goes out, or even prefers her son to go out, given that he tidies his room. If he does do that, he will give his mother something which has utility for her, a tidy room, in exchange for achieving a goal which has utility for him, going out. Notice that this concept of truth for deliberative deontic statements is a subjective one, and indeed depends on the decision theoretic notion of preference, and also that of subjective probability (which we shall discuss below). If the mother foresaw more likely benefit, or less likely cost, in her son staying in than going out after he tidied his room, she would not assert the conditional permission as true. Note also that we are using these terms in a technical sense. To say that a tidy room has more utility for the mother than an untidy one is just to say that she prefers the former to the latter. To say that her son going out is a benefit for the mother, or a cost, is just to say that she prefers the former to the present state of affairs which the son is in, or vice versa.

From the son's perspective, he has to grasp the social context in which he finds himself. His mother has power or authority over him, and can give him benefits or extract costs from him. She is in a position to make obligation or permission statements which he must take account of if he is to achieve his goals. To do that, he must also understand the essentially pragmatic notion of a violation of a rule. He would generally infer pragmatically, from his mother's utterance of the conditional permission, that the only way he could get permission to go out would be by tidying his room. But the mother might add that the son may go out if he does the washing up (or anything else constructive), and then he might adjust his pragmatic inferences accordingly. Moreover, if the house catches fire, he needs to know that he will not violate his mother's rules, along with her presupposed qualifying conditions and underlying goals to do with his safety, if he rushes out without tidying his room or doing the washing up. In technical terms, his deontic reasoning, at least about violations, has to be non-monotonic, and be highly sensitive to context, implicated and presupposed information, and the way benefits and costs for himself and his mother change with changing circumstances.

The evidence we have reviewed implies that subjects can identify themselves with a perspective like that of the son's and make rational$_1$ decisions from it. The subjects, acting as the son, decide to pick just those cards which might reveal a violation by the mother. This violation would be one in which the son suffered a cost, because he tidied his room but his mother did not allow him to attain his goal of going out. It is important for the son to uncover such cases to help him prevent them in the future, by not believing his mother's promises. It could be said that, in this simple case, subjects are acting in a way that would enable them to maximize subjective expected utility from the perspective they adopt. But that does mean that subjects would always act so as to meet such an ideal standard in any deontic reasoning task.

There is, in fact, already some evidence (in Manktelow & Over, 1990) that subjects do far less well in a deontic selection task when violating a rule would bring less benefit than conforming to it, rather than a strict loss from a neutral position, such as might result from being punished by an authority. Classical normative decision theory does not distinguish between benefits and costs in a way which would justify this. Some descriptive decision theories, however, do predict special sensitivity to costs, such as the seminal prospect theory of Kahneman and Tversky (1979) with its notion of a reference point, below which one thinks of oneself as suffering a loss. It can also be argued that, if one's present position is reasonably satisfactory, then being especially sensitive to possible losses is a good, rational$_1$, satisficing strategy. (See Kahneman & Varey,

1991, for recent work on loss aversion, and a discussion of its possible long-term benefits.)

Decision theory and rationality

The deontic reasoning we have discussed is practical reasoning, in which we try to infer which actions we ought to perform or may perform. We have suggested that people try to determine whether to accept or assert deontic rules by considering which states of affairs they prefer to others. After doing this, they can use these rules efficiently to infer what they should or may do in appropriate contexts, as these arise in ordinary affairs. This view sees a deep link between deontic reasoning and decision making, in which preference is the basic notion. But as we have also said, classical decision theory lays down the normative SEU principle, according to which rational action is a matter of maximizing expected utility in one's choices, and this should not be the standard of what it is to have rationality$_1$. We have followed Simon (e.g., 1957, 1983) in rejecting this standard and in speaking instead of bounded rationality. Put in the simplest way, the essential point is (as philosophers say) that *ought* implies *can*; in other words, if we are serious in holding that people ought to conform to some standard, then they should be able to conform to it. But people are often unable to conform to the absolute ideal of classical decision theory, and so it cannot always be the case that they ought to do this.

One particular limitation of classical decision theory we must continue to stress, because this has received so little comment in the psychological literature, is its failure to account for, or take proper account of, people's practical reasoning. Classical decision theory presupposes that people can express their preferences, and that these can be measured in some way, but obviously people's preferences are not always given merely by their basic drives and immediate desires. Preferences are often inferred in sometimes quite complex deontic reasoning, employing perhaps many prudential, social, or moral rules. We must have some account of these inferred preferences in decision making; and yet at the same time, we cannot idealistically assume that people have been able to perform all relevant deontic inferences when they express preferences after some actual deontic reasoning in the real world.

Depending on the circumstances, we might be able to set a reasonable standard for the number and type of deontic inferences people can be expected to perform, if they have rationality$_1$. We could not necessarily require them to perform all relevant deontic inferences, from the rules they accept, and so maximize their subjective expected utility, where this is defined by the ideal preferences they would have if they had the time and mental power to perform all these inferences.

This is just to say that we could only require some degree of bounded rationality$_1$ of them.

Another limitation of classical decision making shows in the standard it sets for probability judgements. It requires that these judgements conform to the principles of the abstract mathematical theory of probability: the probability calculus. We do need good probability judgements in practical reasoning. One option is not necessarily better than another because it may lead to the more highly desired outcome or goal; it can all depend on how probable the different outcomes are. There are powerful arguments for holding that probability judgements should ideally conform to the probability calculus (Howson & Urbach, 1989). None of us, however, can ensure that we conform to the theory's principles in all cases. This is well illustrated by the fact that the probability calculus requires that all logical truths be assigned a probability of 1, although there is in general no effective way of deciding whether or not a proposition is a logical truth.

The probability calculus also requires that the probability of the conclusion of a valid inference given its premises to be 1. But asking people what follows from given premises, which they are in effect to take as certain and definitely not to supplement with anything else they believe, is an unnatural request in itself. People, quite rightly for ordinary decision making, are generally concerned with what follows from their relevant beliefs, and they do not necessarily take even these as certain. For a belief bias effect to limit seriously people's rationality$_1$ it would have to be the case that people often fail to achieve their ordinary goals because they are too confident, or not confident enough, in the conclusions they infer from their beliefs, whether they think of these as certain or uncertain. Note that the uncertainty of a belief is 1 minus its subjective probability, and that the degree of uncertainty of a conclusion validly inferred from uncertain beliefs should not exceed the sum of their uncertainties, according to a basic principle of rationality$_2$ (Adams, 1975; Edgington, 1992). The research we reviewed above on belief bias effects in deductive reasoning does not show that people often depart from this principle in their actual decision making (though see Tversky & Kahneman, 1983, on the conjunction fallacy), nor that if they do in some cases, they often fail to achieve their goals as a result.

So far we have spoken of what people's confidence in the conclusion of a deductive inference should be just given specific premises, which are either to be thought of as certain, or as expressing beliefs which may not be certain. However, degrees of confidence are usually discussed in the body of research on probability judgements and decision making, which unfortunately, as we say, has been seen as distinct from the work on deductive reasoning until recently. In the former body of research, people are said to be overconfident, or underconfident, about some proposition depending on whether the subjective probability they ascribe to it is greater than, or less than, its objective probability, which is usually measured or estimated by the frequency with which events occur in the real world. For example, we may think it highly likely to be sunny on days when it is, in fact, objectively unlikely to be sunny. This difference should show up in a tendency for us to be wrong in our forecasting of sunny days, and we are said to be overconfident that it will be sunny on one of these days. On the other hand, if our subjective confidence that it will be sunny more or less matches the objective probability that it will be, then we are said to be well calibrated on this matter.

Whether people are generally well calibrated obviously has something to do with their rationality, and their is a vigorous debate in progress about the extent to which people are sometimes underconfident and sometimes overconfident, the possible reasons for this, and how far it affects their rationality. (See particularly Gigerenzer, Hoffrage, & Kleinbölting, 1991; and Griffin & Tversky, 1992.) We can only make some brief points here about this issue and rationality$_1$.

The abstract principles of the probability calculus do not themselves specify how the subjective and objective notions of probability should be related to each other. This relation has to be covered by some further rule or rules, such as the main one proposed and discussed by a number of philosophers, usually called the principal principle. (For more on this, and the philosophical issues it raises which we cannot go into here, see Lewis, 1981; Howson & Urbach, 1989; and Earman, 1992.) Suppose we are sure that there is a low (alternatively middling or high) objective probability that it will be sunny on a certain type of day, say, just characterized by the fact that the barometer is falling (steady or rising). Then according to a version of the principal principle, our subjective confidence that it will be sunny on a particular day of just that type should be equally low (middling or high). There are reasons for holding that it is rational$_1$ to conform to this principle generally, though perhaps not invariably, as we will shortly illustrate. However, the problem with testing whether subjects conform to this principle is, again, that it is difficult to be sure that subjects are restricting themselves to just the information they are strictly given by the experimenters, say, that the day is to be characterized by the fact that the barometer is falling and in no other way. This is particularly a problem if we move away from rather abstract questions about matters distant from real life, such as ones about coloured balls in urns, to more realistic ones, to which further information may be relevant, including perhaps what might be pragmatically inferred from the experimental context.

It is very important to note the research which has increasingly found evidence that subjects can sometimes be good at reasoning about objective frequencies (see Cosmides & Tooby, in press; Gigerenzer et al., 1991; Tversky & Kahneman, 1983; but note also Griffin & Tversky, 1992). This is something that they would have to be fairly competent at in order to have a reasonable chance of achieving some of their goals in ordinary affairs. But it is striking that there is sometimes quite a difference, displayed in this research, between what subjects say about the subjective probability of a single case and about the frequency with which something will happen in cases of that type. We would show this difference if we expressed great confidence that it would be sunny on a particular day, yet were also sure that it rained on most days like that. Thus we would appear to violate the principal principle, and this could limit our ability to achieve some of our ordinary goals. If we observe the frequency with which it rains under certain conditions, but do not adjust our degree of belief appropriately to this, then we could tend to get wet when we want to be dry. We would also be in trouble if we did not match our subjective probability judgements about how trustworthy someone was to the frequency with which he broke promises to us.

Our arguments for rationality$_1$ by no means imply the extremely strong conclusion that people are always well calibrated and conform to the principal principle in ordinary affairs. We would not even make this claim, on simple evolutionary grounds, about people living under primitive conditions. No doubt pregnancy is very risky indeed under such conditions, and so it might be adaptive under those conditions to be *overconfident* about one's chances of safely producing healthy offspring. It is at least as hard to argue that being well calibrated about the risks of pregnancy would have led to greater reproductive success than being overconfident.

However that may be, research so far conducted has not shown that there is a widespread tendency to violate the principal principle in ordinary decision making, nor that when it is sometimes violated there, people invariably fail to achieve their goals as a result. Sometimes being overconfident in the technical sense could help to achieve one's goals, by increasing self-confidence in the ordinary sense and keeping doubts from one's mind. A woman who is overconfident about herself having a healthy baby, even though she knows the objective frequency of complications in pregnancy, may be helped by her positive attitude. Griffin and Tversky (1992) rightly give examples in which overconfidence is more of a cost than a benefit, but then we would not claim that people are never irrational$_1$ in particular cases, as there are cognitive constraints to take into account. These can exist alongside a general tendency for human beings to achieve a reasonable number of their goals, which they would have to do to survive any length of time, let alone to create complex societies and advanced technologies.

Conclusions

The notion of rationality which really matters to people is rationality$_1$. People in general do have this to a fair degree, as they do tend to be reasonably good at achieving most of their goals. This is obvious enough, as long as we do not make the mistake of thinking of goals only as grand, distant ends which take special ability or luck to achieve, like becoming a millionaire. We should be impressed enough that people are able to achieve more "mundane" goals, such as all those involved in learning a language, contributing to cooperative group like a family, and generally finding one's way in the world. We cannot yet build intelligent machines which can do any of these things; it is much easier to program them to do formal logic. In experimental set-ups, people do sometimes depart from the normative principles of logic, the probability calculus, and decision theory. But this in itself does not demonstrate that they have pervasive biases and are generally irrational$_1$.

In fact, people sometimes achieve a goal in part because they do *not* try to maximize utility (in the technical sense) or hold coherent and consistent beliefs. With bounded capacities and limited time, people would sometimes miss the chance to achieve a reasonably satisfying goal if they paused to wonder whether their preference relation or their beliefs satisfied abstract normative principles. They can sometimes save precious time by accepting a plausible conclusion without examining closely the logic of its argument, or by being very vague about their preferences.

Of course, to say that people have a reasonable degree of rationality$_1$ is not to say that this can never be profitably improved. Our natural capacity for practical reasoning originally evolved under very different conditions from some of those in which we find ourselves today. In a technological society, having the means to be extremely precise, for example, about profits and losses can be important. Even quite artificial experiments may reveal bounds on our reasoning abilities which sometimes need to be overcome for achieving certain goals. We should thus study when and how logic, statistics, and decision theory can increase rationality$_1$ (see Evans, 1989). But equally we should remember that normative research, particularly on practical reasoning, is far from at an end. Probably the only way to obtain agreed normative principles for this is to study ever more closely the often highly efficient nature of ordinary goal-directed reasoning.

References

Adams, E. (1975). *The logic of conditionals: An application of probability to deductive logic.* Dordrecht: Reidel.

Audi, R. (1989). *Practical reasoning.* London: Routledge.

Baron, J. (1985). *Rationality and intelligence.* Cambridge, UK: Cambridge University Press.

Barston, J.L. (1986). An investigation into belief biases in reasoning. Unpublished Ph.D. thesis, University of Plymouth.

Cheng, P.W., & Holyoak, K.J. (1985). Pragmatic reasoning schemas. *Cognitive Psychology, 17,* 391–416.

Cheng, P.W., & Holyoak, K.J. (1989). On the natural selection of reasoning theories. *Cognition, 33,* 285–313.

Cohen, L.J. (1981). Can human irrationality be experimentally demonstrated? *Behavioural and Brain Sciences, 4,* 317–370.

Cosmides, L. (1989). The logic of social exchange: Has natural selection shaped how humans reason? Studies with the Wason selection task. *Cognition, 33,* 187–276.

Cosmides, L., & Tooby, J. (in press). Are humans good intuitive statisticians after all? Rethinking some conclusions from the literature on judgement under uncertainty. *Cognition.*

Dennett, D.C. (1978). Brainstorms. Cited by Stich, S.P. (1985). Could man be an irrational animal? *Synthese, 64,* 115–135.

Earman, J. (1992). *Bayes or bust: A critical examination of Bayesian conformation theory.* Cambridge, MA: MIT Press.

Edgington, D. (1992). Validity, uncertainty and vagueness. *Analysis, 52,* 193–204.

Evans, J.St.B.T. (1992). *The psychology of deductive reasoning.* London: Routledge & Kegan Paul.

Evans, J.St.B.T. (1989). *Bias in reasoning: Causes and consequences.* Hove, UK: Erlbaum.

Evans, J.St.B.T. (1991). Theories of human reasoning: The fragmented state of the art. *Theory and Psychology, 1,* 83–105.

Evans, J.St.B.T. (1993). Bias and rationality. In K.I. Manktelow & D.E. Over (Eds.), *Rationality.* London: Routledge.

Evans, J.St.B.T., Barston, J.L., & Pollard, P. (1983). On the conflict between logic and belief in syllogistic reasoning. *Memory & Cognition, 11,* 295–306.

Evans, J.St.B.T., Newstead, S.E., & Byrne, R.M.J. (1993). *Human reasoning: The psychology of deduction.* Hove, UK: Erlbaum.

Evans, J.St.B.T., & Perry, T. (1990). Belief bias in children's reasoning. Unpublished manuscript, University of Plymouth.

Evans, J.St.B.T., & Pollard, P. (1990). Belief bias and problem complexity in deductive reasoning. In J.P. Caverni, J.M. Fabre, & M. Gonzales (Eds.), *Cognitive biases.* Amsterdam: North-Holland.

Gigerenzer, G., Hoffrage, U., & Kleinbölting, H. (1991). Probabilistic mental models: A Brunswikian theory of confidence. *Psychological Review, 98,* 506–528.

Gigerenzer, G., & Hug, K. (1992). Domain-specific reasoning: social contracts, cheating, and perspective change. *Cognition, 43,* 127–171.

Grice, H.P. (1975). Logic and conversation. In P. Cole & J.P. Morgan (Eds.), *Syntax and semantics. Vol 3: Speech acts.* New York: Seminar Press.

Griffin, D., & Tversky, A. (1992). The weighing of evidence and the determinants of confidence. *Cognitive Psychology, 24,* 411–435.

Griggs, R.A., & Cox, J.R. (1982). The elusive thematic-materials effect in Wason's selection task. *British Journal of Psychology, 73,* 407–420.

Howson, C., & Urbach, P. (1989). *Scientific reasoning: The Bayesian approach.* La Salle, IL: Open Court.

Johnson-Laird, P.N. (1983). *Mental models.* Cambridge, UK: Cambridge University Press.

Johnson-Laird, P.N. (1993). *Human and machine thinking.* Hillsdale, NJ: Erlbaum.

Johnson-Laird, P.N., & Byrne, R.M.J. (1991). *Deduction.* Hove, UK: Erlbaum.

Kahneman, D., & Tversky, A. (1979). Prospect theory: An analysis of decision under risk. *Econometrica, 47,* 263–291.

Kahneman, D., & Varey, C. (1991). Notes on the psychology of utility. In J. Elster & J. Roemer (Eds.), *Interpersonal comparisons of well-being.* Cambridge, UK: Cambridge University Press.

Klayman, J., & Ha, Y.-W. (1987). Confirmation, disconfirmation and information in hypotheses testing. *Psychological Review, 94,* 211–228.

Lewis, D. (1981). A subjectivist's guide to objective chance, in R. Jeffrey (Ed.), *Studies in inductive logic and probability.* Los Angeles: University of California Press.

Light, P.H., Girotto, V., & Legrenzi, P. (1990). Children's reasoning on conditional promises and permissions. *Cognitive Development, 5,* 369–383.

Manktelow, K.I., & Over, D.E. (1987). Reasoning and rationality. *Mind and Language, 2,* 199–219.

Manktelow, K.I., & Over, D.E. (1990). Deontic thought and the selection task. In K. Gilhooly, M. Keane, R. Logie & G. Erdos (Eds.), *Lines of thinking: Reflections on the psychology of thought* (Vol. 1). Chichester: Wiley.

Manktelow, K.I., & Over, D.E. (1991). Social roles and utilities in reasoning with deontic conditionals. *Cognition, 43,* 183–188.

Newell, A., & Simon, H.A. (1972). *Human problem solving*. Englewood Cliffs, NJ: Prentice-Hall.

Newstead, S.E., & Evans, J.St.B.T. (1993). Mental models as an explanation of belief bias effects in syllogistic reasoning. *Cognition, 46*, 93–97.

Newstead, S.E., Pollard, P., Evans, J.St.B.T., & Allen, J. (1992). The source of belief bias in syllogistic reasoning. *Cognition, 45*, 257–284.

Oakhill, J. & Garnham, A. (1993). On theories of belief bias in syllogistic reasoning. *Cognition 46*, 87–92.

Oakhill, J., & Johnson-Laird, P.N. (1985). The effect of belief on the spontaneous production of syllogistic conclusions. *Quarterly Journal of Experimental Psychology, 37A*, 553–570.

Oakhill, J., Johnson-Laird, P.N., & Garnham, A. (1989). Believability and syllogistic reasoning. *Cognition 31*, 117–140.

Oaksford, M., & Chater, N. (1992). Bounded rationality in taking risks and drawing inferences. *Theory and Psychology, 2*, 225–230.

O'Brien, D.P. (1993). Mental logic and irrationality: We can put a man on the moon, so why can't we solve those logical reasoning problems. In K.I. Manktelow & D.E. Over (Eds.), *Rationality*. London: Routledge.

Over, D.E., & Manktelow, K.I. (1993). Rationality, utility, and deontic reasoning. In K.I. Manktelow & D.E. Over (Eds.), *Rationality*. London: Routledge.

Politzer, G., & Nguyen-Xuan, A. (1992). Reasoning about conditional promises and warnings: Darwinian algorithms, mental models, relevance judgements or pragmatic schemas? *Quarterly Journal of Experimental Psychology, 44A*, 401–421.

Popper, K.R. (1959). *The logic of scientific discovery*. London: Hutchinson.

Popper, K.R. (1962). *Conjectures and refutations*. London: Hutchinson.

Revlin, R., Leirer, V., Yopp, H, & Yopp, R. (1980). The belief bias effect in formal reasoning: The influence of knowledge on logic. *Memory & Cognition, 8*, 584–592.

Savage, L. (1954). *The foundations of statistics*. New York: Wiley.

Simon, H. (1957). *Models of man: Social and rational*. New York: Wiley.

Simon, H. (1983). *Reason in human affairs*. Stanford: Stanford University Press.

Slote, M. (1989). *Beyond optimizing*. Cambridge, MA: Harvard University Press.

Stevenson, R.J. (1993). Rationality and reality. In K.I. Manktelow & D.E. Over (Eds.), *Rationality*. London: Routledge.

Stich, S.P. (1985). Could man be an irrational animal? *Synthese, 64*, 115–135.

Tversky, A., & Kahneman, D. (1983). Extensional versus intuitive reasoning: The conjunction fallacy in probability judgment. *Psychological Review, 90*, 293–315.

von Winterfeldt, D., & Edwards, W. (1986). *Decision analysis and behavioural research*. Cambridge, UK: Cambridge University Press.

Wilkins, M.C. (1928). The effect of changed material on the ability to do formal syllogistic reasoning. *Archives of Psychology*, No. 102.

Name Index

Subject Index

problem-based learning, in medical
  training, 104
procedure invariance, procedure of, 18
propositional connectives, inferences
  based on, 45
protagonists, and counterfactual
  reasoning, 57–8
pseudo-diagnosticity, 51–2, 102, 103,
  104, 105, 113, 116
psychologists, crosstalk with
  philosophers, 1

quantifiers, 42

random selection, 14
rationality₁, 165, 168, 169, 184; and the
  achievement of goals, 165, 167, 184–5;
  and belief bias, 170, 173–5; and
  deontic reasoning, 178–81; and
  rationality₂, 178
rationality₂, 165, 168, 169–70, 178, 182
rationality, 165–87; bounded, 174, 181,
  182; and decision theory, 181–5; and
  practical inference, 168–70
reason-based choice, 11–36; between
  two equally attractive options, 14–15;
  non-valued features in, 31–2; reasons
  pro and con, 15–18; under conflict,
  18–26
'representative heuristic' judgment:
  under certainty, 137; under
  uncertainty, 156

satisficing, 169
scientific research, and belief bias, 175
scientists, domain-specific training, 99
selection tasks: and deontic reasoning,
  176–7, 178, 179, 180; *see also* Wason
  selection task
selective scrutiny model, 172
self-analogy, in jurors' decision making,
  148, 149, 150, 152, 158

semantic networks, 42
SEU (subjective expected utility), 166,
  168, 181
similarities: contrast model of, 93;
  negative, 93, 94
similarity coverage model, 72–6, 77, 83,
  92, 93, 94
single-premise arguments: and the gap
  model, 84–5, 90; and similarity
  coverage, 74–5
social accountability in choice, 35
social contract theory, 50, 177
social judgement, confirmation bias in,
  58
spatial inference forms, 137
statistical heuristics, 98
statistically prescribed judgments, 97
stimulus generalization, principle of, 77
stories: certainty principles in, 129–30;
  construction of by jurors, 125–8;
  matching to jurors' verdicts, 126,
  128–9; reasoning to construct
  representations, 130–4; *see also*
  narratives
subjective expected utility (SEU), 166,
  168, 181
subjective probability: and confidence,
  182–3; and deontic reasoning, 179;
  and uncertainty of a belief, 182
sure-thing principle, 29, 34
syllogistic reasoning: bias effects in, 165,
  170–5; figural effect in, 46

temporal analogy, in jurors' decision
  making, 149
temporal inference forms, 137
theoretical reasoning, and rationality,
  165, 169
three-premise arguments, and the gap
  model, 90
tradeoff contrast, in reason-based
  choice, 25–6